The Truth of the Ancient Ways

A Critical Biography of the Swordsman Yamaoka Tesshū

Anatoliy Anshin

Kodenkan Institute

ISBN: 0984012907
ISBN-13: 9780984012909
Library of Congress Control Number: 2011938616

Published by Kodenkan Institute, New York, NY.
Printed in the United States of America.

General enquiries: enquiry@kodenkan.info
http://www.tesshu.info

Cover design is based on a color woodblock print triptych copied by famous Ukiyoe artist Tsukioka Yoshitoshi in 1877 (the name of the original author is unknown). The triptych depicts a notorious robber Fujiwara-no Yasusuke (Hakamadare) attempting to kill a court noble Fujiwara-no Yasumasa, an episode from the mid-Heian era. The story appears in *Konjaku monogatari shū* (*Stories of the past and present*, late Heian period). The original image is taken from the Rare Books Image Database, the National Diet Library of Japan.

The Truth of the Ancient Ways

A Critical Biography of the Swordsman Yamaoka Tesshū

Yamaoka Tesshū (1836–1888)[*]

* Source: Ushiyama 1937.

Disclaimer

This book is meant only to present research into the biography of Yamaoka Tesshū and, in the broader sense, the cultural history of the Japanese warrior class and its military arts. *None of the practices described in this book should be imitated.* Neither the author nor the publisher is responsible for death, injury, or any other harm or damage that may result from readers' attempts to follow practices or philosophies appearing in this book.

Contents

Conventions

- Dates prior to the adoption of the Gregorian calendar by the Meiji government on January 1, 1873, are lunar. For stylistic reasons, English month names are used for the months of the corresponding number in the calendar (e.g., "May" for the fifth month, "June" for the sixth month, and so on). The letter "*i*" indicates an intercalary month. Where dates appear after journal or newspaper articles, they are expressed in year/month/day format. The conversion of Japanese hours is approximately correct for the seasons under discussion; however, one or two hours of leeway must be taken into consideration. The tables in Nojima 1987 were used for converting dates and time.

- Japanese names are presented in traditional order, first name following surname. To avoid confusion, I use the most widely recognized form of a name to designate an individual at all phases of his or her life, even when this is historically inaccurate.

- The ages of Japanese people are given according to the inclusive Japanese method *kazoedoshi* (at the point of birth, a person is considered to be already one year old).

- All measurements are converted into US units.

- Titles of Japanese literary works appear in the original form. Their English translations are offered in parentheses immediately following the first mention of a title.

- Diacritical marks are omitted for Japanese names and terms commonly used in English, such as Tokyo, shogun, daimyo etc.

- Readings of Chinese titles, terms, and names are given in the Pinyin system.

- Indian equivalents of Japanese names of Buddhist deities appear in parentheses with diacritical marks omitted.

- Japanese historiography avoids using the term *samurai* when referring to Japanese warriors. This book generally follows the Japanese academic convention of using the term *bushi* instead.

- The term "pre-Tokugawa" in this book refers to the *bushi* culture from 1185 to 1603, from the time when the professional warrior class grasped political power in Japan and established the first shogunate until the dawning of the peaceful Tokugawa era.

- The term "military arts" in this book describes sophisticated physical skills in the use of various kinds of weapons for killing and self-protection, skills that required long-term training to acquire. This term refers to the skills of the *bushi* of both the pre-Tokugawa ages and of the Tokugawa era, regardless of the removal of the latter from the realities of actual combat.

- With regard to military arts, the English term "school" (*ryū*) is used to refer to formal organizations communicating martial skills to society. The term "training hall" (*dōjō*) is used to refer to their physical location.

- The term *musha shugyō*, referring to the *bushi* martial training that served as a means for the cultivation of spiritual values specific to the warrior class, is retained in its original form for the reasons explained in Chapter 1.

- In nineteenth-century Japan, the terms *rōshi* and *rōnin* were used in a broad sense to refer not only to warriors without a master but also armed commoners, rogues, gamblers, and other dangerous elements of society. That is why to translate this term into English as "masterless warrior" is inappropriate. In this book, the term *rōshi* is used in the sense it was used in the period in question, without English translation.

- The Tokugawa Bakufu formally ceased to exist after surrendering political authority voluntarily to the imperial government in October of 1867. However, the Bakufu apparatus as such and its retainer corps continued to exist for at least half a year after that. For stylistic reasons, the term "Bakufu" is also used to refer to what might be better described as the "former Bakufu" in the period following October of 1867.

Japanese Historical Era Names[*]

Nara: ca. AD 701–794

Heian: ca. AD 794–1185

Kamakura: ca. AD 1185–1333

Nambokuchō: AD 1336–1392
(sometimes included in the following Muromachi era)

Muromachi (Ashikaga): ca. AD 1392–1573

Azuchi-Momoyama: ca. AD 1573–1600

Tokugawa (Edo): ca. AD 1603–1867
(also referred to as the Great Tokugawa Peace)

    Bakumatsu period: ca. AD 1853–1868

Meiji: AD 1868–1912

---

[*] According to *Nihonshi kōjiten* (1997).

Old Provinces and Domains of Japan Appearing in This Book

Modern Prefectural Equivalents of Old Provinces

Awa—the southern part of Chiba Prefecture
Hida—the northern part of Gifu Prefecture
Hitachi—the biggest part of Ibaraki Prefecture
Kai—Yamanashi Prefecture
Kōzuke—Gumma Prefecture
Mikawa—the eastern part of Aichi Prefecture
Musashi—Tokyo, Saitama, and part of Kanagawa Prefecture
Suruga—the central part of Shizuoka Prefecture

Tokugawa-era Domains and Their Location in Modern Prefectures

Bizen (Okayama)—the southeastern part of Okayama Prefecture
Chōshū—the northwestern part of Yamaguchi Prefecture
Fuchū (Suruga, Shizuoka)—the central part of Shizuoka Prefecture
Hikone—the northern part of Shiga Prefecture
Hizen (Saga)—part of Saga Prefecture and part of Nagasaki Prefecture
Jōsai—the midwestern part of Chiba Prefecture
Katsuyama (in Awa Province)—the southern part of Chiba Prefecture
Kumamoto—most of Kumamoto Prefecture and part of Ōita Prefecture
Mito—the north-central part of Ibaraki Prefecture
Satsuma—the western part of Kagoshima Prefecture, and most of Okinawa
        Prefecture
Shōnai—the northwestern part of Yamagata Prefecture
Tosa—Kōchi Prefecture
Yanagawa—the southern part of Fukuoka Prefecture

Introduction

Previous Studies of Yamaoka Tesshū

Among circles engaging in the practice of Japanese military arts, calligraphy, or Zen studies, there are few who do not know the name of Yamaoka Tesshū (1836–1888). He was a leading figure among Japanese swordsmen of the second half of the nineteenth century, and his name is still associated with particularly conservative and severe methods of training. He also left a vast number of calligraphy works that are still highly valued today. Yamaoka is known for his pursuits of Zen enlightenment through the practices of the Rinzai Zen sect, and he contributed to the reconstruction of Buddhist temples early in the Meiji era, in the "age of Buddhism persecution" in Japan, to the degree that he has been called a "great benefactor of Japanese Buddhism."[1]

Yet Yamaoka's accomplishments during his lifetime were not limited to the fields of swordsmanship, calligraphy, and Buddhism. He played a crucial role in the bloodless surrender of Edo Castle, which was one of the most important events in the Meiji Restoration (1868). He held important posts in the prefectural governments of Shizuoka, Ibaraki, and Saga, as well as in the Imperial Household Ministry after the Restoration, and served as a chamberlain of Emperor Meiji. As an informal educator, he exerted spiritual influence on many prominent figures in the politics, economy, and culture of Meiji Japan, including the third mayor of Kyoto, Kitagaki Kunimichi; the famous master of comic storytelling, San'yūtei Enchō; the founder of the first oil company in Japan, Ishizaka Shūzō; the founder of the first private bank in Japan, Hiranuma Senzō; and Emperor Meiji himself.[2]

Either because of his somewhat monastic personality, religious pursuits in Zen Buddhism, or the combination of the two, Yamaoka never strove for fame.[3] However, Meiji society did not let his accomplishments go unnoticed, and largely against his own will, Yamaoka became famous during his lifetime and remained so after his death. Admirers included him in the famous trio—the so-called Three Boats of the Bakumatsu Period (*Bakumatsu no sanshū*). The other two "boats" are the famous spearman and Yamaoka's brother-in-law Takahashi Deishū and a prominent statesman, Katsu Kaishū. All three were retainers of the Tokugawa Bakufu. The trio derives its name from the pseudonyms of each, which end with the character *shū*, meaning "boat."[4]

For over a century, Yamaoka's name has appeared in newspapers and books. He has been popularized as a hero of novels and Kabuki theater plays.[5] Nowadays, he continues to be presented by his admirers as an "exemplary Japanese" and an incarnation of the Bushidō spirit in certain periodicals.[6] Furthermore, Yamaoka is listed among 350 Japanese who most influenced the formation of modern Japan and who are presented on the online exhibition "Portraits of Modern Japanese Historical Figures" on the Web site of the National Diet Library of Japan.[7] Yamaoka has remained popular with many prominent figures in Japan's politics and economics; for example, the former prime minister of Japan, Nakasone Yasuhiro, is his ardent admirer and is known for having practiced Zen meditation regularly at Zenshōan Temple in Tokyo, which was built by Yamaoka in 1883.

The startling fact is that despite such a faithful following among politicians and businessmen, as well as popular writers, there had been virtually no full-fledged research on Yamaoka, either in Japan or overseas. For over a century, Yamaoka's figure has presented a contrasting combination of broad popularity with the absence of critical biographies and the lack of verified data. Several factors have contributed to this neglect. First, many Japanese and Western scholars have not overcome what Conrad Totman terms the "Meiji bias," which impels them to focus on those who successfully overthrew the Tokugawa Bakufu during the Meiji Restoration.[8] Individuals from the defeated side have been generally overlooked, Yamaoka Tesshū, as the shogun's retainer, being one of them.

Another reason lies in Yamaoka's personality. He never publicized or talked about his deeds and feats, preferring to stay in the shadows. Several years after Yamaoka's death, his disciples wrote in *Shumpūkan eizoku shu'isho* (Prospectus relating to the preservation of Shumpūkan training hall, 1890) that he consistently avoided fame and gain during his life, and they had to abandon the idea of erecting a big monument commemorating his name because that would be equal to profaning Yamaoka's philosophy.[9]

Ogura Tetsuju, who was a live-in disciple (*uchideshi*) in Yamaoka's swordsmanship training hall, Shumpūkan, was one of the very few contemporaries of Yamaoka who left memoirs about him. He recalled:

> Yamaoka is great. He used to say: "My name will go up in the world in five hundred years." ...Because my teacher sought recognition in five hundred years, all those opportunists puttering about for the sake of their worldly goals must have seemed to him farcical and pitiful.[10]

And on another occasion:

> I believed it would be really a pity if such a hero's feats were to fall into oblivion. Fortunately, a friend of mine, Sakura Magozō...was a skillful writer, and I thought of having him write my teacher's autobiography before it was too late. But when I proposed the idea to my teacher, he said, "There is no need to do this. If an unwritten thing remains, it will remain for future generations. What is not supposed to remain will disappear however much in detail you write about it...[11]

Thus, unlike other prominent people of the time, such as Saigō Takamori or Katsu Kaishū, Yamaoka did not leave much primary material—no autobiography, diaries, or literary works—that could shed light on his thinking or the facts of his life. His numerous calligraphy pieces, *waka* and *haiku* poems, as well as his private notes on swordsmanship provide only a hint about his philosophy.[12]

To make the situation even more complicated, there are not many contemporary secondary sources, and except for Murakami Yasumasa's *Ittō Shōden Mutō-ryū kaiso Yamaoka Tetsutarō-sensei nempu* (Chronological record of daily life of Yamaoka Tetsutarō-sensei, the founder of Ittō Shōden Mutō-ryū, 1999), there has been no attempt to discover such sources.[13] After Yamaoka's death in 1888, his admirers published numerous biographies, books, and novels that usually do not demonstrate a critique of sources and, instead, are full of anecdotes, legends, and products of the authors' imaginations. They tend to provide a picture full of unexplained contradictions and, more often than not, do not even allow us to date the events in Yamaoka's life with any certainty.

Largely relying on the above popular sources, the few Japanese academic works and swordsmanship histories that touch on Yamaoka do not provide any new information.[14] The only English biographical book about Yamaoka is *The Sword of No-sword: Life of the Master Warrior Tesshu* (1984) by John Stevens. It merely copies the Japanese admirers' tradition of adoring Yamaoka and treating him virtually as a superhuman figure.[15] Other Western scholars' discussions of Yamaoka, such as those of Winston King and Cameron Hurst, are based entirely on Stevens's book.[16]

At present, the articles of Shima Yoshitaka on Yamaoka's calligraphy and religious pursuits in Zen are a rare exception that at least partially allow us to grasp the real image of Yamaoka.[17] For example, Shima showed that there was little possibility that Yamaoka reached the final stage of Zen enlightenment.[18] This is contrary to the popular image of Yamaoka as a warrior whose superior sword skills were backed by Zen-Buddhist mental training, an idea that has long been uncritically accepted not only by Yamaoka's admirers but also by scholars.[19]

In my earlier articles, I attempted to create a basis for the study of Yamaoka's role in the bloodless surrender of Edo Castle by addressing several of his handwritten documents, as well as *Masamune tantōki* (The record of tempering the Masamune sword, 1883) narrated by the prominent statesman Iwakura Tomomi. I also attempted to overcome the confusion with secondary sources produced by later generations of his admirers. From this, as well as an intense scrutiny of the most misleading secondary sources, it became clear that Yamaoka's life had been grossly misinterpreted.[20] At the beginning of the twentieth century, a certain Abe Masato, whose background is absolutely unknown, published numerous books on the Three Boats of the Bakumatsu Period.[21] He claimed that one of the books, *Bushidō* (1902), was a compilation of records of Yamaoka's several lectures on the warrior ethos Bushidō and that another one, *Tesshū zuihitsu* (Essays of Tesshū, 1903) was a reprint of Yamaoka's original writings. I have demonstrated that these and other books of Abe Masato that were allegedly ascribed to Yamaoka are mostly counterfeits and have no relation to Yamaoka.[22] Unfortunately, the publishing activity of Abe Masato has not been scrutinized for a century, and his books are still reprinted by such well-known publishers as Kadokawa Shoten, Kokusho Kankōkai, and Daitō Shuppansha.[23] These books have greatly distorted Yamaoka's image, and many authors who wrote about Yamaoka drew heavily on Abe's works, unaware of their fraudulent nature.

Likewise, in an article from 2007, I identified a problem with Yamaoka's most famous biography, *Yamaoka Tesshū-sensei seiden: ore no shishō* (My teacher: the true biography of Yamaoka Tesshū-sensei, 1937) compiled by Ushiyama Eiji.[24] The biography includes the narrative of Yamaoka's live-in disciple Ogura Tetsuju. It is the only memoir from one of Yamaoka's contemporaries from which we can gain some valuable information.[25] However, when editing this biography, Ushiyama included parts from other previously published biographies of Yamaoka and other materials, including Abe Masato's counterfeits. To make things worse, Ushiyama almost never provides references to his sources, and as a result, everything looks as if it comes from Ogura's memoirs. This biography also contains many inaccuracies and mistakes with regard to historical facts, ages of persons, and personal names. Nevertheless, in the majority of cases, it is possible for an informed and careful scholar of the field to discern Ogura's memoirs from the other content and utilize them efficiently for the study of Yamaoka's life.

Book Structure

This book is based on my doctoral dissertation[26] and is the first critical study of the life and deeds of Yamaoka Tesshū. The conventional approach to studying historical figures is to consider them within the cultural, social, and political context of their time. Naturally, a scholar studying Yamaoka Tesshū would be tempted to consider him within various historical frameworks of the late Tokugawa era. However, in the case of Yamaoka, such an approach would result in a serious misinterpretation. I paid due attention to contemporary context, but what must be taken into account is that Yamaoka was, in a sense, a maverick, largely apolitical and stubbornly going against major cultural trends in the warrior society of his time; a study of Yamaoka based merely on conventional approaches would be insufficient and superficial. Although Yamaoka's accomplishments were diverse, the first context in which he should be studied is swordsmanship, as this was the field in which he invested most of his time and energy. Until his death, Yamaoka's self-perception was that of a "swordsman," and this is how he identified himself to others. As he used to say, swordsmanship was his proper sphere.[27]

As Yamaoka's writings show, however, swordsmanship for him was much more than the art of killing. It was a tool for developing his character and spirit through the exhausting bodily practice that regularly turned him face-to-face with what he perceived as the centuries-old martial tradition and that served as a means for the maintenance and reinforcement of his warrior (swordsman) identity. Late in his life, he explained the cultural meaning of this training in a certificate that he issued to his disciples when they reached the first level of skill in his swordsmanship school. The document is titled *Ittō-ryū heihō jūni kajō mokuroku* (The twelve-item list of Ittō-ryū military art). Explaining why the term *heihō* ("military art") and not *kenjutsu* ("swordsmanship") appears in the title of the certificate, he wrote:

> "Military art" (*heihō*) in the title of the scroll means the Way of the Warrior (*budō*). *Heihō* is the universal term for [all kinds of] martial skills (*bugei*). *Heihō* is used instead of *kenjutsu* in order to convey the broader meaning. It means to apply the [fundamental] principle of one art to a myriad of things.[28]

Here, Yamaoka points to his belief that the practice of military arts was supposed to constitute the very foundation of *bushi* existence and identity. From his viewpoint, in all aspects of his life, the warrior was supposed to base his judgments, words, and deeds on what he had acquired during the process of training in the military arts.

I hope that throughout this book, it will become clear for the reader that Yamaoka's whole life, coinciding with the end of the Tokugawa era, was an uncompromising quest for a swordsmanship school preserving the warrior skills and the system of warrior values of the pre-Tokugawa ages. In a broader sense, it was a quest for what he perceived to be the authentic warrior culture, which, from his point of view, had been largely lost by his time. That being said, in order to grasp the meaning of Yamaoka's activity in the field of swordsmanship in the second half of the nineteenth century, it is imperative that one first comprehends the historical change of Japanese warrior culture prior to his time. It is no exaggeration to say that without the correct comprehension of the foundations of this culture before the Tokugawa era and their change after its dawning, understanding of Yamaoka's life path is practically impossible. These topics do not seem to have been addressed straightforwardly and properly enough in the literature and the outline given in Chapter 1 is designed to fill in this gap.

Chapter 2 deals with Yamaoka's boyhood and youth in Edo and Takayama. It focuses on the development of his scholarship, thought, and religion and attempts to trace the early influences of Yamaoka's elders. It also addresses the beginning of his training in swordsmanship; his encounter with spearmanship master Yamaoka Seizan; his subsequent adoption into Seizan's family; and his work for the Bakufu Military Institute (Kōbusho).

Records convey only two instances of Yamaoka's involvement in turbulent political events prior to the Meiji Restoration—that is, his complicated relationship with an anti-Bakufu radical, Kiyokawa Hachirō, and the Society of the Tiger's Tail established by Kiyokawa, as well as his participation in the Rōshigumi affair. These two episodes have been a source of great confusion in attempts to understand Yamaoka's thinking and position on the politics of Bakumatsu Japan. Chapter 3 is dedicated to analyzing and creating a more realistic understanding of the driving force behind Yamaoka's actions in this period.

Chapter 4 explains the events of Yamaoka's life that induced him to start the quest for what he believed to be the genuine swordsmanship of the pre-Tokugawa ages. Yamaoka believed that this swordsmanship was supposed to combine sword skills practicable in actual combat with the highest standards of spirituality and morality expressed in the notion of the "life-giving sword." Chapter 5 reconsiders the importance of Yamaoka's role in the bloodless surrender of Edo Castle. An analysis of the historical evidence, so far either largely overlooked or ignored by historians, points to the fact that without Yamaoka, this event would hardly have been possible. Another contention of this chapter is that the actions of the swordsman Yamaoka Tesshū in preventing a national disaster were guided by the spiritual and physical training he obtained during his quest for the pre-Tokugawa warrior culture and the ideal of the "life-giving sword."

Finally, Chapter 6 will address the theme of how Yamaoka, late in his life, attempted to return Ittō-ryū, one of the "three root lineages" of Japanese swordsmanship, to the pre-Tokugawa standards of combat practicability, an undertaking unheard of both before and after him. It will analyze how Yamaoka, putting an enormous amount of time and effort into the practice of this warrior tradition, finally came to establish his own swordsmanship school, Ittō Shōden Mutō-ryū, which, as its name indicates, was supposed to embody the "correct transmission of Ittō-ryū."

Notes on Sources

There are two primary locations where materials related to Yamaoka Tesshū are preserved: in Zenshōan Temple, Tokyo, and in a collection called Shumpūkan Bunko, in Tamagawa Library, Kanazawa City (the collection was presented by Murakami Yasumasa, the sixth headmaster of Ittō Shōden Mutō-ryū). These materials consist largely of Yamaoka's personal belongings, letters, calligraphy works, swordsmanship treatises handcopied by Yamaoka or his own private notes on swordsmanship, and so on. In addition, a portion of the swordsmanship materials related to Yamaoka is also preserved in the National Diet Library of Japan. The National Archives of Japan contain a great number of official documents mostly coming from the period when Yamaoka served in the Imperial Household Ministry. A number of his personal belongings, letters, and of course, calligraphy pieces are in the possession of private collectors.

Many of these materials are still waiting to be disclosed to the general public. Those that I have seen in the above locations do not contain the kind of primary data that would shed a fresh light on the facts of Yamaoka's life or help us interpret anew the primary material that has already been published. Many of Yamaoka's private notes on swordsmanship preserved either in Zenshōan Temple or Tamagawa Library appeared in published form in the twentieth century in biographical works by Maruyama Bokuden (1918b), Ōmori Sōgen (1970), and others. In this book, I have extensively used Yamaoka's writings on swordsmanship when dealing with his activities and thinking in this field, and I mostly cited from the published versions, not originals, as more often than not, the latter do not have any title or record number that would allow one to make a clear reference.

In the virtual absence of more general primary material that could shed light on the facts of Yamaoka's life, one is forced to rely on the available secondary sources. These materials are used in the book mostly as a source of particular data, such as dates, places, and the general development of events, and only after the accuracy of these facts has been cross-checked as far as possible. The previously mentioned chronology of Yamaoka's life by Murakami Yasumasa, as well as a memoir of Ogura Tetsuju were of great value to my work.

In closing, I should note that this book is far from being a comprehensive biography of Yamaoka Tesshū, encompassing equally all spheres of his existence. However, touching upon major landmarks in his life, it concentrates on the aspect that was most important for Yamaoka—swordsmanship. In this, the book gives a rather exhaustive analysis that is different both in essence and form from all previous biographies of Yamaoka. Furthermore, through the study of Yamaoka's life path, this book also intends to provide a more accurate and sober understanding of the cultural history of the Japanese warrior class, including its military arts.

Chapter 1

Prior to His Time

The Foundations of Japanese Warrior
Culture before the Tokugawa Era

The Origins of the Professional Warrior Class

The *bushi* were the professional warrior class that ruled Japan for almost seven hundred years, from the end of the twelfth until the middle of the nineteenth century. Until recently, the common theory on the origins of the *bushi* stated that they emerged from a new class of feudal lords who armed themselves for the purposes of self-defense as local administrations loosened. Presently, the prevailing view among historians is that *bushi* first appeared as a conglomerate of special military nobility, hunters, and other classes of people whose main profession was killing. From the end of the Heian era (ca. 794–1185), these men began to transform into local feudal lords and thus came to take on the features of landowners.[1]

By the beginning of the twelfth century, poor internal security forced the Japanese imperial court to hire these professionals, who also had their own retainers, and delegate police and military responsibilities to them. This reliance on professional warriors resulted in the rise of the *bushi* as key players on the national scene. By the middle of the twelfth century, numerous members of the *bushi* clans Taira and Minamoto, who claimed noble descent from emperors, occupied government posts and received revenue from manors. More and more, they acted principally as military figures employed by civilian authorities.[2]

During the 1150s, *bushi* played crucial roles in violent factional clashes at court, and in the aftermath, the ambitious *bushi* Taira-no Kiyomori emerged and seized political power, establishing the first warrior rule in Japanese history. Members of the Taira clan came to occupy all major posts in the government. However, Kiyomori's bold ambitions and harsh punishment of those who resisted him produced a counterreaction. The Taira were overthrown in a series of civil unrests, and their majority was exterminated in 1185 by the rival Minamoto clan led by Minamoto-no Yoritomo. Yoritomo established the first shogunate (the Bakufu), a form of warrior regime in which political power formally belonged to an individual *bushi* to whom the emperor granted the title of *sei'i taishōgun*, or the "great barbarian-subduing general."[3]

The relationship between members of the *bushi* class was based on a peculiar master-subordinate bond in which subordinates were expected to exercise absolute loyalty to their masters, and the latter offered pay and protection in return. However, the real character of this relationship depended on the historical period. In the beginning, when the class was still forming, *bushi* often changed masters at their discretion, and it was only with time that this relationship became relatively rigid. It is also necessary to bear in mind that the *bushi* class was a society that placed the highest value on power and force. If the master's position became weak, not only could the master-subordinate relationship be broken, but the subordinate could overthrow his master.[4]

The Intangible Warrior Culture

As Dipesh Chakrabarty noted, ideas acquire materiality only through the history of bodily practices. They work not simply because they persuade through their logic but because they are also capable, through a long history of cultural training of the senses, of making connections with our glands and muscles and neuronal networks.[5] Regardless of the historical period, and as long as they claimed to be military men by birth, the phenomenon of the *bushi* is hardly comprehensible without paying close attention to their bodily practices and related mental attitudes, which constituted the major part of what I call the "intangible warrior culture." Intangible culture is in an indissoluble union with tangible culture, as for example weapons and skill in their handling. The two constitute both sides of what is generally referred to as "warrior culture." In the eyes of the *bushi*, who aspired to achieve what they perceived as an immutable standard of the "true warrior," it was the intangible culture that was supposed to constitute the existential foundation of the professional warrior class of premodern Japan and to guide their every thought and action.[6]

Before the dawning of the Tokugawa era (1603–1867), which was characterized by about 260 years of tranquility and peace, the basic elements of the *bushi* intangible culture were the warrior etiquette, the state of constant alertness for a surprise attack or other kinds of danger, practical knowledge applicable to virtually all aspects of a warrior's life during peace and war, the cult of the blade, and training in the military arts. These elements were inseparably linked with each other and at the same time interwoven in the everyday process of preparation for death.[7]

Etiquette demanded that the warriors constantly express their attitudes and system of moral values—in other words, sustain their warrior identity—through the correct "form," that is, bodily practice. Numerous mentions of how the body should be used for etiquette can be found in pre-Tokugawa warrior house rules and precepts, including the oldest warrior precepts in Japan surviving from the thirteenth century—*Rokuhara-dono go-kakun* (The house rules of His Highness Rokuhara) and *Gokurakuji-dono go-shōsoku* (A letter from His Highness Gokurakuji) written by a military commander of the Kamakura era Hōjō Shigetoki.[8] Thus, in the case of the *bushi* class, not only the "contents" (the system of moral values, such as loyalty and filial piety) were important, but so was the "form" through which these were expressed and cultivated. Whether one expressed his attitude through the appropriate form (bodily practice) or not defined the crucial difference between the warrior and the commoner, as well as between what was regarded as the "true warrior" and he who did not merit this description. The etiquette also worked to restrain mundane violence among those whose social status required the constant wearing of swords and other weapons and the possession of considerable skill in handling them.[9]

Maintaining the state of constant alertness for a surprise attack or other kind of danger was the second fundamental element of the *bushi* intangible culture. This was another feature that distinguished *bushi* from commoners. A very early mention of such a mental attitude can be found in *Yoshisada-ki* (Records of [Nitta] Yoshisada) of the first half of the fourteenth century. The document, citing "house records," emphasizes the necessity for a warrior to always stay on alert and refers to the state of constant alertness as a "custom of the past," the past that long predated even the fourteenth century.[10]

A *bushi* was expected to maintain the state of constant alertness to care not only for his own safety, but also for that of his lord. The state of constant alertness cultivated among the *bushi* can be divided into two types: one pertaining to the constant preparedness for danger in daily life, the other pertaining to constant preparedness for larger-scale military operations. The former was a quiet readiness to resort to self-defense in an appropriate manner. It was aimed at avoiding a situation when one's unpreparedness or carelessness could be exploited by a potential enemy in a surprise attack, that is, opening oneself up to any sort of hazard. The latter was expressed not only in the possession of all the necessary armory but also in keeping it in excellent condition.[11]

The state of constant alertness was the inner attitude that superseded outward symbols of the warrior and that was demanded of all members of warrior society, regardless of whether they were in service or not. It should be noted, however, that there was nothing artificial or unnaturally strained in the maintenance of such a mental attitude. Instead, it was based on the awareness that life is a ceaseless struggle for survival and that all other creatures in the world live in the same state of alertness. War was deemed to be a natural state of life, and the "true warrior" was not even to consider the dual notions of "war" and "no war."[12]

Care for one's armory had a further meaning that is related to the third fundamental element of *bushi* intangible culture: practical knowledge, or the "know-how" of the hereditary warrior houses. Early mentions of this know-how can be found in the above mentioned oldest warrior precepts in Japan that survived from the thirteenth century.[13] Practical knowledge of the *bushi* pertained to virtually all aspects of life during peace and war and underlay the rest of the elements of their intangible culture. In the case of armory, its regular care implied constant attention to the structure of armor and weapons, and this attention naturally reinforced the knowledge of their weak and strong points. This allowed the warrior to use them in the most efficient way on the battlefield.[14]

The cult of the blade was the fourth element of the *bushi* intangible culture. When outdoors, Japanese warriors constantly wore a long sword and a short sword or dagger. They were not supposed to detach the short blade from their waist even for a moment; this was the manifestation of the state of constant alertness within the broader context of everyday preparation for death. Everyday life was intended to be but a constant preparation for one's death, with the proper spirit expressed, once again, through the proper "form," the body. Preparation for death was not conducted in a morbid manner but, rather, was accompanied by a positive attitude that was achieved by setting a goal that was meaningful in a warrior's life. This meant neither awaiting nor fearing death, not the desire to die irresponsibly at any convenient chance, but constant readiness to sacrifice one's life for his cause.[15]

It should be noted that the reverence for the sword was not unique to Japan's warrior class. It was shared by the wider masses of Japanese people long before the *bushi* grasped political power in the country (still, the former, of course, did not espouse the same warrior ethos). The pair of long and short blades was given to young men upon their accession to manhood as a sign of their male independence. Furthermore, in Japan, the blade was treated as a sacred item, because it was associated with purity and the process of purification. This made it suitable for symbolic usage in religious and magic practices in Shintō, esoteric Buddhism, and the Shugendō religion.[16]

Military Arts

It is essential to note that the previously mentioned four elements of the *bushi* intangible culture could not work on their own. They required cultivation and reinforcement, and this could be done only through the process of regular training in military arts. This cause-and-effect link should not be overlooked—it was not the bodily etiquette nor the state of constant alertness but, more than anything, the training in military arts that, in combination with all the other fundamental elements, distinguished the *bushi* from the other strata of Japanese society.

A very early mention of the necessity for a warrior to train without rest every day in archery can be found in the letter of the shogun's regent in the Kamakura Bakufu, Hōjō Yasutoki (1183-1242), to a military commander, Hōjō Tokiuji.[17] Even *bushi* of the highest social standing were expected not just to practice military arts but also to set an example with this practice for their retainers.[18] Training methodologies of the hereditary warrior houses were premised upon many years of exhaustive practice that had to begin from early childhood so that, by the time *bushi* reached adulthood, they were a full-fledged military force.[19] Needless to say, such a practice was mixed with a kind of "on-the-job training" at war that reinforced all the skills and knowledge previously acquired.

By the tenth to eleventh centuries, hereditary lines of martial specialists had become firmly fixed, and anyone who wielded a bow or sword without being from a warrior house was widely scorned. The reason for this appears to lie in a social ethos that denigrated the practice of military skills by those who could not comprehend a warrior's honor and customs.[20] The *bushi* came to espouse their own concept of values, which was inseparably linked with specific bodily practices aimed at maintaining all aspects of their existence as warriors during times of incessant war and unrest. In this regard, the *bushi* society before the peaceful Tokugawa era can be described as a "society of will." Its members were not military men who exercised self-discipline and willpower only when on duty and made a distinction between "military" and "civil" where their lifestyle was concerned. *Bushi* generally were not supposed to have dualistic notions of "civil" and "military," in the same way as they did not have dualistic notions of "war" and "no war." A *bushi* had to exercise incessant self-discipline and willpower all his life, regardless of his physical or mental condition.[21]

Besides acquiring combat capabilities for fulfilling the warrior's primary duty on the battlefield and making the other fundamental elements of the *bushi* intangible culture work, training in military arts served several other important functions for the *bushi*. Professional warrior groups transmitting complex training methodologies functioned as repositories of this culture, providing the means for sustaining and reaffirming the warrior's identity through regular "revisiting" of centuries-old traditions, that is, maintaining the vital link with the warrior's past. Systematic martial training was also indispensable for cultivating the self-discipline and willpower that determined the practical realization of values peculiar to the *bushi* class.[22]

Until about the fourteenth century, historical mentions of the systematic dissemination of military skills by formally established organizations are scarce. In the eighth century, there were already hereditary warrior houses that specialized in military science, such as the Ōtomo, Saeki, or Sakanoue.[23] Such a hereditary specialization required long-term, methodical training as well as a system of transmission of warrior skills and knowledge from generation to generation. This intangible warrior culture left few traces in historical documents because its practice was limited to exclusive kinship groups of military men and its knowledge was transmitted mostly orally.[24]

Two of the most famous archers of the Heian era—Tomo-no Wataketamarō and Ki-no Okimichi—are said to have developed archery styles that were passed on to members of the *bushi* class. There were also several noted archers among the military commanders of the Sakanoue clan, especially Tamuramarō, who won fame in campaigns against the Emishi people in northeastern Japan. In later times, it was common to speak of the Tomo, Ki, and Sakanoue "schools" of archery, but most historians do not consider them formalized schools; others regard them as a type of court ceremonial archery, not to be confused with combat skills.[25]

Japanese swordsmanship shows even earlier accounts of organizations that allegedly engaged in the dissemination of sword-related skills. Both academic and popular sources, as well as Japanese swordsmanship histories, often mention that from around the eighth century, Shintō priests of the Kashima Jingū Grand Shrine in Eastern Japan taught swordsmanship. This is sometimes referred to as Jōko-ryū or Chūko-ryū (the Ancient School) or Kashima no Tachi (the Sword of Kashima), which further gave birth to seven schools of swordsmanship called Kashima Shichi-ryū or Kantō Shichi-ryū (all seven may sometimes be generically referred to as Kashima-ryū).[26]

It is not clear whether these Shintō priests had any relation to the hereditary warrior houses. In any event, these accounts seem to be based on what is more a legendary tradition than on hard evidence, and historians to date have avoided making clear-cut assertions in regard to this topic. Even if such warrior training entities existed, they taught the skills of using the straight sword until around the tenth century AD, when curved blades were introduced in Japan.[27] It is also worth remembering that these claims are made in regard to the period of Japanese history when the sword was only an auxiliary weapon on the battlefield.

Apart from Eastern Japan, we also encounter such terms as Kyō Hachi-ryū (Eight Swordsmanship Schools of Kyoto), Kyō-ryū (the Kyoto

School), and Kurama Hachi-ryū (Eight Swordsmanship Schools of the Kurama area), which are said to have been transmitted by Buddhist monks and other individuals from Kyoto. These relate to much later ages, most probably around the twelfth century, because they are often associated with the military commander Minamoto-no Yoshitsune. However, there is no information about the founders of these schools and their lineages, and it has been suggested that these terms were merely exploited for fame and gain by later generations of swordsmen from Western Japan.[28]

The earliest attempt to transmit martial skills (apparently with the emphasis on cold steel) through a formally established "school" (*ryū*), most commonly referred to as Nen-ryū, is attributed to a monk and ex-warrior of the fourteenth century called Jion, also known as Nen Ami (1350-?).[29] There are also accounts of Chūjō-ryū, which traces its lineage back to Chūjō Nagahide (?-1384). Nagahide allegedly studied both sword and spear with Jion and later formed Chūjō-ryū, a school combining techniques he learned from Jion with his own family's tradition of martial skills (the family was based in Kamakura and held important posts in the Bakufu). After several generations in the Chūjō family, the school was inherited by the Toda family, and from then on, it has been referred to interchangeably as Chūjō-ryū and Toda-ryū.[30]

However, neither of these schools survived to our times in their original form. Furthermore, there is confusion and uncertainty over some of the most basic facts of the lives of both Jion and Chūjō Nagahide and of their school lineages.[31] There are only legends, no historical materials on Jion, and as Japanese swordsmanship historian Tominaga Kengo noted, Jion's biography, appearing in various sources, more resembles a plot from popular fiction.[32] Presently, historians regard Tenshinshō-den Katori Shintō-ryū, established by Iizasa Chōisai in the middle of the fifteenth century, as the oldest attested military arts school in Japan.[33] The school is also known as the root of the majority of Japanese old martial traditions transmitted in the form of formalized schools. With regard to swordsmanship, Tenshinshō-den Katori Shintō-ryū, Ittō-ryū, and Shinkage-ryū are usually referred to as the "three root lineages" of Japanese swordsmanship, although Tenshinshō-den Katori Shintō-ryū has never specialized exclusively in swordsmanship, and the two other lineages probably also transmitted other arts before the Tokugawa era. Depending on the source, sometimes the lineages from which

Ittō-ryū and Shinkage-ryū are said to have sprung are counted among the "three root lineages." Nen-ryū, Chūjō-ryū, or Toda-ryū may appear instead of Ittō-ryū, and Kage-ryū may appear instead of Shinkage-ryū.

Formalized schools of military arts were expected to teach techniques that would allow a smaller or weaker opponent to defeat a superior one or how to efficiently use shorter weapons against longer ones; therein lay the value of such a technical system for someone seeking to learn martial skills.[34] The founder of such a school had to possess exceptional combat capabilities in order to maintain his school through all the challenges of a time of incessant wars. Such individuals were rare, and this is the reason why there were few formalized schools of military arts in Japan before the peaceful Tokugawa era. Additionally, the founder had to possess an outstanding mind. Besides the development of superb techniques in the art of killing, he also had to create a distinctive and complex methodology of teaching, codify the techniques in predetermined patterns of movement (*kata*), lay the foundations for the continuity of his lineage through generations, and at the same time, develop methods that would preserve the secrecy and integrity of his system.

It is not a coincidence that the first formalized schools of military arts appeared in the Muromachi era (ca. 1392–1573); this was a part of the broader phenomenon of the advent of "schools" (referred to in Japanese most often as *ryū*, *ryūgi*, or *ryūha*), a mode of transmission seen not only in the field of the Japanese military of old, but also in painting, music, dance, theater, and other art forms.[35] They possessed structured training curricula, a system of cultural and technical inheritance through generations of headmasters, school names, names of predetermined patterns of movement (*kata*), a formal system of disciple gradation, and other outward attributes.

The process of transmission in military arts schools was accompanied by an atmosphere of rigid traditionalism and secrecy aimed at the preservation of skills and knowledge that had been tested on numerous battlefields and survived in the long process of historical natural selection as the most effective means of waging war. Needless to say, the primary goal of keeping the warrior arts secret was to avoid giving an advantage to potential enemies. It was also aimed at maintaining the integrity and authenticity of the tradition, as well as preventing its misuse.

Measures directed at maintaining secrecy included having all new disciples seal in blood a nondisclosure pledge upon entrance.[36] The greater part of military teachings was transmitted only orally, in direct communication between teachers and disciples. Texts were deliberately written so that their content could not be properly understood in the event they fell into the hands of outsiders. Esoteric arts and special sciences that pertained to the field of practical knowledge were taught only to those disciples who had reached a certain level of combat skill and, as a rule, were inaccessible to beginners. The training was held in venues hidden from the eyes of outsiders.[37] Moreover, it was structured so that even if an outsider could peep in, he or she would not understand how the techniques could be applied in real combat. This measure was also taken against those who, under the pretext of training, entered military arts schools to "steal" their skills, as well as to prevent these skills from leaking outside through unfaithful disciples. This is why junior disciples also did not know the true essence of the skill they learned.[38]

The formalized schools of military arts were only the tip of the iceberg of military skills and training methodologies transmitted in pre-Tokugawa hereditary warrior houses. However, the technical curriculum of those schools that managed to survive to the present through the Tokugawa era relatively unchanged, allows us to make reasonable assumptions about martial skills and methods of their acquisition among the *bushi*. One of the key points in the pre-Tokugawa training methodologies was that the warrior had to master both unarmored and armored modes of combat. Knowledge of the armor structure was indispensable for the latter. Although Japanese armor is very difficult to cut through, its designers sacrificed full protection of the body for the sake of greater mobility. As a result, it had a number of openings, and some vital points of the human body were left unprotected, such as veins on the inner side of the arms and legs, the waist, and the armpits. That is why *bushi* skills included a large number of techniques designed specifically for targeting exposed areas of an armored opponent's body with various kinds of weapons.[39]

Another important point was that the warrior had to be proficient in all kinds of military arts and handle a wide range of distances associated with various kinds of weapons, because actual combat was unpredictable. This generally included skills in handling the spear, bow, staff, glaive, long sword, short sword, and both the long and short swords simultaneously, as well as spike throwing, unarmed combat, horsemanship, swimming, techniques of tying captives with ropes, and others. The teachings and esoteric practices of Shintō, Buddhist esoteric sects, and Shugendō were also incorporated into the curriculum. These practices dealt directly with the deliberate change of the state of mind and were employed by pre-Tokugawa *bushi* to achieve performance unattainable by ordinary people under critical circumstances.[40]

The vast curriculum of such skills did not signify shallowness of their mastery. The warrior was supposed to be equally skillful in all kinds of military arts. Yet this does not mean that the warrior had to begin from scratch every time he learned a new type of skill; as long as they were transmitted and learned within the same professional warrior group, the underlying principles of using the human body were the same. One more aspect of such universality was that all kinds of martial skills were inseparably linked and composed the whole whose parts could not be separated—that is, every single art reinforced all the others. Such military systems were hierarchically structured, and military strategy, tactics, and logistics could be learned only after a *bushi* reached a level at which he was irreproachable in terms of training in all kinds of individual combat skills.[41]

During the training, the *bushi* used either wooden imitations of weapons or blunt blades. The goal behind every movement was either to kill or mortally wound the opponent or protect oneself from being killed. The practice, constantly accompanied by the danger of serious injury, was aimed at achieving the physical capacity in which movements combined blinding speed, power, and precision.[42]

Musha Shugyō

In premodern Japan, as well as in other countries of East Asia, the process of martial training did not presume simply a kind of military drill or the mechanical repetition of certain movements. This training was based on the notion that physical practice should serve as a means for the cultivation of spiritual values specific to the warrior class. Such a notion is known in Japanese as *musha shugyō*—a cultural phenomenon that is not unique to Japan but that, in the view of David Waterhouse, acquired its own special characteristic there.[43] Waterhouse does not explain what he means by this, but the "special characteristic" of Japanese *musha shugyō* should be sought in the fact that cold steel was perceived as a sacred and symbolic object linked to Shintō and Buddhist deities, as well as in an ancient belief that Japanese martial skills descended from the Shintō gods of war, namely Futsunushi no Ōkami and Takemikazuchi no Ōkami.

Musha shugyō does not have any concise equivalent in English. Yuasa Yasuo noted the difficulty that Western translators encounter when they have to translate the term *shugyō* into English. He argued that the common English translation "cultivation" does not reflect the Japanese meaning in full.[44] It does not convey the nuance of practicing warrior arts not only for their own sake but also as a form of austerity indispensable for ascending the path of perfection and purifying one's spirit.

Another way to translate *shugyō* into English is "askesis," as for example in the work of David Waterhouse, who translated *musha shugyō* as "warrior askesis."[45] Here, we face another problem: although this translation conveys the meaning of austerity, it may mislead those Western readers who are not familiar with East Asian culture. "Askesis" is a term rooted in Christian culture, which treats the human body as a source of sin and requires self-torment for the sake of liberating the spirit. It presumes a direct opposition of body and spirit. However, this has never been the case in East Asian cultures. *Musha shugyō* presumed the oneness of body and spirit, and neither could be sacrificed for the other.

To avoid the weaknesses of these two translations, this book will retain the phrase in its original form. However, what must be understood is that *musha shugyō* implies the simultaneous cultivation of body and spirit by a warrior through constant, arduous physical practice. It further should be noted that although the term *musha shugyō* could be used in premodern Japan in the meaning of wandering of the country (from several months to several years) with the aim of tempering one's body and spirit,[46] that was not the only form of such practice; it could also mean seclusion on the grounds of Shintō shrines or Buddhist temples or an austere training at one's place of residence.[47] Moreover, even before the Tokugawa era, it did not necessarily presume dueling, as some specialists maintain.[48] In this book, *musha shugyō* is used not in the narrow sense of intensive training or austerity within a limited time frame, but to refer to a paradoxical, lifelong process of seeking spiritual perfection through polishing skills in the art of killing.[49] This perspective will help us understand how Yamaoka Tesshū, a warrior of the end of the Tokugawa era, inherited and strove to preserve memories of the *musha shugyō* of the pre-Tokugawa ages.[50]

The "True Warrior": Between Good and Evil

In the quest for spiritual perfection, some descendants of the hereditary warrior houses came to develop a philosophy emphasizing humanistic values more than anything else. It is worth emphasizing that the notion of pursuing one's humanity through *musha shugyō* appeared in the times of Japan's worst wars and unrest, long before the dawning of the Great Tokugawa Peace. For a number of pre-Tokugawa *bushi*, aspiring for practical realization of this philosophy, weapons, and skill in their handling acquired a transcendental meaning (which in no way meant that they were removed from the realities of actual combat), and their cultural perception of training in military arts did bear a dualistic character: it could be both constructive and destructive for the *bushi* and those around him.[51] The two extremes of "good" and "evil" of the warrior profession were ultimately expressed in the paramount concepts of "the killing sword" (*setsunintō* or *satsujinken*) and "the life-giving sword" (*katsujinken*) that can be found in the teachings of some military arts schools in Japan. As is often the case, these concepts and terms were adapted from Buddhism. However, the notion of the weapon (sword) that destroys evil and brings peace and order to people and the nation can also be found in ancient Shintō mythology. Most relevant here is the famous myth about relinquishing the Izumo Land (*Izumo no Kuni yuzuri*), which is related to the very roots of the mythical divine creation of the Japanese state,[52] and the legend about the conquering of the east by Emperor Jimmu.[53]

It appears that Tenshinshō-den Katori Shintō-ryū, established in the middle of the fifteenth century and deeply connected with esoteric Buddhism, is the earliest example of the usage of the terms the "killing sword" and the "life-giving sword" in regard to Japanese military arts. The school emphasizes the importance of training in military arts as a means for character formation, and according to the school's teaching, training in military arts with a malevolent heart is perceived to be destructive, a mind-set referred to as "the killing sword." Training with the proper attitude, aimed at quelling hostilities and finding peaceful solutions, is referred to as the "life-giving sword." The process of *musha shugyō* is directed at the practitioner's awakening to the concept of "the life-giving sword" and his fulfillment as a human being. The training is aimed at gaining unparalleled superiority and strength over the enemy; however, it is a kind of strength that must not be revealed on the surface.[54]

In Japan, *musha shugyō* gave rise to the term "saint swordsman" (*kensei*), which was used to refer to individuals who, in the eyes of others, combined unequalled mastery in swordsmanship with the wisdom and moral character of great sages (in reality, the martial proficiency of *kensei* was not necessarily limited to swordsmanship). However, interpretations of the means and goals of *musha shugyō* varied considerably. The term "saint swordsman" was applied to individuals whose qualities of moral character were not only different from but even at opposite extremes to each other.

Moreover, these qualities could even contradict some of the core humanistic values. We can find warriors of the pre- and early Tokugawa eras who pursued only "the killing sword," casting aside any humaneness under the pretext of *musha shugyō*. An extreme case that must be mentioned is the famous founder of the Niten Ichi-ryū school (which also may be referred to as Nitō Ichi-ryū, Emmei-ryū, and other names), Miyamoto Musashi (1582–1645). Musashi is said to have murdered all his opponents in more than sixty duels in a quest for victory over others.[55] In spite of this, he has been raised to an icon of the *bushi* by numerous uncritical academic and nonacademic writers.[56]

A reassessment of Musashi's warrior status is long overdue. First, it is necessary to establish an objective historical fact: Musashi did not kill his opponents in the righteous cause of, for example, defending his land against foreign aggressors or fighting for his lord's interests on the battlefield. His obsession with bloodshed was revealed through "polishing" his sword skills by challenging others to individual duels. Musashi's distorted notion of *musha shugyō*, or "self-perfection," brought nothing but misfortune to his victims and their families. During his life, he received "guest swordsman" (*kyakubun*) treatment from several daimyos. However, his stipend was always much lower than that of other swordsmen in a similar position. He apparently sought to affiliate himself with the Bakufu central government but without success.[57] This can be viewed as a social rejection of Musashi's cruelty, which was regarded as excessive even in the early Tokugawa era.[58] To the critical eye, Musashi's reckless striving for duels may be seen as a form of psychotic addiction to bloodshed, like that of a serial killer. In this, none of the aspects of his personality should be treated on equal terms with those of Yamaoka Tesshū, as some authors attempt to do.[59]

Japanese Warrior Culture in the Tokugawa Era

Military Arts Schools: Quantity and Quality

Compared to the pre-Tokugawa ages, which were marked by incessant wars and unrest, the peaceful Tokugawa era (1603–1867) is characterized by two waves of decline in the standards of the military practicability of the *bushi* martial skills. The first occurred in the beginning of this era and is commonly referred to as "flowery training" (*kahō*), meaning the ritualization and embellishment of movements during training in predetermined patterns of movement (*kata*). The second wave occurred in the middle of this era as a result of the proliferation of sparring with the bamboo sword and body protectors, which removed *bushi* training even further from the realities of actual combat. Such an estrangement from the direct experience of a real fight gave birth to a large number of psychological theories of combat (*shimpō-ron*) in Tokugawa-era military arts schools. One of the most influential myths, which was created in this period and has survived to the present, was the "unity of the sword and Zen" (*ken-Zen ichinyo, ken-Zen itchi*, etc.). There were only a handful of formalized schools of military arts, all established during the time of wars and unrest, that deviated from these major trends and managed to preserve the practical value of their skills throughout the Tokugawa era.

From the standpoint of *bushi* military history, the first four decades of the Great Tokugawa Peace were an extension of the previous age of unrest,[60] although, as we shall see, the first "flowery training" appeared exactly at this time. After the suppression of the peasant-Christian rebellion in Shimabara in 1638, Japan saw no large-scale wars for over two centuries. The long-lasting peace did not result in the abolishment of the warrior class. However, it brought inevitable changes to the foundations of its intangible culture, the culture that was initially centered on martial skills and mental attitudes developed and accumulated by hereditary warrior houses for over half a millennium. The first distinctive feature of this period is the rapid extinction of the military systems of the hereditary warrior houses combined with a sharp increase in the number of formalized military arts schools, a phenomenon that may be called a *"ryū-ization"* of the *bushi* military skills. By the end of the Tokugawa era, there were 718 swordsmanship schools, 52 archery schools, 148 spearmanship schools, and 179 schools of unarmed combat.[61] There were also numerous schools of other kinds of military arts, such as spike throwing, glaive, staff, swimming and water combat, gunnery, and also military strategy.

Yet, as is often the case, quantity does not necessarily mean quality. These schools could be either older lineages taught under different names by former disciples or their breakaway factions, schools established by epigones, or schools that, as a military scholar of the first half of the eighteenth century Matsushita Gunkō said, were "a mere assemblage of technical elements of other schools with a few new twists added."[62] The majority of them taught skills that were not practical in actual combat. Their training was based solely on prearranged patterns of movements (*kata*) using wooden imitations of weapons or blunt blades. However, this training differed greatly from that of schools established prior to the Tokugawa era in its loss of speed of action, in its extreme formalization and ritualization, and in its movement embellishment. It was also much less physically demanding and exhausting. The main goal of establishing such organizations in the Tokugawa era was to make one's living. This phenomenon originated in the mass "daimyo purge" conducted by the first three Tokugawa shoguns, which produced tens of thousands of unemployed *bushi*, many of whom found a way to support themselves through the teaching of poorly developed martial traditions.[63]

At first glance, the situation presents a contradiction: in a time of peace, one would expect the demand for military skills to diminish considerably, and there would seem to be no reason for the birth of so many military arts schools. However, the cause for this phenomenon is not difficult to understand. As contemporary critics wrote, training in military arts was done for the sake of looking like a *bushi*.[64] This demand not only failed to show signs of declining but increased and led to the creation of numerous new traditions that then endured for many generations. It was in the Tokugawa era that it first became possible to establish special facilities for indoor training, the training halls (*dōjō*), and engage exclusively in the lifelong teaching of military arts, thus receiving an income through private teaching. Such a situation was not possible in the time of medieval wars; although the demand for practical military skills was far greater, they were mostly taught within hereditary warrior houses for the purpose of physical survival, and the teaching process was not associated with commercial gain. Furthermore, the litmus test of actual combat served to filter out any ineffective forms of teaching, leaving only the tried and tested in existence.

Warriors, Skills, Schools: Narrow Specialization and Social Discrimination

Another dominant trend among military arts schools established in the Tokugawa era was narrow specialization and discrimination of disciples according to their social status. There were several reasons for the narrow specialization of military arts schools. As just mentioned, beginning from the second half of the seventeenth century, training in military arts became more of a formality indispensable for the demonstration of *bushi* social status. The universality and quality of martial skills was less important than simply attending the training, and this led to the appearance of many unqualified or narrowly specialized teachers of military arts who exploited this demand to make their living.

However, the social structure of warrior society in the Tokugawa era was decisive in creating this narrow specialization of both military arts schools and the *bushi* themselves. With the end of wars and large-scale unrest, the warrior society turned into a rigid vertical system consisting of multiple subclasses, between which various kinds of social discrimination were exercised. This vertical system was based on a military hierarchy that, in a time of peace, had lost its original meaning. The structure of the system, as well as the way *bushi* subclasses were treated, depended on a particular domain, but in general, discrimination was exercised through such things as etiquette, speech, and clothes, as well as social and financial privileges.[65]

In the same manner, discrimination toward *bushi* subclasses was revealed in subclass symbols and the kinds of military arts that the *bushi* were or were not encouraged to study. The long sword and especially the combination of the long and short swords became the exclusive property of the *bushi* class beginning with Toyotomi Hideyoshi's "sword hunt" of 1588, which was aimed at the formal separation of warriors from the other strata of Japanese society by expropriating the blades from the latter. In the Tokugawa era, while the long and short swords continued to distinguish the *bushi* class from the commoners, other kinds of weaponry served as symbols for distinguishing and governing subclasses within the *bushi* in daily life. The military system of domains was supported by narrowly specialized military arts schools, where such symbols bore a special meaning rooted in the social context of severe class discrimination.[66]

Thus, in the Tokugawa era, with the exception of swordsmanship, the kinds of military arts that the *bushi* could study were directly linked to the subclass to which they belonged. As a rule, only top retainers of domains studied military strategy and tactics; only high-ranking *bushi* studied archery and horsemanship; gunnery was usually studied regardless of the subclass, while skills in arresting, tying with ropes, spike throwing, and staff were studied by *bushi* of the lowest ranks whose job was in the field of civil administration, which included arresting criminals. Swordsmanship was the most widely practiced military art in the Tokugawa era[67] and was studied by all *bushi*. However, the swordsmanship school that a *bushi* could attend depended on the subclass to which he belonged.[68]

The Dissonance between Means and Goals: The Birth of a Cultural Phenomenon

The degradation of actual combat utility in the military arts in the early Tokugawa era was accompanied by conceptual speculation concerning the principles of these arts, an emphasis on practice for the sake of character perfection, and the development of psychological theories of combat.[69] The quantity of psychological theories and their sophisticated arguments actually signified their divorcement from the realities of combat in the same manner that the quantity of newly established military arts schools signified the degradation of the combat utility of *bushi* physical skills. A mainstream product of such psychological theorizing was the invented cultural myth that is usually referred to as the "unity of sword and Zen." This myth has been so strong that it turned into a sort of generally accepted historical reality rarely challenged even by historians.[70] As Karl Friday notes, in the twentieth-century West, Suzuki Daisetsu[71] and Eugen Herrigel[72] are probably the two authors most responsible for creating the association of Japanese military arts with Zen. Most subsequent Western works seem to have accepted this association uncritically.[73] In Japan, however, this myth has walked on its own for about four centuries, misleading the majority of academic and popular authors, with Suzuki Daisetsu being just one of them.

Such a situation originates in an overreliance on well-known early Tokugawa-era authors, such as the Zen monk Takuan and the warrior-swordsmen Yagyū Munenori and Miyamoto Musashi. Another reason should be sought in an uncritical treatment of the Yagyū Shinkage-ryū school of swordsmanship, which, as will be discussed later, was the first military arts school in Japan to introduce "flowery training" early in the Tokugawa era and which also appears to be the first to create swordsmanship theories centered around Zen. The fame and authority of this school, which taught the Tokugawa shoguns for many generations, have made it immune to questioning about the practicability of its skills and the validity of its philosophical and psychological doctrines in the context of actual combat.

Shinkage-ryū, which is one of the "three root lineages" of Japanese swordsmanship, was established in the middle of the sixteenth century by Kōizumi[74] Ise no Kami (1508?–1577), who is said to have received the full transmission of Kage-ryū skills under a certain Aisu Ikōsai.[75] Kōizumi also studied Zen from his youth, and his surviving writings contain many Zen terms.[76] However, as Ōmori Nobumasa notes, these writings are not swordsmanship treatises; they contain mainly simple lists of techniques and are not evidence of the connection between Kōizumi's sword skills and Zen. Some technique names might have symbolized Kōizumi's Buddhist views, but these pertained to those doctrines that are universal in all Buddhist sects, not just Zen.[77] Furthermore, Buddhist terminology adapted for many swordsmanship writings was, as a rule, used in a different, non-Buddhist sense,[78] and we cannot exclude the possibility that Kōizumi was merely doing the same.

Shinkage-ryū was inherited from Kōizumi by the Yagyū family; hence, the school is more often referred to as Yagyū Shinkage-ryū or Shinkage Yagyū-ryū. The second headmaster of the school from this family lineage, Yagyū Munenori (1571–1646), taught swordsmanship to the first, second, and third Tokugawa shoguns and was eventually promoted to the rank of daimyo.[79] The marriage between Japanese swordsmanship and Zen occurred as a result of what can be called a joint work of Munenori and his friend, the Zen monk Takuan. Takuan, who <u>was not</u> himself a swordsman, wrote *Fudōchi shimmyōroku* (*The marvelous record of immovable wisdom*, ca. 1632) for Munenori, and it became a basis for the latter's swordsmanship treatise *Heihō kadensho* (*The book on the family-transmitted military arts*, 1632). Discussing swordsmanship from a Zen point of view, both writings contain abstract theorizing on the psychological state necessary to face an opponent, and their philosophy is elevated above the realities of actual combat.[80] However, its appeal lay in the fact that it was most suitable for the "flowery swordsmanship" practiced by the Tokugawa shoguns in the time of peace.

The ideas in both writings have had an impact on the theory of Japanese military arts ever since.[81] They spread all over Japan because Yagyū Shinkage-ryū, enjoying the most privileged position among all other schools in the country, became one of the most famous and widely practiced swordsmanship lineages in the Tokugawa era, and this inevitably influenced many other schools of military arts.[82]

Here, a reservation should be expressed. The above discussion is not intended to negate the adherence of a part of the pre-Tokugawa *bushi* society to Zen teachings. In such warrior documents as *Tako Tokitaka kakun* (Tako Tokitaka's house rules, ca. 1544), *Shingen kahō* (The house law of [Takeda] Shingen, 1558), and *Kuroda Nagamasa chakushi Tadayuki kunkai shojō* (Kuroda Nagamasa's letter with admonitions to his son Tadayuki, 1614) we can find exhortations to study Zen as a way to comprehend the meaning of life and death or reincarnation[83] (the same could be studied in other

Buddhist sects through different means). However, these advocate Zen only as a philosophy of life, not a form of mental training indispensable for the <u>practical</u> aspects of the military. It is a distinction that does not appear to have been appropriately recognized in both scholarly and popular literature.

Thus, in the early Tokugawa era, we can observe a broad sociocultural phenomenon in the warrior society: the appearance of a gap, or contradiction, between the spiritual side (self-perfection in the context of the Tokugawa-era warrior ethos and psychological theories of combat) and physical practices that were supposed to support it. The problem with this gap was that the character *bu* ("martial") and other terms with a similar connotation, as well as claims of the actual martial value of "flowery training," never disappeared from the rhetoric about self-perfection and moral character building. It was a form of cultivating the spirit by those who claimed military status by birth through means that were impractical in actual combat, yet seemingly without any awareness of their ineffectiveness. This dissonance between means and goals persisted through the Tokugawa era and has survived to the present.

The Introduction of Safe Training Equipment and Free Sparring in Swordsmanship

The pair of long and short swords became an exclusive symbol of the *bushi* class only in the Tokugawa era. This symbol was so important that the loss or theft of even one of the swords sometimes resulted in the careless possessor's entire family line being deprived of its surname and elite status, which in the perception of the Japanese of the time was equal to the family's extinction.[84] The paradox is that the veneration of this symbol was in direct proportion to the decline in the skill necessary for its handling in actual combat. "Flowery training" continued to be the prevailing trend in swordsmanship schools until the first half of the eighteenth century. At this point, it was discovered that turning swordsmanship into a sport centered on free sparring with the use of safe training equipment could open new business opportunities and bring even more financial prosperity.

Sporadic usage of body protectors in swordsmanship and spearmanship began early in the Tokugawa era.[85] The first usage of the bamboo sword is attributed to the Yagyū Shinkage-ryū school. According to various secondary sources and Yagyū Shinkage-ryū itself, it was the founder Kōizumi Ise no Kami who introduced the bamboo sword for training in swordsmanship. This round bamboo sword, called *hikihada shinai*, was made of a set of thinly cut straight bamboo strips inserted in a leather casing. It was soft and flexible and caused little pain at the point of impact. However, training in Yagyū Shinkage-ryū was not conducted through free sparring as yet. The bamboo sword was used only for training in predetermined patterns of movement, and there were no body protectors.[86]

Training with uncurved, round substitutes of the sword, which gained particular popularity starting from the second half of the eighteenth century, resulted in an even greater decline of the combat capabilities of the *bushi*.[87] It is very unlikely that Kōizumi Ise no Kami, who himself had numerous military exploits and was praised as "the number-one spearman of Kōzuke Province,"[88] would have introduced such training equipment at a time when war was still an everyday matter in Japan.[89] It is more probable that it was an innovation of the Yagyū family that added visual appeal to movements and introduced *hikihada shinai* to make training for the shogun and other members of his family safe and amusing. It can be said that the Yagyū family pioneered the introduction of "flowery training" in Japanese swordsmanship, producing one of its finest forms.[90]

The first school to switch from training based on predetermined patterns of movement (*kata*) to free sparring with the use of the bamboo swords and body protectors was Jikishinkage-ryū, which introduced this method of training late in the seventeenth to early in the eighteenth century. Body protectors were used in this school from the time of its sixth headmaster, Takahashi Danjōemon. They were improved in the time of the seventh headmaster, Yamada Heizaemon, who is said to have been disappointed with the low morale and lack of enthusiasm among *kata* practitioners. He made the switch to uninhibited free sparring with the use of equipment that prevented injuries.[91]

Still, up to this point, Jikishinkage-ryū does not seem to have used the new method of training as a means for active commercial self-promotion. It was the school's eighth headmaster, Naganuma Kunisato (1688–1767), who, as a pragmatic businessman, understood that the fresh sensation of the new safe sport could make Jikishinkage-ryū a trendsetter and bring lucrative commercial opportunities. So far, scholars and swordsmanship historians, perhaps striving to preserve the "sacredness" of modern *kendō* swordsmanship, have not addressed the commercial character of its prototype, although Naganuma's reforms of Jikishinkage-ryū reveal this very clearly. Naganuma apparently realized that, instead of teaching a limited number of students for a long time for a higher tuition fee, profits and benefits in terms of cash flow, fame, and geographical influence for his school could be greatly increased by multiplying the number of disciples paying lesser fees. Perfecting the training equipment further, Naganuma simplified the traditional multilevel disciple gradation system, leaving only three ranks. Also, whereas the teaching had been conducted only by the headmaster (the highest authority) of the school, Naganuma now authorized those disciples who had reached the *menkyo* rank not just to teach on behalf of the school but to carry out the "full transmission" of the school's skills.[92] The first of these measures promised to save disciples their money, because, according to tradition, they were supposed to pay every time they were promoted to a higher rank. However, in actuality, it was aimed at attracting more disciples by reducing the costs. The second measure was aimed at the geographical expansion of the school through the creation of a horizontally structured organization with multiple intermediate chains of instruction.

Thus, it was during the Hōryaku years (1751–1764) that safe swordsmanship sparring gained particular popularity and spread all over Japan. The innovations resulted in rapid geographical expansion and a large influx of new disciples to Jikishinkage-ryū, which reached the peak of its prosperity during the time of Naganuma Kunisato. Simultaneously with Naganuma, swordsmanship sparring was employed and promoted even more widely for fame and gain by the second headmaster of Nakanishi-ha Ittō-ryū, Nakanishi Tsugutake. The rise in demand for cultural activities among commoners in this period also facilitated the spread of the new sport.[93] Training based on free sparring, proliferating rapidly throughout the country, stimulated further factionalism within swordsmanship schools, giving birth to an even greater number of newly established schools, factions, and branches.[94] As we shall see, however, one of the major problems with the safe swordsmanship sparring was that, like the "flowery training," it was often perceived by its practitioners not as a sport but as a skill applicable in actual combat.

Proliferation of Interschool Matches and Employment of the "New Schools" at Domain Colleges

From the second part of the eighteenth century, training in Japanese swordsmanship was divided into three currents: predetermined patterns of movement with use of the wooden sword (in the majority of cases it was the "flowery training"), free sparring with the use of the bamboo sword and body protectors, and a mix of both. Over time, the first type of training declined considerably while the latter two became dominant. The process and timing of the introduction of training based on free sparring depended on the personal views of the headmasters of swordsmanship schools, as well as on the specific circumstances in particular domains.

There were essentially two different ways of studying swordsmanship in the Tokugawa era: a *bushi* could either train at a town training hall or at the domain college as part of his broader educational curriculum.[95] Initially, free sparrings were, as a rule, limited only to practitioners of the same swordsmanship schools. Schools maintained the atmosphere of utmost secrecy and strictly prohibited their disciples from engaging in matches with practitioners of other traditions. Besides the ban on information disclosure and participation in interschool matches, schools also often prohibited the simultaneous study of swordsmanship of other traditions.[96] The same bans were also common in schools of other kinds of military arts.

It is important to note that the secrecy of military arts schools established in the Tokugawa era and the secrecy of those of the pre-Tokugawa ages were fundamentally different. Prior to the Tokugawa era, the preservation of secrecy was a matter of life and death. In the Tokugawa era, when the skills of the majority of military arts schools became impractical and commercialized, the reclusiveness of military arts schools was preserved for its own sake in order to maintain the profitability of a certain family lineage. Interschool matches producing winners and losers were dangerous for the well-being of these families, and the ban on interschool matches was aimed at protecting their commercial and social status.

Furthermore, in the Tokugawa era, swordsmanship schools' secrecy was also reinforced by overlapping policies of the Bakufu and domains. From the Bakufu's standpoint, distance between the various domains, if not outright hostility and distrust, better served the shogun's hegemony, and training confined to the domain's borders was a better way to control the activities of the *bushi*. On the other hand, domains adhered to a policy of self-sufficient local units and were reluctant to hold interschool matches, because it could lead to a leakage of information about the internal state of their affairs.[97]

The situation changed dramatically early in the first half of the nineteenth century, when the so-called new schools, such as Shintō Munen-ryū, Shingyōtō-ryū, Kōgen Ittō-ryū, Kyōshin Meichi-ryū, Hokushin Ittō-ryū, and others, were the first to begin engaging actively in matches with disciples of other schools.[98] Historians refer to them as "new schools," not because they were established anew (the majority of them had appeared in the eighteenth century), but because they did not hesitate to break old traditions and customs and were the first to employ interschool matches. An interesting fact is that all of the new schools initially appeared and functioned in rural areas and in the majority of cases were managed by peasants and rural warriors.[99]

The motives for interschool matches by the new schools are not difficult to understand. They were very similar to the case of Jikishinkage-ryū and Nakanishi-ha Ittō-ryū in spreading the use of the bamboo sword and body protectors; the new schools were driven mostly by commercial considerations. Unlike pre-Tokugawa warriors who fought for their lords' interests in mortal combat on battlefields, representatives of swordsmanship schools of the early nineteenth century engaged in relatively safe interschool matches in training halls to expand the popularity of their schools and so gain financial prosperity.

In the Bakumatsu period, international and domestic crises forced the Bakufu and domain officials to implement military reforms directed at employing European weaponry and methods of army and naval warfare. However, swordsmanship and other native military arts continued to occupy an important place in the military training of the *bushi*.[100] This is when the Bakufu and domain officials turned their eyes to the new schools whose methods of training based on free sparring and active engagement in interschool matches <u>seemed</u> more practical and promised to provide what conservative schools lacked most: physical mobility, speed, stamina, higher morale of practitioners, and the possibility to test and polish one's swordsmanship skills in sparring with practitioners of other traditions.

The timing of the authorities' turn to the new schools depended on a particular domain, and in a great many cases, its progress was not smooth. Conservative schools that adhered to the "flowery training" strongly opposed any use of the new schools and their methods of training for domain retainers. The exclusive character and traditionalism of conservative schools was so strong that even domain authorities could not intervene easily in their activities. Considerations of secrecy of the domain inner affairs also hindered swordsmanship reforms. Another barrier was the social order and discrimination—as mentioned above, the new schools functioned in rural areas, and incorporation of a "new school" in the domain military training system meant that it was necessary to employ people from outside the *bushi* class as teachers; this was only possible by granting them the status of domain retainer with all concomitant privileges. It also meant that people from outside the *bushi* class, as well as low-ranking *bushi*, would be put in teaching positions over middle- and high-ranking *bushi*. As a result, they would engage in free sparring and might prevail over them. As Fuse Kenji suggested, the danger of loosening the rigid social class system was evident.[101]

However, national security issues prevailed over all other considerations. The Mito Domain became one of the pioneers in the employment of new schools. The main driving force behind the domain's decision was the formation of the idea of "practical swordsmanship." This idea was an outcome of the domain's policy of "national defense and war preparedness" that made military readiness its first priority and necessitated the cultivation of a healthy and strong body and spirit among its retainers, who were prone to be weak. As a result, such new schools as Hokushin Ittō-ryū and Shintō Munen-ryū were employed by the Mito Domain in 1841 when its domain college, Kōdōkan, was tentatively opened.[102]

Eventually, the new schools were employed at domain colleges throughout the country. Domains started to gather both new schools and conservative schools committed to the "flowery training" under one roof at public training halls or at the training facilities of domain colleges.

Conservative schools were forced to remove the ban on studying the swordsmanship of other traditions, as well as the ban on interschool matches, and they also had to start training in free sparring. Needless to say, representatives of the new schools were more proficient in this method and quickly proved their superiority over conservative schools (still, only in matches with the use of the bamboo sword and body protectors), thus gaining great popularity among domain retainers.[103]

As a general rule, regardless of time and space, free sparring with the use of safe equipment usually conditions its practitioners to be preoccupied solely with a superficial victory. The proliferation of interschool matches in Japanese swordsmanship led to the invention of extralong bamboo swords that allowed one to reach an opponent more easily from a greater distance. The first use of such a sword substitute is ascribed to Ōishi Susumu of the Yanagawa Domain; he is said to have used a bamboo sword over five feet long and defeated swordsmen of almost all training halls in Edo during the Tempō years (1830–1844). It is accepted by historians that the large-scale proliferation of long bamboo swords began under Ōishi's influence, although bamboo training substitutes longer than the standard length of the real sword but shorter than Ōishi's were used even before him.[104]

The New Methods of Training and the Bushi Intangible Culture

As we can see, in the Tokugawa era the training methodologies of the hereditary warrior houses, directed at achieving maximum efficiency on the battlefield, were largely forgotten. The phenomenon of "flowery training," in which the formal repetition of movements removed from the realities of actual combat was accompanied by excessive emphasis on psychological and technical theories, signified the collapse of the former warrior culture. From the second half of the eighteenth century, swordsmanship training halls with their free sparring and interschool matches created the illusion of practicability and at the same time accelerated this decline.

The only positive effect among practitioners of free sparring (at least those who trained intensely) was supposedly improved stamina due to strenuous sparring and the revival of a kind of martial spirit. It was this that gave the impression of "practicability" to the Bakufu and domain authorities. Their enthusiasm for the new methods of training was based primarily on the higher mobility, speed, and freedom of movement of the practitioners of the new schools, as well as their seemingly higher morale compared to those of conservative schools that adhered to the "flowery training."

However, all these qualities had already belonged to the sphere of safe sport. The training of ardent practitioners of free sparring with the use of the bamboo sword and body protectors was, as ever, the practice of inefficient military skills for the sake of cultivating a kind of martial spirit and warrior ethos without awareness of what harm the former could bring in actual engagement. The character *bu* ("martial") continued to be used unreservedly in regard to swordsmanship sparring, and claims about the latter's martial value persisted. It was an extension of the dissonance between means and goals originating in "flowery training." Testimonies of participants of nineteenth- to twentieth-century armed incidents involving usage of the Japanese sword are sufficient to comprehend the degree to which sparring with the bamboo training substitute of the sword was meaningless in actual combat.[105]

In the Tokugawa era, *musha shugyō* lost its meaning in the context of "flowery training" and free sparring. Swordsmanship schools of both currents could still advocate the development of the virtuous character and the "life-giving sword." However, the new context rendered these concepts empty since, as we have seen, they were not backed by the physical and spiritual practices comparable to those of the pre-Tokugawa ages. The sportive environment of training halls that produced winners and losers and inflated egos with considerations of fame and gain was in direct conflict with the pre-Tokugawa spirit of *musha shugyō*. Traveling around the country and engaging in sparring with practitioners of other training halls became quite popular after the proliferation of interschool matches in the first half of the nineteenth century. Yet, although this kind of training was still referred to as "*musha shugyō*," it differed radically from the pre-Tokugawa form of wandering that could cost a warrior his life. This traveling in the Tokugawa era included elements of tourism, and training and matches were far from being intensive. Instead, they were held in a relaxed atmosphere and were accompanied by "after-hours" wining and dining.[106]

In this regard, it should be noted that some authors tend to seek more martial value in Tokugawa-era "duels" (*taryū jiai*) than they actually deserved. These authors argue that such matches never disappeared completely, as accounts of celebrated duels during the middle and late Tokugawa era attest.[107] However, they fail to mention that these were not the mortal duels of the pre- and early Tokugawa era and that they rarely, if ever, resulted in a fatal outcome. Neither do they mention the fact that mortal duels were practically impossible under Tokugawa law.[108] That is why, although *dōjō yaburi* ("destroying" a training hall of a military arts school through an interschool match to build up one's fame) became common by the end of the Tokugawa era, it cost one nothing but his reputation and, usually, only a moderate injury.

Finally, one more distinctive feature of the Tokugawa era is the rise in the number of generalized writings on the warrior ethos, Bushidō. They were intended not for practical spiritual guidance of retainers of certain hereditary warrior houses during the time of wars and unrest, but for a broad audience of *bushi*, the majority of whom turned into bureaucratic administrators during the Great Tokugawa Peace. Characterized by extreme academic moralizing on "what a warrior should be," these writings made little sense precisely because their values and ideas could no longer be supported by the corresponding bodily practices and mental attitudes. Of course, the cultural and social trends varied depending on a particular domain, but in general, the meaning of training in military arts, which was supposed to constitute the foundation of the *bushi* intangible culture, was distorted to the degree that the "military art," or "military training" in its original sense, ceased to exist. This demise took with it the rest of the fundamental elements of the intangible warrior culture described in the beginning of this chapter. Likewise, the cult of death became largely extinct, and from the middle of the Tokugawa era, the tradition of belly-cutting (*seppuku*), which was unique to the *bushi* as a class and underlay this cult, lost its substance. In many cases, it turned into a mere execution by decapitation during which *bushi* were beheaded by the "assistant" at the very moment they were receiving a dagger for cutting their belly. Sometimes, they were given wooden daggers or fans just to imitate the belly cut.[109]

Chapter 2

Boyhood and Youth

Note: Yamaoka Tesshū used two proper names during his life—Tetsutarō and Takayuki. Tesshū was his main pseudonym. Murakami Yasumasa identified the earliest usage of this pseudonym in a swordsmanship treatise hand-copied by Yamaoka on September 23, 1866.[1] To avoid confusion with Yamaoka Seizan, Yamaoka Tesshū will be referred to as Tesshū until the moment when he was adopted into Seizan's family to become its heir.

Tesshū's Childhood—Family, First Training, and Relocation to Takayama

Tesshū was born the fourth son in the Ono family on June 10, 1836 in the capital of Edo. The Ono family, which descended from the ancient and powerful clan of Tachibana, originated in Mikawa Province, and from the time of Ieyasu, the founder of the Tokugawa Bakufu, its members from generation to generation were direct retainers of the shogun. One of its ancestors, Ono Takahiro, was rewarded and promoted several times for his outstanding service to the second Tokugawa shogun, Hidetada. He particularly distinguished himself during the Osaka Summer Campaign in 1615, being one of the first warriors to storm Osaka Castle and take an enemy's head. Tesshū's father, Ono Takatomi,[2] was a high-ranking official with an annual stipend of six hundred *koku*.[3] At the time of Tesshū's birth, he held the post of magistrate of the rice storehouse in Asakusa, from which the Bakufu paid rice stipends to its retainers, and he received an additional salary of two hundred *koku* per year for his service.[4]

Besides the stipend, the Ono family also held a fief in Hitachi Province. The fief was managed by a Shintō priest, Tsukahara Iwami, who served in one of the most famous shrines in Japan, Kashima Jingū.[5] Ono Takatomi, after his first wife died of a disease, married Tsukahara's daughter Iso in 1835. Iso gave birth to six boys, the first of which was Tesshū. Tesshū also had three elder brothers and several sisters, the children of Ono Takatomi's first wife. As the first son born to Iso, Tesshū was constantly given special treatment in the Ono family. In spite of the fact that Ono Takatomi had already decided to make the eldest, although adopted, son, Takaaki, his successor, Tesshū received the childhood name Tetsutarō, which was traditionally given in the family only to heirs. He was educated in accordance with his noble descent and in line with the warrior ideal of the "unity of literary and military arts," meaning a well-balanced combination of scholarly education and military training. With regard to the latter, Tesshū began training as early as at the age of nine in Shinkage-ryū swordsmanship under a man called Kusumi Kantekisai.[6] In less than a year after that, Tesshū's father was promoted and appointed to be the twenty-first intendant of Hida Province, a territory held directly by the shogun. In August 1845, almost the whole Ono family, leaving only Tesshū's two elder brothers in Edo, moved to Takayama, where the administrative office of the province was located.[7] In Takayama, Tesshū continued his training in Shinkage-ryū swordsmanship, as well as spearmanship under a student of Kusumi Kantekisai. He also studied archery and horsemanship. At the age of fifteen, Tesshū started to participate in local military exercises, which his father organized.[8]

Tesshū appears to have been particularly gifted in swordsmanship. In January 1851, at the age of sixteen, he received a document (*kirigami*) certifying his proficiency in Shinkage-ryū.[9] However, a year later, he switched to one of the most famous swordsmanship schools in the Bakumatsu period, Hokushin Ittō-ryū. The teacher of this school, Inoue Hachirō, came to Takayama on the invitation of one of Tesshū's elder brothers and other practitioners of swordsmanship in the area. Thirty-six-year-old Inoue Hachirō was one of the best disciples of the founder of Hokushin Ittō-ryū, the renowned Chiba Shūsaku.[10]

It is necessary to keep in mind that military arts schools had (and often still have) certain mannerisms that were a side effect of the specific physical training of each school and were revealed unconsciously in movement. Bringing a mannerism of one school into the practice of another was not allowed, and the switch demanded an enormous effort by the disciple to shed the mannerisms of the previous school and adopt those of the new school. In other words, one had to become a beginner again and start training from scratch. This is why there had to be a very serious reason for the switch, a reason that justified the negation of Tesshū's seven years of training with all of the unconscious mannerisms he had accumulated as he came to possess one of the highest ranks in Shinkage-ryū. However, records do not provide us with an explanation of why the swordsmanship practitioners in Takayama made this switch. The only apparent fact is that it was a group switch, not Tesshū's personal decision. Still, it brought him into contact with Ittō-ryū, one of the three root lineages of Japanese swordsmanship, albeit through its faction at this time. He would continue to practice the swordsmanship of the Ittō-ryū lineage all his life.

Scholarship, Thought, and Religion

In Takayama, Tesshū's education revolved around writing and the customary reading aloud of Chinese texts without understanding their meaning under the guidance of Tomita Sessai. In addition, Tesshū attended public lectures on Chinese classics. By nature, Tesshū was quite bad at academic pursuits, but there was one exception: calligraphy. Taught by the headmaster of the Jubokudō style, Iwasa Ittei (1779–1858), Tesshū revealed an extraordinary talent and learned very quickly. Within months, Iwasa made Tesshū his successor and the fifty-second headmaster of the Jubokudō style, granting him the license of full transmission of the tradition and the pseudonym Ichirakusai.[11] During his life, Iwasa taught Jubokudō calligraphy to about twenty-four disciples. Tesshū was the last one, and it appears that no other disciple received from Iwasa any rank or license.[12] Tesshū had probably revealed a remarkable talent and diligence in calligraphy, to the extent that Iwasa Ittei, who was already seventy-two years old and did not have any successors yet, set his hopes on Tesshū's future and decided to make him the fifty-second headmaster of the Jubokudō school in spite of his young age and quite short time of study.[13]

It is likely that during his stay in Takayama, Tesshū was under the influence of early modern Japanese nationalism to some extent, as represented by the philosophical National Learning School. The school appeared at the end of the seventeenth century and, mainly through the study of Japanese classical literature, sought to restore what it believed to be the pure Japanese culture and spirit of old as they existed before Confucianism and Buddhism were introduced to Japan. National Learning flourished in Hida Province because of the teaching activity of Hida native Tanaka Ōhide, a disciple of one of the pillars of the school, Motoori Norinaga. Young Tesshū would have been exposed to this ideology because his main teachers in Takayama, Tomita Sessai and Iwasa Ittei, had close ties with Tanaka; Tomita was Tanaka's disciple, and Iwasa was his close friend.[14] Also, during Tesshū's pilgrimage to the Ise Jingū Grand Shrine in March of 1850, his only travel while staying in Takayama, he is said to have accidentally met Fujimoto Tesseki, a zealot of the nationalistic "Revere the Emperor, Expel the Barbarians" movement ("barbarians" meaning "foreigners"). Fujimoto is said to have opened Tesshū's eyes to Japan's international environment,[15] that is, the growing pressure on Japan from Western powers to open itself to the outside world. After that, during a short stay at Ise Jingū, Tesshū met a renowned scholar of the National Learning School, Ajiro Hironori, who was the shrine's priest. It is said that Ajiro taught Tesshū Japan's history in the light of the school's philosophy.[16]

Rather than politics, however, Tesshū's world view was most influenced by Buddhism. As early as the age of eight, Tesshū developed a deep worship of bodhisattva Kannon (Avalokitesvara), the Buddhist deity of mercy.[17] He retained this worship throughout his life and finally established Zenshōan Temple in Tokyo in 1883 with the principal image of Kannon. Tesshū's teacher of calligraphy, Iwasa Ittei, was also an ardent follower of Buddhism to the degree that he was even called "Buddha Ichiemon" (Ichiemon was Iwasa's common name).[18] From Tesshū's letters to Iwasa, we know that they exchanged Buddhist sutras,[19] and it is highly probable that Tesshū's interest in Buddhism was inflated by Iwasa, as well as by the Jubokudō calligraphy, which traces its origins to Kōbō-daishi, the founder of the esoteric Buddhist sect Shingon in Japan.

Foreign Pressure and Swordsmanship Training in Edo

In July 1852, Tesshū returned to Edo from Takayama together with his five brothers after his mother and father died of disease in September 1851 and February(i) 1852 respectively. They settled in Koishikawa Ward in the house of Ono Takakata, who had already been recognized by the Bakufu as the heir of the Ono family. Tesshū and his younger brothers became dependants of Ono Takakata; however, Takakata was indifferent to his siblings,[20] and it was Tesshū's teacher of swordsmanship, Inoue Hachirō, who took care of them. Inoue returned to Edo several months after Tesshū, in November 1852.[21] All this time, he was busy wrapping up the Ono family's pending affairs in Takayama.[22] While teaching swordsmanship there, Inoue had gained the trust of Tesshū's father, who, shortly before his death, had entrusted Inoue with some family assets and asked him to take care of his children. Tesshū and his younger brothers were told to regard Inoue as their own father.[23] At the beginning of 1853, Inoue Hachirō realized that there was no hope of obtaining even minimal help from Ono Takakata, and, seeing the deplorable condition of Tesshū and his brothers, he decided to arrange for their adoption into other families.[24]

From November 1852, Tesshū resumed training in Hokushin Ittō-ryū under Inoue Hachirō in the Gembukan training hall of Chiba Shūsaku.[25] Only a half year later, in June 1853, this training was interrupted again by the appearance of American "black ships" under the command of Commodore Matthew Perry, who came to demand Japan open itself to the world. Tesshū wrote to his teacher of calligraphy in Takayama, Iwasa Ittei, shortly after Perry's arrival in Uraga Harbor:

> In troth, I have so many many things to do because of this American affair. Now I go out every day to different places to study military science and on other business, and this bustle really troubles me...[26]

The Bakufu declared measures to guard the coastal districts, and although Perry stayed only long enough to leave his letter with a promise to return the following year, the defense preparations continued frantically after his departure. In March 1854, the Bakufu signed the Treaty of Peace and Amity with Perry and disbanded the emergency forces; however, the general impression was that war was imminent.[27]

The consciousness of danger from foreign countries only strengthened the faith in the might of the traditional weapons among the *bushi*.[28] Tesshū was no exception, and the sense of crisis stimulated him to even more rigorous training in swordsmanship. His writing of 1857 reveals his mood and determination in the years following the opening of Japan by Commodore Perry. Urging the Bakufu authorities to make retainers of the shogun train more diligently in military arts, he wrote:

> The state of the country should be renewed and the military should be strengthened. We should wait [for an emergency] counting day by day. If those who lack in resolution and are satisfied with the present state of things vainly waste their time and do not make their decision now, the time will definitely come when they will be eating their hearts out.[29]

Tesshū's earnest training brought its results soon: in March 1855 he was granted the middle-level rank (*chūmokuroku menkyo*) in Hokushin Ittō-ryū by Inoue Hachirō, and in 1856, he was employed at the Bakufu Military Institute as an assistant instructor of swordsmanship.[30] Still, already at this time, it seems there was something in Tesshū's training that constantly disturbed him. As a gifted swordsman, he would have possessed intuition that pushed him to seek in swordsmanship something besides perfection in the art of killing. Specifically, he could not find a strong spiritual background in Hokushin Ittō-ryū. Its founder, Chiba Shūsaku (1794–1855), has been treated by scholars and swordsmanship historians as a "great swordsman," who made Japanese swordsmanship "practical" through its "modernization" and "rationalization."[31] However, a more critical inspection of the evidence shows that the reality was quite different. Chiba was not originally a *bushi* but a peasant with the mind of a pragmatic businessman. Similar to Naganuma Kunisato (Jikishinkage-ryū) of the first half of the eighteenth century, he understood that profits and benefits through the teaching of sportive swordsmanship could be increased by multiplying the number of disciples paying lesser fees. Mirroring the Naganuma pattern, Chiba simplified the traditional eight-rank system of the original Ittō-ryū lineage and left only three ranks.[32] This was done in order to attract more disciples through cheapness. Chiba also authorized those disciples who reached the middle rank to teach on behalf of the school. Furthermore, he simplified the sword skills and thereby created an illusion of easy practice and fast progress. He also made the terms of study shorter. Thus, a rank achieved in other schools after at least three years of practice, in Hokushin Ittō-ryū, could be achieved within one or one and a half years. To make swordsmanship look even simpler, Chiba conducted its "rationalization"—that is, in effect, he removed from this art all of its spiritual, philosophical, and esoteric aspects.[33]

Yet what distinguished Chiba's business initiative from the Naganuma pattern was its scale. Chiba's "reforms" in swordsmanship were similar to the business model of modern hypermarkets that focus on high-volume, low-margin sales. He managed the largest training hall (Gembukan) in Japan, which, at the peak of its heyday, took the space of almost four square miles in the O-Tamagaike District of Kanda Ward. Chiba is said to have had five or six thousand disciples, the record in the history of Japanese swordsmanship.[34]

Tesshū was still far from questioning the practicability of Hokushin Ittō-ryū's sportive swordsmanship in actual combat; like the majority of other young men, he followed the prevailing trend in Tokugawa-era swordsmanship. It would take him years to realize that training aimed at achieving practical results in actual combat should be done in a way different from that of sparring with the bamboo sword. At this point, Tesshū was dissatisfied only with the absence of deep spirituality in Hokushin Ittō-ryū, and he had no choice but to start looking for it somewhere else. This is when he encountered Yamaoka Seizan.

The "Virtuous Spear" of Yamaoka Seizan

As far as free sparring with the use of the bamboo sword and body protectors was concerned, already at the age of nineteen (1854), Tesshū's skill was such that he was sure of victory over any opponent.[35] He even received the nickname "Devilish Iron" (Oni Tetsu, a slightly changed pronunciation of his abbreviated name Ono Tetsu). Focusing on constant training rather than his appearance, he dressed in rags and looked like other street teenagers of Edo despite his noble descent. For this, he received another nickname: Boro Tetsu, or "Ragged Iron."[36] This unkempt appearance contrasted with his moral character: already at this age, Tesshū is said to have demonstrated indifference to rivalry, fame, and gain. He was taciturn and had the reputation of a young man who always kept his word.[37]

In 1854, Tesshū moved to the Dōshin-chō District of Koishikawa Ward in Edo and entered a nearby spearmanship school of the Yamaoka family.[38] The family had served the Bakufu for generations; its head, Yamaoka

Seizan, who was also the headmaster of the spearmanship school, is said to have been one of the greatest spearmen of his time. However, it was Seizan's personality that attracted Tesshū most.[39]

The only document shedding light on the personality of Yamaoka Seizan is his short biography, which was written by Nakamura Masanao, the future drafter of the Meiji government's Imperial Rescript on Education (Kyōiku Chokugo, 1890).[40] The biography gives a rare example of a Bakumatsu *bushi*, who preserved the memories of *musha shugyō* of the pre-Tokugawa ages. This *bushi* taught spearmanship that had not lost its practicability in actual combat and had retained spiritual teachings characteristic of some pre-Tokugawa schools of military arts.

According to the biography, Seizan was exasperated at how the long-lasting peace of the Tokugawa era had weakened the morale of the *bushi* class, and he made up his mind to become like the warrior of antiquity and prepare himself for a time of crisis. To this end, he made it a rule that every year, on cold midwinter nights, he would tighten a rope around the bottom of his abdomen, throw cold water mixed with pieces of ice over his whole body, bow to the East in the direction of Tōshōgū Shrine,[41] and pray in silence with his forehead pressed to the floor. Around two o'clock in the morning, he would begin practicing one thousand thrusts with a heavy twenty-pound training spear. He would continue to do this for thirty nights on end. During the year, he taught his disciples in the daytime and at night practiced spear thrusts thousands of times. Sometimes, he would spend the whole night practicing, doing thirty thousand thrusts in total[42] (obviously with a spear of the usual, lesser weight).

The numbers above are no doubt exaggerated. As the following citation shows, however, the author of this biography, Nakamura Masanao, was aware of the difference between the "flowery training" and practical pre-Tokugawa skill, and perhaps he deliberately exaggerated them in an attempt to convey the rigor and energy of Seizan's training. Already at the age of twenty-two, Seizan had achieved great fame as a spearman, which had spread far and wide because of the practical value of his methods in combat. As Nakamura states:

Spearmanship of our age is [practiced in the form of] "schools" (*ryū*). [These "schools"] have lost the vigor and the ability to move actively, and have forgotten the realities of bloody battles; if those who uselessly engage in "flowery training" and seek only embellishment of movements, are compared to Sensei,[43] what they do is truly no better than a childish game.[44]

In his lectures on military arts, Seizan stressed that the goal of training in military arts should be the tempering and perfection of one's character. He stated:

If you want to be superior to others, first of all, you must master virtue in yourself. The enemy will submit if you excel him in virtue. This will be the true victory. Trying to gain victory by technique or fighting is a great mistake. If you want to excel in your technical skill, first, you must prohibit drinking and debauchery to yourself. One should always put his spirit into the techniques, and all his deeds should come from a sincere heart—this is the ultimate mindset one must strive for.[45]

If we accept that the contents of the biography are broadly accurate, Seizan was the inheritor of a spear skill that was preserved from the pre-Tokugawa age and that, unlike the majority of Tokugawa-era schools, avoided the dissonance between means and goals. Seizan's philosophy of building the virtuous character was backed by a deadly art.

Tesshū esteemed Seizan as his teacher, even though Seizan was only six years older than Tesshū at the time of their encounter. It appears that Seizan and the Yamaoka family also gave Tesshū special treatment, recognizing in him an extraordinary talent and a spirit similar to Seizan's. However, their relationship was not destined to last long. Approximately eight months later, on June 30, 1855, the twenty-seven-year-old Yamaoka Seizan died of disease. The story is that Seizan was suffering from beriberi and was lying at home when somebody brought news that his teacher of swimming was going to be assassinated by jealous mates. In spite of the serious disease, Seizan is said to have rushed to rescue his teacher and died of heart failure in Sumidagawa River while swimming. To avoid the Bakufu investigation, the official version of the circumstances of Seizan's death maintained by the Yamaoka family for a long time was that Seizan died of the disease at home.[46]

Seizan's untimely death left the Yamaoka family without an heir. Seizan was the eldest of the three Yamaoka brothers. The middle brother Shinkichi was also very skillful in spearmanship, but he could not become the heir because he was dumb from birth. The youngest brother, Kenzaburō, had already become the heir of his mother's family line, taking the surname of Takahashi. Later, he would also gain a reputation as one of the most skillful spearmen in Japan, take the pseudonym Deishū, and become another of the famous Three Boats of the Bakumatsu Period.[47]

In the absence of an heir, the Yamaoka family decided to take a successor from outside who would marry the eldest daughter of the family, the sixteen-year-old Fusako. They regarded Tesshū as an ideal candidate, and in about half a year he married Fusako, despite his social status in the Bakufu hierarchy, which was much higher than that of the Yamaoka family. From this time, Tesshū began to use the surname Yamaoka.[48]

The Bakufu Military Institute

While Yamaoka Tesshū was immersing himself primarily in swordsmanship training, the top Bakufu officials began to take measures in response to the foreign threat. Besides triggering the inner political turmoil that finally led to the overthrow of the Tokugawa family, the arrival of Commodore Perry shook off the Bakufu's last illusions that foreign powers would bypass Japan. The Bakufu embarked on strengthening its national defense, and in 1856 it established in the Tsukiji District of Edo the Military Institute (Kōbusho), an institution that became the base for the later Meiji army.[49] The Military Institute was not the first attempt of the Bakufu to provide its retainers with systematic military training. Such attempts had been made since the end of the eighteenth century; in 1792, the first gunnery drill of the Bakufu retainers was organized in the Tokumaru plain of Musashi Province and was held regularly there from that time. The Bakufu attached importance to firearms, and in 1843, 1844, and 1852 it opened three gunnery training sites in Edo. However, all these attempts were directed at training retainers in narrow fields of military science, mainly Western gunnery. The Military Institute became the first educational institute of the Bakufu where retainers could learn all kinds of military skills.[50]

The planning and construction of the Military Institute began in 1854. The major figures behind its establishment were the Bakufu senior councilor Abe Masahiro and several senior inspectors as well as the daimyo of the

Mito Domain, Tokugawa Nariaki.[51] The Military Institute was opened with Abe Masahiro's announcement: "According to the recent generous intention of the shogun, it was ordered to build the Military Institute for training in gunnery, swordsmanship, spearmanship, swimming, and other arts. The building of the Military Institute's facilities in Tsukiji is finished, and all officials, shogun retainers, lesser liege vassals, their sons, and dependants should train there earnestly…"[52]

The main goal in the establishment of the Military Institute was to teach Bakufu retainers modern methods of combat as well as revitalize their martial spirit. However, the Bakufu officials still had only a vague idea of what these methods should be, and the sole "modern" curriculum item at the time of its establishment was Western gunnery. The rest of the curriculum items were mostly Japanese and included swordsmanship, spearmanship, swimming, unarmed combat, horsemanship, the military strategy of the Yamaga-ryū school founded by Yamaga Sokō in the seventeenth century, and even ancient Chinese strategy.[53]

The creation of the Military Institute had one more purpose. The Bakufu was facing a serious youth problem: mass unemployment among young retainers of the Bakufu (especially younger sons of direct retainers and lesser liege vassals who could not become heirs of their families) produced many delinquents. The Military Institute was supposed to provide a good military training to young men regardless of their rank, prevent them from becoming delinquent, and allow them to develop their talents. Still, this did not mean that admission to the Military Institute was limited only to Bakufu retainers. Anyone who wished to study was accepted, including rear vassals of the Bakufu retainers and even masterless warriors. Neither was there any upper age limit, and men over fifty years old were allowed to enter.[54]

To attract more people and encourage serious study at the Military Institute, the Bakufu offered many privileges. Training at the institute was free of charge, free meals were served in the afternoon, and the full range of training equipment was available for borrowing. Those who achieved outstanding results were granted financial rewards, employment, and promotion within the Bakufu hierarchy. The Bakufu also offered students an opportunity to demonstrate their skill before the shogun during the annual military arts demonstrations that were held for the shogun several times a year at the Military Institute.[55]

Young men were not required to master all the military arts taught at the Military Institute. Instead, they were encouraged to achieve proficiency in at least one art. They were also free in the choice of their teacher. In line with the general trend of the Bakumatsu period, the Military Institute gathered several schools of swordsmanship under one roof, established the same standard for their training equipment, and encouraged training mostly in free sparring. Senior teachers and instructors were allowed to bring their students to the Military Institute both for training and for assistance. Among instructors who were officially appointed in March 1856 were people close to Yamaoka Tesshū: Takahashi Deishū (spearmanship) and Inoue Hachirō (swordsmanship).[56]

The same year, twenty-one-year-old Yamaoka Tesshū became an assistant of swordsmanship (*sewa kokoroe*) at the Military Institute through the recommendation of Inoue Hachirō.[57] From this point, Yamaoka's training became even harder; he practiced both at the Military Institute and the Gembukan training hall at the same time.[58] His effort was noticed, and he was chosen to participate in the military arts demonstration held in November 1856 before the shogun Tokugawa Iesada at the institute. The shogun rewarded and promoted participants on this occasion, and those of the assistant rank, including Yamaoka, received a piece of valuable material.[59] His name is also on the list of swordsmanship assistants who were recommended for demonstration before the shogun in May 1858.[60]

In spite of all the favorable conditions offered by the Bakufu to trainees at the Military Institute, its education did not influence young retainers as the Bakufu had expected. Furthermore, because the Bakufu did not limit admission to the institute only to its retainers, it gathered people with various backgrounds, which resulted in serious organizational disorder. According to the records, trainees lacked discipline, tended to forget their personal belongings, and sometimes even mistakenly took others' swords home. Incidents, including theft, were not rare.[61] In a petition that Yamaoka Tesshū submitted to the Bakufu officials in 1857,[62] he expressed his frustration:

From autumn, the curriculum of training in spearmanship and swordsmanship has been set, and [efforts are made] to make warriors...polish their skills and not neglect [their military duties]. I truly cannot express my gratitude for your thoughtful and kindhearted teaching of these warriors. However they themselves do not realize the preciousness of their seniors' teaching. They addict themselves to dissipation and licentiousness, and hanker after fame and gain. There are no more than two or three people in one unit who do their utmost to polish their military skills. What will the rest do if an emergency arises? All this is very frustrating. Still, there is a way to encourage them for the proper action. What is it?...Let us assume that we have a [contemporary] brave warrior and a cowardly warrior who are led to the edge of a deep cleft. They are told that they will be rewarded with one hundred gold coins if they jump to the opposite side of the cleft. The brave warrior goes ahead and jumps to the opposite side to obtain one hundred gold coins. The cowardly warrior hesitates, but suddenly he sees a fierce tiger behind him, forgets all his fears, and jumps over the cleft regardless of the reward. Is there any difference between bravery and cowardice in the latter case? [The true] brave warriors are warriors of the ancient times. Cowardly warriors are warriors of the present. One hundred gold coins is a reward. The fierce tiger is a punishment. Therefore the reward for the [contemporary] brave warriors and the punishment for cowardly warriors is enough to make them all jump together to the opposite side of the cleft. Thus, persons of pleasure will become diligent and hard-working, the cowardly and weak will become brave.[63]

Yamaoka's observations of the Bakufu Military Institute can be confirmed by the report of one of the inspectors of this organization who noted that most people at the Institute trained in a perfunctory manner, that the overall number of trainees and the number of skillful warriors was declining, and that the perfunctory attitude was seen even among the teaching staff for many of whom attendance at the institute on the prescribed number of days was a mere formality necessary to obtain promotion to an official rank or other benefits.[64]

This early writing by Yamaoka already demonstrates his longing for the ideal of the "true warrior" of the pre-Tokugawa ages. It is indicative that, in his own *musha shugyō*, Yamaoka set up standards of the "true warrior" and did his best to approximate himself to them. The statement "[the true] brave warriors are warriors of the ancient times. Cowardly warriors are warriors of the present" shows that, in Yamaoka's view, true warriors were motivated by virtue, not rewards. He further points out that the only measure to improve the morale of his contemporaries was punishment and reward. It is hard to say from whom Yamaoka Tesshū inherited his sense of these standards. The influence of his spearmanship teacher Yamaoka Seizan certainly was strong. Still, some earlier influences also undoubtedly existed, since his quest for a military arts school with spiritual teachings corresponding to the pre-Tokugawa standards began even before his encounter with Seizan.

Yamaoka was aware that the very basis underlying the standards of the "true warrior" was the culture of death, and his petition implicitly criticizes its absence among the young retainers of the Bakufu, whose understanding of loyalty was already limited to the mere exchange of service for pay. This kind of contractual relationship between lords and warrior retainers appeared in the Tokugawa era within the broader context of the developing consumer culture.[65] Late in the 1850s, Yamaoka appears to have come to realize that this kind of relationship was more a product of the time of peace and, furthermore, that it emerged as a result of the extinction of the cult of death. He took the same view as warrior-writer Daidōji Yūzan (1639–1730), who wrote that all *bushi* who received a stipend from their lords must not think that their body and life belonged to themselves. Daidōji noted that, although servants of the warrior houses worked without rest by engaging in physical labor for a small stipend, they were not obliged to do the most important thing: sacrifice their life for their lord. This was why no one could censure them for running off or behaving in a cowardly manner on the battlefield, the place perceived as the most important "worksite" of the warrior class. Rather, they were just servants who lived by selling their labor. In contrast, the *bushi* were those whose most important commitment to their lords was sacrificing their lives. They might not necessarily engage in everyday physical labor as servants; however, they were supposed to die readily for their lords whenever the need arose. This was the reason why their stipends were much higher than those of the servants.[66] Yet it is necessary to emphasize that, for such as Yamaoka, the noncontractual bond between the lord and retainer was different from the excessively emotional tie depicted in Yamamoto Tsunetomo's *Hagakure* (*Hidden in the Leaves*, ca. 1716). It was rather a deliberate realization of values pertaining to the skill of handling arms in the broader process of *musha shugyō*.

Yamaoka was not an intellectual, but he perceived flaws at the core of the Bakufu military and in a broader sense, contemporary warrior culture. Eleven years later, the Bakufu would lose the Boshin Civil War to the imperial army precisely because of the reasons foreshadowed in Yamaoka's writing: low morale and lack of organization.[67] At this point, the Bakufu did not heed Yamaoka's petition and take adequate measures to improve the morale of the shogun's retainers at the Military Institute. Furthermore, the retainers were misled in their military training by personal preferences and the mistaken judgment of a few top officials. In February 1860, the Military Institute moved to the Ogawa-chō District, and some changes occurred in the training curriculum. The most surprising change was the introduction of Japanese archery, which already at that time was a complete anachronism in Japan. However, there were political reasons for such a seemingly irrational move. After the death of the Military Institute's founder and an advocate of Western gunnery, Abe Masahiro, in June 1857, the conservative Ii Naosuke became the new senior councilor, and his policy was the opposite of his predecessor's: Ii was against Westernization and emphasized the revitalization of the "pure Japanese spirit" at the cost of defensive capabilities. As a result, when the Military Institute moved to its new building in Ogawa-chō, archery, which had been one of the symbols of the Japanese warrior class since ancient times, became the most important item of the curriculum, and at the same time some gunnery instruction was abolished.[68] The introduction of archery in the Bakufu Military Institute was another indication of the dissonance between means and goals, i.e. the practice of inefficient military skills for the sake of cultivating the spiritual side of the *bushi*.

Chapter 3

Expel the Foreigners, Protect the Shogun

The Society of the Tiger's Tail

In the Bakumatsu period, private swordsmanship training halls provided good opportunities for establishing personal contacts and networking among people from different parts of the country. Many of them turned into centers of fraternization for the advocates of the nationalistic "Revere the Emperor, Expel the Barbarians" movement, whose friendships later deepened into political brotherhoods and secret societies.[1] In 1857, the same year Yamaoka submitted his petitions to authorities of the Bakufu Military Institute, he met for the first time the twenty-seven-year-old Kiyokawa Hachirō in the Gembukan training hall.[2] Kiyokawa was a rural warrior from Shōnai, one of the northernmost domains of Japan, and he was seven years older than Yamaoka.

Yamaoka is said to have recognized in Kiyokawa at first sight an unusual man with aspirations similar to his own.[3] Indeed, later Kiyokawa would turn out to be an exceptional *shishi* (Meiji Restoration activist), who, having no official rank or title, greatly influenced important decisions of both the Bakufu and the imperial court. Kiyokawa was highly educated and was remarkably talented at writing. In his youth, he traveled to Edo many times, where he studied Confucianism and other areas of Chinese scholarship, as well as Hokushin Ittō-ryū swordsmanship at the Gembukan training hall. After a period of intensive study and training and two attempts to open his own private academy in Edo (both were thwarted by accidental fires), he opened a private academy in July 1859 in the O-Tamagaike District of Kanda Ward, where he taught Chinese scholarship, calligraphy, and swordsmanship.[4]

There were aspects of moral character common to both Yamaoka and Kiyokawa but also major differences. Some of these differences were complementary. Kiyokawa had what Yamaoka lacked most: an excellent scholarly training, a breadth of intellectual knowledge, and networking ability. To Kiyokawa, Yamaoka was a retainer of the Bakufu who would go to any extreme to accomplish his commitment, who was ready to sacrifice himself for a just cause, and who could always be relied upon. The crucial difference that separated them, however, was that, although Kiyokawa also trained at the Gembukan training hall and even taught Hokushin Ittō-ryū swordsmanship for some time, he was not devoted to *musha shugyō* through the practice of military arts to the same degree as Yamaoka, and what is most important, unlike Yamaoka, he was not concerned about ethical questions of the application of martial skills.

For Kiyokawa, all ethical questions took second place to the radical "Revere the Emperor, Expel the Barbarians" ideology, which in his mind was inseparably linked with the forceful overthrow of the Bakufu. At the age of seventeen, Kiyokawa is said to have been influenced greatly by a prominent advocate of this ideology, Fujimoto Tesseki, who strengthened Kiyokawa's resolve to leave his home to travel and study. Kiyokawa felt indignation over the Bakufu position in negotiations with foreign powers, especially when the former arbitrarily entered into a treaty of amity and commerce with the United States (1858) without obtaining the imperial court's permission and repressed political opposition with brutal force. About half a year before the assassination of the Bakufu senior councilor Ii Naosuke (March 1860), Kiyokawa had already predicted that the Bakufu would collapse from within in five or six years. He believed that in a time of severe political repression, there was no other way but to go underground and wait for change. However, Ii's assassination altered his attitude dramatically. After that, he understood that the Bakufu's days were numbered and the time had come for "heroes" to rise and resort to decisive action.[5]

The "Revere the Emperor, Expel the Barbarians" movement turned into one of the main currents of thought of the time. The movement was a radical reaction to the Bakufu policy of opening Japan's ports and trade with the foreigners, and it gradually turned into opposition to the Bakufu itself. The reasons underlying the movement were not only nationalistic; the trade with the foreigners caused a great discontent among many people—export of raw silk and other goods threw markets in Eastern

Japan into disorder and caused inflation of prices.[6] However, Kiyokawa did not recklessly object to the trade with foreign countries. He just did not want to see them treating Japan in the same arrogant manner as they did India and China. Kiyokawa could not tolerate the Bakufu stance, which from his point of view did everything to please the foreigners and at the same time was incapable of helping its own people, who were suffering because of inflated prices and other adversities brought by the trade with the "ugly barbarians."[7] The opening of Japan was acceptable to Kiyokawa if foreign powers negotiated with it on equal terms and its people were content.[8]

Kiyokawa opened his academy in the period when Japan faced a turning point in its inner and foreign politics. This period was marked by the sharp decline of Bakufu power and a wave of killing and wounding of foreigners in the streets of Edo and Yokohama that followed the opening of Yokohama Port in 1859.[9] Kiyokawa's charismatic personality attracted many persons of like mind, and soon, his private academy in Edo turned into a "Revere the Emperor, Expel the Barbarians" society named Kobi no Kai, or the Society of the Tiger's Tail. The name originated in the traditional belief that a tiger's tail symbolized danger.[10] The Japanese expression "to step on a tiger's tail" is close to the English "grab a tiger by the tail" with the connotation of revealing one's courage by resorting to dangerous action. The society was also referred to by its members as the Society of Heroes (Eiyūkai).[11]

At the point of its establishment, there were no more than fourteen to fifteen regular members of the Society of the Tiger's Tail. If sympathizers are added, the number would be about forty men. The society was financed by Kiyokawa, who received money from his family in the Shōnai Domain. Discussion during the society's meetings was extremely heated and emotional, and none of the members knew when the collision of opinions would erupt into a fight.[12] The main goal of the society was the overthrow of the Bakufu at all costs, and indeed, it was a very risky gathering since it functioned in Edo, right before the Bakufu's eyes.

It may seem strange that such a loyal retainer of the shogun as Yamaoka Tesshū joined the Society of the Tiger's Tail as all his biographers write. By the time the society was established in the middle of 1860,[13] Yamaoka had already been in one of the highest teaching positions at the Bakufu

Military Institute—he was an acting senior teacher (*shihan yaku nami*) of swordsmanship.[14] In view of his senior position within this organization, his anti-Bakufu activity could not go unnoticed, especially taking into account the fact that the Bakufu had a developed system of secret informers.

Furthermore, the majority of biographical sources about Yamaoka and Kiyokawa state that, as a Restoration activist, Yamaoka was busy day and night with "national affairs" along with Kiyokawa. However, all of them consistently fail to specify exactly what kind of activities he performed. The most disturbing fact about Yamaoka is that we do not know what he did because no concrete information has survived. From the abundant historical and biographical data on Kiyokawa Hachirō, including the most detailed studies by Suda Koryū and Oyamatsu Katsuichirō, we can know a lot about the thoughts and actions of Kiyokawa's associates in the Society of the Tiger's Tail, such as Imuta Shōhei, Azumi Gorō, Murakami Shungorō, Masumitsu Kyūnosuke, Ishizaka Shūzō, and others, but nothing specific about Yamaoka Tesshū.

The only conclusion that can be derived from the available information, or more precisely, from its absence, is that Yamaoka was not an active member of the society. It seems that the only thing that compelled him to occasionally participate in its gatherings was a hatred of foreigners. On the question of how to treat the Bakufu, however, Yamaoka maintained a distance from Kiyokawa and other members. Kiyokawa acknowledged this in one of his writings related to the period of October 1861 (after the Society of the Tiger's Tail was disbanded, most of its members were put in jail, and Kiyokawa was hunted by the Bakufu) referring to Yamaoka as a man who could be "likened to our like-minded brethren."[15] Kiyokawa clearly was aware that Yamaoka was far from full solidarity with the society.

In this regard, it is necessary to mention a popular myth of the existence of the Party for Revering the Emperor and Expelling the Barbarians (Sonnō Jōi Tō) with Yamaoka Tesshū as its main founder. Maruyama Bokuden, the third priest of Zenshōan Temple, was responsible for creating the myth.[16] The myth has been particularly popular among Yamaoka's admirers. In actuality, Maruyama was misled by a scroll titled *Sonnō Jōi hokki* (The establishment of the [movement for] revering the Emperor and expelling the barbarians), which is preserved in the temple. A part of this document is handwritten by Kiyokawa Hachirō and is related to his radical activities.

Another part is a list of the members of Kiyokawa's Society of the Tiger's Tail handwritten by Yamaoka. Maruyama probably referred to the society by the name "Party for Revering the Emperor and Expelling the Barbarians"; however, historically, such a formal party never existed. And as Maekawa Shūji demonstrated, Yamaoka created the list late in his life on the occasion of a large-scale commemoration of all those who fell in the turbulent 1860s. It merely includes the names of those members of the Society of the Tiger's Tail who were killed at that time.[17]

For a warrior like Yamaoka, his relationship with Kiyokawa posed an ethical dilemma. He was a loyal retainer of the shogun on the one hand, yet he did not betray his friends on the other. In spite of the fact that their activity was directed at overthrowing the Bakufu, he assisted them in the most difficult moments, even when the Bakufu was after them. For a century and a half, such an ambiguous and seemingly contradictory stance has puzzled Yamaoka's contemporaries, biographers, and admirers. However, Yamaoka, like the members of the Society of the Tiger's Tail, understood that the Bakufu's days were numbered, and his stance can be explained if we assume that Yamaoka distinguished between vassal loyalty to the Tokugawa family and loyalty to the political apparatus expressed in the abstract notion of the "Bakufu."

Both Yamaoka Tesshū and Kiyokawa Hachirō were *bushi*, who invested considerable time and effort in becoming skillful in swordsmanship, which they perceived as the art of killing (although, as discussed in Chapter 1, what they learned at the Gembukan training hall of Chiba Shūsaku was largely removed from the realities of actual combat). However, the motives that guided the two in the question of whether to resort to violence or not were different. In the case of Yamaoka, he was opposed to the terrorist activity of "Revere the Emperor, Expel the Barbarians" zealots that actively sought to participate in inner politics and resorted to reckless violence. His stance toward the developments in the country can only be explained as a form of semi-underground military preparation for a possible large-scale war with foreign powers. In this, he remained a *bushi* who was absolutely loyal to the Tokugawa family.[18]

By contrast, Kiyokawa and the young members of the Society of the Tiger's Tail were not obviously concerned with the value of human life and apparently did not care if innocent people were caught up in their terrorist actions. They believed that their countrymen would welcome the merciless killing of foreigners, who treated the Japanese as barbarians, did not observe Japanese customs, and threatened Japan with superior technologies and military might.[19]

The only foreigner to die at the hands of the society was Henry Heusken, a Dutch interpreter for the US envoy in Japan, Townsend Harris. He was slashed to death on December 5, 1860 in the Akabane area of Edo. It was Imuta Shōhei of the Satsuma Domain who wounded Heusken fatally. The action was well planned, and the Bakufu failed to find the perpetrators. Heusken's assassination, the fifth in a series of incidents with foreigners that followed the opening of Yokohama, brought some results. Since the opening of Yokohama in 1859, legations of foreign powers had been quartered in temples in the Shinagawa area of Edo; however, the assassination of Heusken forced them all, except the American envoy Townsend Harris, to move to Yokohama.[20]

Kiyokawa was convinced that assassination was a legitimate political weapon, but he quickly realized that the murder of one foreigner or high-ranking Bakufu official would not bring him closer to his ultimate goal. In January 1861, Kiyokawa came up with a new scheme to fundamentally change the balance of power between Japan and foreigners. At the initial stage, this involved a complete extermination of the resident foreigners by burning down their settlements in Yokohama.[21] Yamaoka knew about Kiyokawa's plan, and he attempted to prevent the members of the Society of the Tiger's Tail from implementing it by pointing to the fact that their reckless violence would harm innocent people; however, his attempts at persuasion were in vain.[22] Yamaoka took a much more sober and balanced view of the developments in the country and understood well that any attempt to "expel the barbarians" would bring catastrophic consequences for both the Bakufu and Japan.[23]

The radicals, such as those of the Society of the Tiger's Tail, sought to exclude foreigners from the country, and for the later generations, their exclusionist position might look like an emotional and irrational fantasy, but until 1863, loyalism and exclusionism, combined in the slogan "revere the Emperor, expel the barbarians," were taken seriously by many young men. They were motivated by hatred of foreigners, which in their minds was inseparably linked with veneration for the emperor and the imperial court.

Lacking responsibility for negotiation and government, full of enthusiasm for the martial values of their own culture, and not having much knowledge about the might of the West, these men were willing to trust in the strength of their traditional weapon and spirit to repel the Westerners.[24] Kiyokawa's use of violence, however, was more deliberate. For him, the terrorist activity against the foreigners was a means to provoke a major conflict between the Bakufu and foreign powers that would accelerate the Bakufu's early collapse.[25] The evidence suggests that Kiyokawa did not have any real concern about the catastrophic consequences that would follow large-scale war between Japan and foreign powers, and in this, he was a typical Restoration activist, who tended to think only of immediate goals. It was the special ability of these men to create disorder in which others might come to the fore, but they themselves were often little prepared with alternatives.[26]

Details of Kiyokawa's scheme to murder all foreigners in Yokohama were discussed in the winter and spring of 1861 at the regular meetings of the society. During the final meeting, held sometime in the middle of May 1861, the following plan was worked out: after the extermination of all foreigners in Yokohama in August or September of the same year, they would issue a call to action and gather men of like mind from all over Japan. They would kill anyone who stood in their way, be it the shogun or a daimyo. Next, they would appeal to the emperor, stand under the Brocaded Banner symbolizing the emperor's punitive expedition against "the enemies of the imperial court," dictate terms to the whole country, and as Kiyokawa always liked to say, "turn the Realm upside down," that is, restore the imperial rule. If they failed, they would go on a violent rampage around the whole of Eastern Japan, gather more like-minded men, and pursue their goal until their death.[27]

It was decided that from that point on, they should direct their efforts at rallying more like-minded men and at the same time dissolve the Society of the Tiger's Tail for a while because its regular meetings could attract unnecessary attention.[28] Unfortunately for the society, and fortunately for Japan and the Bakufu, their decision to disband was a little late. There was a buckwheat-noodle shop near Kiyokawa's private academy whose owner was a Bakufu informer.[29] This man saw the gatherings of strange-looking men who spoke different dialects. He sent his adopted son to overhear what was going on in Kiyokawa's academy and reported everything to the Bakufu authorities.[30]

Seeing that the activity of Kiyokawa and his fellows had started to assume serious dimensions, to the degree that it threatened national security, the Bakufu authorities made a decision to take urgent measures to prevent the group from realizing its scheme. Since the information overheard by the son of the informer was insufficient to arrest the whole group at one stroke, they made up a plan to provoke them into a violation of law. However, on May 20, 1861, everything ended with the killing of another Bakufu informer who, under the disguise of a drunk craftsman, was sent to provoke Kiyokawa when he, with his six associates, was returning from a meeting with Restoration activists from the Mito Domain. Kiyokawa cut off the commoner's head right in the street but managed to escape arrest. Within a few days after the incident, several members of the Society of the Tiger's Tail fled to other domains, but most of them, as well as Kiyokawa's mistress, O-Hasu, were put in jail. On May 21, Kiyokawa left Edo, and from that time for a year and a half, he was in hiding from the Bakufu and Shōnai Domain authorities, traveling incognito all over the country and continuing his radical activities.[31] At this point, the Society of the Tiger's Tail ceased to exist.

Besides Yamaoka Tesshū, there were two other retainers of the shogun who attended the meetings of the Society of the Tiger's Tail. One of them was Matsuoka Yorozu (Shōichirō); the name of the other is unknown.[32] It is interesting that after the disbandment of the society, none of them went into hiding, was arrested, or was even scrutinized.[33] Two petitions submitted by Yamaoka and Matsuoka to Bakufu authorities shortly after the killing incident show that not only did Yamaoka and Matsuoka keep their distance from the other members of the society, but to a degree, they also secretly cooperated with the Bakufu authorities, conducting surveillance of the activity of the society, although the latter was probably done largely against their own will.[34] According to one of the petitions, the Bakufu was going to make Yamaoka and Matsuoka testify face-to-face against the arrested members of the society at its supreme court using an insignificant note of the two as evidence. However, their attempts at persuasion appear to have brought results: there was no trial or testifying against the members of the society at the Bakufu supreme court. Furthermore, neither Kiyokawa nor any other member of the society ever found out that Yamaoka and Matsuoka had spied on them, and they remained on good terms.

As noted earlier, Yamaoka Tesshū distinguished between loyalty to the Bakufu and loyalty to the shogun and the Tokugawa family, and these two petitions prove this once again clearly. The distinction between the two loyalties explains why Yamaoka conducted surveillance against the members of the Society of the Tiger's Tail and at the same time supported them before and after the killing incident. He saw the root of evil in the country in the bureaucratic apparatus of the Bakufu and realized that its end was near, but as the direct retainer of the shogun, he strove to do his best to preserve the well-being of the Tokugawa family. Yamaoka was not alone in such thinking; many *bushi* of other domains also preferred to believe that their lord, who might temporarily be the victim of bad advice or wicked councilors, was really on their side.[35]

The Rōshigumi Affair

For a short period of time, from December 1862 to April 1863, Yamaoka served as one of the Bakufu supervisors of the Rōshigumi group.[36] The Rōshigumi consisted of several hundred *rōshi* (warriors without a master, armed commoners, rogues, gamblers, and other dangerous elements of society). It was gathered by the Bakufu on the eve of the Shogun Tokugawa Iemochi's visit to the imperial court in Kyoto, which was going to be the first such visit in 230 years. The visit was intended to be the final step toward the realization of the unity of the imperial court and the Bakufu in order to stabilize the political situation in the country. Besides the shogun, all the top officials of the Bakufu had to be in Kyoto, which presented an extremely hostile environment for them; the terrorist activity of Restoration activists in the old capital reached its peak at the time and was accompanied by brutal assassinations of Bakufu supporters.[37] Under these circumstances, the regular Bakufu troops were not sufficient to stop the activists. A special force like the Rōshigumi was needed to deal with the activists in the same inhumane and guerilla manner they dealt with Bakufu supporters.[38]

To gather the *rōshi*, the Bakufu cooperated with Kiyokawa Hachirō, who was amnestied in January 1863 after a year and a half of hiding following the killing incident. It was Kiyokawa who suggested to the Bakufu that dangerous elements of the society (the *rōshi*) could be used for the Bakufu's benefit if properly manipulated. It appears that, at this point, Kiyokawa had temporarily abandoned the idea of the forceful overthrow of the Bakufu and had started to believe sincerely in the Bakufu's promise to "expel the barbarians" (drive all foreigners out of Japan), which it had given to the imperial court in October 1861.[39] After a period of hesitation (the employment of *rōshi* by the Bakufu was an unprecedented matter), the top Bakufu officials decided to follow Kiyokawa's advice and recruited the Rōshigumi, advertising the higher goals of serving the national cause in a time of crisis and "expulsion of the barbarians," which broadly corresponded to Kiyokawa's long-cherished idea of the large-scale extermination of foreigners.

However, quite soon, Kiyokawa realized that the Bakufu's true intention was the oppression of his allies in Kyoto with the help of the Rōshigumi. Kiyokawa felt this gave him no option but to resort to acting independently of the Bakufu and in defiance of its policy. On February 29, 1863, after the Rōshigumi had already been in the old capital, he managed to get an edict from the imperial court exhorting the Rōshigumi to "expel the barbarians." The case was unprecedented: the imperial court gave its edict to the men employed by the Bakufu without consulting with the Bakufu first.[40] Both the Rōshigumi and its informal leader, Kiyokawa Hachirō,[41] became untouchable by the Bakufu because they were protected by the imperial edict. Kiyokawa could openly proceed to the realization of his scheme to exterminate foreigners in Yokohama, and the Bakufu was powerless to restrain him.

Upon the Rōshigumi's return to Edo,[42] Kiyokawa immediately proceeded with the realization of his plan to massacre the foreigners in Yokohama, the start date for which was scheduled for April 15, 1863. His plan presumed a massive assault by several hundred members of the Rōshigumi on Yokohama, after which they were supposed to attack the Bakufu army headquarters in Kanagawa, take money, provisions, and ammunition; then they would go to Kai Province and capture Kōfu Castle, making it their base. From there, they were going to issue a call to the whole country under the coverage of the will of the imperial court and recruit more people of like mind. The retaliation of the foreign powers would force the Bakufu into war, and all the Restoration activists of Japan were supposed to become the "demons guarding the sacred traditions of Japan."[43]

Kiyokawa's activity ended with his assassination on April 13, 1863 by order of the Bakufu.[44] Political assassination was a rather common practice in other domains at the time; however, it was an unusual measure in the case of the Bakufu. In a sense, Kiyokawa had not left the Bakufu any other choice: he was under the cover of the imperial court, and at the same time, his reckless terrorist activity presented danger not only to the Bakufu but to the whole country. From the point of view of the Bakufu officials, there was no other way but to eliminate him physically.

Further actions of the Bakufu were quick and resolute. On April 15, all Kiyokawa's closest associates were arrested. The Rōshigumi was turned over to the Shōnai Domain, renamed Shinchōgumi, and put in charge of helping Shōnai troops patrol the streets of Edo. The same day, the Rōshigumi supervisor, Yamaoka Tesshū, and the Rōshigumi superintendent (*rōshi toriatsukai*, the highest post in the Rōshigumi), Takahashi Deishū, were relieved of their duties and put under house arrest.[45]

Yamaoka did not leave any materials that could shed light on his involvement in the Rōshigumi affair. Neither are there any materials that would help us understand how he became a Rōshigumi supervisor. There is no doubt that Yamaoka was aware of the Bakufu's reason for sending the Rōshigumi to Kyoto. However, in this case, it appears that his loyalty to the Tokugawa family overrode all other priorities, even those that pertained to his moral principles. Yet some insight into his motives in the affair can be gained from the recollections of his wife's brother, Takahashi Deishū, whose way of thinking seems to have been very close to Yamaoka's. Takahashi became the Rōshigumi superintendent on the eve of the group's return to Edo from Kyoto. At the time, he was an acting senior teacher of spearmanship at the Bakufu Military Institute, and he opposed the idea of the creation of the Rōshigumi from the very beginning.[46] After Kiyokawa Hachirō obtained the imperial edict, the Bakufu for its part took measures to strengthen its control of the Rōshigumi on the way back to Edo. Ironically, on March 7, 1863, Takahashi, who had objected to the creation of the Rōshigumi, was appointed to be another *rōshi* superintendent, largely against his will. Takahashi saw clearly what consequences the whole

Rōshigumi affair as well as Kiyokawa's affiliation with it would bring, and his prediction that "I will not serve even for a month by any possible contingency…Because I will either incur suspicion from the Bakufu senior councilors, or the *rōshi* will take off my head…"[47] was very precise: just a little more than a month after his appointment, Takahashi was dismissed and put under house arrest along with Yamaoka.

It is natural to suppose that, like Takahashi, Yamaoka also knew well that his supervisory role in the Rōshigumi would not bring him any good. However, he accepted it either against his own will as Takahashi did, or as a kind of self-sacrifice on his part for the sake of the Tokugawa family's cause. In contrast to the interpretation by all of Yamaoka's biographers of his role in these events, his involvement in fact led him to play a decisive role in the Rōshigumi's undoing. Yamaoka did this by taking the most valuable thing for Kiyokawa—the original of the imperial edict. Kiyokawa took all possible measures for the edict's safekeeping, and he was always accompanied by bodyguards. Yamaoka knew that Kiyokawa would show the document to him because they were close friends, and one day, while they were still in Kyoto, Yamaoka asked Kiyokawa if he could read its contents. It is not clear whether Yamaoka did this of his own accord or he was given an order. Whatever the case, Kiyokawa gave the edict to Yamaoka readily and never saw it again. Yamaoka passed it to the *rōshi* superintendent Udono Kyūō, who refused to return the edict to Kiyokawa under the pretext that it was addressed not to a particular individual but to the Rōshigumi as a whole. It is said that Udono gave the edict to the Bakufu senior councilor Itakura Katsukiyo in Kyoto. Thus, the imperial edict to the Rōshigumi was hushed up, its contents were lost, and it did not survive to our time.[48]

As a result of the Rōshigumi affair, Yamaoka spent eight months under house arrest. On the evening of November 15, 1863 a fire broke out in Edo Castle. Yamaoka and Takahashi left their houses without permission, gathered other Bakufu retainers living in the neighborhood, and rushed to guard the castle outside its gates. They were risking their lives because the breach of house arrest could be punished by death. However, the Bakufu officials recognized the revelation of utmost loyalty in their conduct, and in December 1863 the two were released.[49]

Chapter 4

"The Truth of the Ancient Ways"— The Beginning of the Quest

Ten Fists

Yamaoka's stance on the turmoil in the internal politics of the Bakumatsu period may be characterized as aloofness, and the only evidence of his involvement in political events of the time was his minor affiliation with the Society of the Tiger's Tail (1860–1861) and his short-term participation in the Rōshigumi affair (December 1862 – April 1863), which were discussed in the previous chapter. Instead, in the late 1850s and 1860s, he devoted as much time as possible to his own *musha shugyō*, as well as to teaching swordsmanship at the Military Institute. Yamaoka's aloofness with regard to politics may be explained by his belief that participation in political struggles and intrigues would inevitably put him at risk of misusing his swordsmanship skills with the consequent unnecessary loss of human life. This was against his moral principles (and religious conscience) and contradicted the very foundations of his *musha shugyō*, which strove for the ideal of the "life-giving sword." Yamaoka does not appear to have ever explicitly used the term "life-giving sword," but, in one of his writings on swordsmanship, he stated that "a swordsman who pursues the [ultimate] truth of swordsmanship" must avoid bloodshed.[1] Furthermore, the fact that there is no evidence that, as a senior swordsman, he was entangled in any kind of bloodshed in the Bakumatsu turmoil may be regarded as the direct realization of the concept of the "life-giving sword."

As noted earlier, Yamaoka held the *chūmokuroku menkyo* rank of Hokushin Ittō-ryū swordsmanship. This gave him the right to establish his own branch training hall and have disciples. However, he chose to reject this. By this time, he had already started to question the practicability of Hokushin Ittō-ryū sword skills in actual combat. From Yamaoka's point of view, Chiba Shūsaku's "modernization" and "rationalization" now seemed to be nothing more than a distortion of the original Ittō-ryū tradition. In another writing on swordsmanship, Yamaoka even criticized Chiba's famous match with Ōishi Susumu, which took place in the early 1830s. Implicitly pointing to the fact that Chiba's whole technical system was removed from the realities of the battlefield, he wrote:

A match between Ōishi Susumu and Chiba Shūsaku was held. They say that Ōishi used the bamboo sword of more than five *shaku* long,[2] and to oppose him Chiba used as a guard of his bamboo sword a lid of a large barrel.[3] Their match was a mere lark, and was not what I call "swordsmanship."[4]

Written criticism of the founder of a contemporary swordsmanship school, especially a school that was one of the most famous in the Bakumatsu period and early Meiji era, was extremely rare. This shows the degree to which Yamaoka was upset with what he saw as the deviation of Hokushin Ittō-ryū from his standards of the genuine warrior culture.

Nor was Yamaoka satisfied with what he saw at other private swordsmanship training halls or the Bakufu Military Institute, and his criticism was directed not only toward Hokushin Ittō-ryū but also toward the way Japanese swordsmanship in general was taught and learned by his contemporaries. In the following private note, he expressed his view as follows:

Since great antiquity ten fists (*totsuka*) has been considered standard for the length of the sword.[5] Ten fists is half the length of our body. This is why, if we combine the sword with the half of our body, it will become a part of us when facing an enemy...Since ancient times all those who acquired fame in the world with swordsmanship and transmitted their schools through their family lines, used sword training substitutes[6] ten fists long or less. However, in the Tempō years, there was a man in the Yanagawa Domain whose name was Ōishi Susumu. He was the first one to make the bamboo sword more than five *shaku* long because he strove recklessly for victory in matches. He came to Edo, engaged in matches in all training halls and was extremely victorious...Since that time most practitioners of swordsmanship schools do not know the truth of the ancient ways anymore. Following the general trend around them, they think that the long bamboo sword gives an advantage. The shallowness of their practice and absence of knowledge should be lamented. Those who want to study swordsmanship at all should not seek meretricious victories...Nowadays the one who wants to revive the Way of the Sword should first of all make the bamboo sword according to the ancient method and use it to acquire the ability to handle the real sword in actual combat.[7]

In another writing Yamaoka unreservedly states that all swordsmanship schools, including Shintō Munen-ryū, Shingyōtō-ryū, and the factions and branches of Shinkage-ryū and Ittō-ryū, had abandoned the legacy of their original founders and fallen into using the extralong bamboo swords, which made them mere descendants of Ōishi Susumu.[8]

Why was the length of the "ten fists" so important? As Yamaoka points out, the "ten fists" length of the Japanese long sword historically was deemed as best fitting the physique of Japanese people. The first mention of this ideal length can be found in *Kojiki* (*A Record of Ancient Matters*, AD 712) and *Nihon shoki* (*Chronicles of Japan*, AD 720). Here, the sword appears in various mythological scenes under the name of *totsuka no tsurugi*, or "ten fists long sword"[9] (this term is not a proper noun and refers to different swords in different myths[10]).

Yamaoka emphasized that the length of the long sword measured in "ten fists" allowed a swordsman to feel it as an inseparable part of his body. This measurement was referred to as *jōsun*, the "standard length," and was employed by most military arts schools all over Japan from the pre-Tokugawa ages. For example, this length is preserved in the oldest military arts school in Japan, Tenshinshō-den Katori Shintō-ryū, which was established in the middle of the fifteenth century. The school teaches that one has to consider the sword as an extension of the body and command it as if manipulating one's own fingers. The school also warns against using excessively long and heavy weapons, because it leads to a loss of speed in actual combat.[11]

The length of the long sword also relates directly to one of the most fundamental principles in Japanese swordsmanship—"distancing" (*maai*). This principle refers to the constant awareness of the proper distance that a swordsman must maintain between himself and his opponent to be able to reach the opponent's body and yet protect his own. The majority of those who trained with long bamboo swords in the Bakumatsu period continued to wear real swords of the "ten fists" length in their daily life. Needless to say, it was hardly possible to switch between the sense of distance with the long bamboo sword developed during many years of training and the sense of distance with a much shorter, real sword when actual combat erupted. Furthermore, shorter distances require faster movement and shorter reaction times, which cannot be developed without the appropriate training.

Accounts of inefficient distancing on the battlefield can be found in historical records. Many Japanese who used the real sword during the second Sino-Japanese War (1937–1945) testified that, in the beginning, they could not reach their Chinese opponents' bodies even with the sword tip. This was because of their improper sense of distance. It took them time (i.e., repeat failures) to gain the proper sense.[12] These Japanese were fortunate because their enemy did not oppose them with swords. Otherwise, one such failure would have almost definitely cost them their lives. In overlooking such matters, Japanese scholarship and swordsmanship historiography have consciously or unconsciously hushed up a simple fact: that all those who engaged in free sparring with the long bamboo sword from the time of the Bakumatsu period were poorly qualified for using the real sword in actual combat.[13]

It appears that, in the Bakumatsu period, Yamaoka Tesshū was one of the few individuals who demonstrated a real concern about the length of the *bushi* traditional weapon and actually applied the traditional length to his sword-training substitute.[14] However, there is no evidence that the majority of other swordsmanship practitioners of the time questioned the discrepancy between the length of the real sword and its training substitute. The long-lasting Great Tokugawa Peace resulted in a near universal oblivion of both the realities of actual combat and the proper use of arms in warrior society from the lowest strata to the highest. This is particularly evident from the Bakufu's decision to limit the length of the bamboo sword to *san shaku hassun* (3.8 feet) for the training of its retainers at the Military Institute.[15] The Bakufu was worried about the widespread use of extralong bamboo swords. Nevertheless, *san shaku hassun* was still about seven inches longer than the average length of the real sword worn in daily life. The discrepancy remained far too great in Japanese swordsmanship, where just one inch of improper distancing in real engagement could lead to fatal consequences.[16]

A Farewell to Interschool Matches

Yamaoka Tesshū was not alone in his criticism of the ways of swordsmanship training. Another prominent swordsman of the Bakumatsu period, Kubota Sugane (1791–1866) of Tamiya-ryū school, criticized all schools of swordsmanship for losing touch with the skills of handling the real sword.[17] However, it appears that Yamaoka went further than his fellow contemporary critics by pointing specifically to the harm that engagement in interschool matches was bringing to their practitioners. This is clear from the following document, written by Yamaoka early in the Meiji era, when he had already opened his Shumpūkan training hall.

[In the distant past], when founders established their schools, they developed training methodologies based on their refinements in swordsmanship. At present there is no one who preserves these methods of training or truly practices them. In general, people merely pursue victory with the long bamboo sword. When I think of the reason for this, there is no one who knows the fundamental truths of swordsmanship, and everyone just follows fads and is preoccupied with outward embellishment of their movements. That is why, when it comes to using the real sword in actual combat, even if they win, it is by luck, and it is hard to say that they gained a real and self-evident victory. My point of view is different. I maintain that, regardless of outward appearance, one should achieve peace of mind through the true principles [of handling the sword] and the natural victory. If you want to master the truth of this Way, it is my rule that the beginner should enter and train in my school for three years and develop his body well [according to the principles of the school]. That is to say, when tempering your body, it should be done in the natural way…You will build the "swordsmanship body" and achieve the level when you do not deviate from the principles of my school, even when confronting a practitioner of some other school. If you really want to train in swordsmanship, [you should keep in mind that] for three years I prohibit those who join my school to go to other swordsmanship training halls, so popular nowadays, and recklessly engage in matches there. This is not because I do not want to send people who entered my school to other training halls. This is because I do not want them to negate their efforts to build the body according to the principles of my school. In no way can I welcome in my training hall those who do not pursue the true training in swordsmanship. I do not like useless waste of effort. Since ancient times all schools prohibited interschool matches. They did not allow this to their practitioners unless they were at the *menkyo* level of swordsmanship. This is how founders of all schools, who went through extreme hardship, contrived their Ways and developed their training methodologies. If you do not swear that you are The One who pursues the true training in swordsmanship, do not come to my training hall.[18]

These lines were written by a man who himself spent a great part of his life in interschool matches and finally realized the futility of training that was not based on the pre-Tokugawa methodologies developed exclusively for handling a real sword in actual combat.[19]

As we can see, besides the length of the bamboo sword, Yamaoka Tesshū's criticism, unlike that of his fellow swordsmen, included what he regarded as senseless engagement in interschool matches. However, even Yamaoka with his critical approach still exhibited certain forms of bias, especially in his belief that both free sparring and use of the bamboo sword and body protectors were necessary for training.[20] The same kind of belief was common to a handful of other more general contemporary critics of Japanese swordsmanship, such as the previously mentioned Kubota Sugane.[21]

Logically, the warfare methods invented during the Great Tokugawa Peace in the safe environment of training halls could not be more effective than those invented in times of constant wars. In the second half of the nineteenth century, when pre-Tokugawa training methodologies were practically forgotten, none of the critics of Japanese swordsmanship, including Yamaoka, appear to have taken into account the probability that, if the training in free sparring with the use of the bamboo sword and body protectors had been practical and led to outstanding performance in actual combat, it would have been invented long before the Tokugawa era.

Searching for Practical Swordsmanship and the Encounter with Asari Yoshiaki

As Yamaoka's writings indicate, he believed that the swordsmanship of his time had lost all connection with the realities of combat and had been turned into a kind of competitive sport or entertainment with excessively long bamboo swords. In a broader sense, he lamented the loss of the *bushi* intangible culture, which he considered to be based on a set of sacred and immutable standards belonging to the pre-Tokugawa ages, standards that were molded in life-and-death situations.[22]

Thus, Yamaoka Tesshū presents an exceptional case of a *bushi* who, in the end of the Tokugawa era, was convinced that Japanese swordsmanship deviated considerably, both technically and spiritually, from its original roots in the pre-Tokugawa ages. His own gift in swordsmanship and his intuition, combined with his awareness of the crisis in the country, undoubtedly played a major role in the way he perceived contemporary warrior culture. From Yamaoka's point of view, only the "ancient ways" (*kohō*) contained the truth. It is remarkable how often Yamaoka used such terms as "the ancient ways," "the truth of the ancient ways" (*kohō no shinri*), "antiquity" (*jōko*), or "since ancient times" (*korai*) in his writings. Yamaoka retained this longing for the past all his life, and later, when he was a prominent figure in the Meiji government, it distinguished him from the rest of the Meiji statesmen, who were far more prone to copy "Western" and "modern" ways.

Yamaoka did not confine himself to conceptual criticism. By trial and selection, he strove to acquire sword skills that would correspond to the standards of the pre-Tokugawa ages, as he perceived them. In 1859, at the age of twenty-four, he had already contrived his own method of training in free sparring that was aimed at making the training as close to the physical and mental realities of actual combat as possible. He called it "all-day-long withstanding sparrings" or "all-day-long multiple sparrings" (*shūjitsu tachikiri shiai* or *shūjitsu kazu shiai*). The idea was to train for the endurance required on the battlefield by engaging in two hundred free sparrings from early morning to late at night for seven successive days; this would total 1,400 incessant sparrings in just one week. He described his approach:

> Swordsmanship is the art that determines whether you stay alive or die on the battlefield. These days, people think that swordsmanship is a sport, and they are preoccupied only with competition; I have not seen anyone who would exert one's powers [during the training] as if he really were on the battlefield...If you train [in many successive sparrings], in the beginning, you may think that it is like the usual sparring, but after you have gone through sparrings with several hundred opponents, you will feel as if you are really on the battlefield. This is when the [true] spirit is born...This is the real swordsmanship. If you

do not train with this attitude, [your skills] will be useless on the battlefield, even though you may train for tens of years.[23]

Although this training was aimed at acquiring enormous physical stamina, it had a much more important goal: tempering one's spirit through training beyond the normal limits of the body's endurance. This was achieved through reaching the point where it was impossible to continue by mere physical effort and one could persevere only through the power of the spirit making the body work as if it were fresh and full of energy. In one of his private writings on swordsmanship, Yamaoka, who was not known to brag about his accomplishments, claimed that, in his youth, he used his spiritual power so well that he did not feel tiredness or weakness by the end of the seventh day.[24]

Still, Yamaoka remained concerned that his innovations in methodologies of swordsmanship training might not allow him to resurrect the "ancient ways" and, in failing, might actually lead him in a false direction. It appears that, up to this point, he had completely dismissed training in predetermined patterns of movement (*kata*) with the use of the wooden sword, which he contemptuously called the "dead method."[25] It is not difficult to understand why Yamaoka referred to this kind of training with such disdain—by his time, the majority of those schools that still wholly or partially used wooden imitations of weapons were characterized by ritualization, movement embellishment, and loss of speed during the training in *kata*. In no way could this "flowery training" satisfy Yamaoka. However, he had already started to feel that the handling of the sword in actual combat of the pre-Tokugawa ages must have been much more sophisticated than what was taught in the majority of Bakumatsu swordsmanship schools through free sparring with use of the bamboo sword and that the training methodologies aimed at achieving this sophistication must have been different.

In 1860, Yamaoka started to look for a new swordsmanship teacher.[26] At this stage, he was unaware of a fact that he would come to realize much later in his life: that what he was looking for was transmitted not in factions and branches of Ittō-ryū but only in its main line represented by the Ono family. He did not know that already in the first half of the Tokugawa era, a Confucian scholar, Ogyū Sorai, referring to factions and branches of Shinkage-ryū and Ittō-ryū, had written that "the fact that now they are exceedingly preoccupied with the beauty of their theatrical fighting techniques is [a sign of] the spirit of the peaceful time."[27] Probably lacking detailed knowledge of the history of Japanese swordsmanship, Yamaoka ironically chose Nakanishi-ha Ittō-ryū, the faction of Ittō-ryū that spread the kind of sportive swordsmanship he was desperately trying to escape. After a four-year search, during which he visited numerous training halls, in the spring of 1864, he encountered Asari Yoshiaki, the headmaster in the fifth generation of this school.[28] Yet Asari appears to have differed greatly from his predecessors and possessed, to a degree, sword skills practicable in real combat. In line with the secrecy of pre-Tokugawa schools of military arts, he preferred to stay in the shadows all his life. His small training hall of almost ten yards long and a little over three yards wide was located on the premises of the Katsuyama (Awa Province) Domain daimyo's residence in Edo and was concealed from the eyes of outsiders.[29] This is how Yamaoka described his first impression of Asari:

> I made every effort to find a man with the true understanding of swordsmanship. I searched everywhere but could not find such a man at all. It so happened that I heard about Asari Matashichirō[30] of Ittō-ryū. People said that he was...a master who had inherited the tradition of Itō Ittōsai. I felt delight upon hearing this, went to [Asari's place], and asked for a match. Indeed, his skill was much different from swordsmanship so fashionable in the world: behind his seeming softness was concealed inner strength, his spirit and breath were one, and he saw chances to win before the engagement...He really was a master with the true understanding of swordsmanship. Since then, every time I practiced with Asari, I had to admit to myself that my level was far from his.[31]

Actually, there is an eyewitness account of the first match between Yamaoka and Asari.[32] This account suggests the level of skill of the two in free sparring with the bamboo sword did not differ so much. However, according to the same eyewitness account, Yamaoka could not match Asari in a special kind of training in handling the wooden sword in low positions (*gedan jiai*). It was not free sparring, nor was it a predetermined pattern of movement (*kata*), but a special kind of training that avoided reckless competition and, at the same time, allowed for some freedom of action. The requirement was to constantly keep the hilt of the wooden sword at the center of one's body, near the abdomen. This prevented the swinging movements so characteristic of sparring with the bamboo sword that were equal to opening oneself up and exposing one's vital points to an opponent trained in the proper usage of the sword.[33] For Yamaoka, it was a new kind of training, and it made him re-evaluate *kata*-based methods of training that he had dismissed as "dead methods." He was forced to recognize that not all such methods ended so disappointingly and that it was not the training in *kata* itself that posed the problem but the oblivion of the pre-Tokugawa training methodologies that underlay them. It appears that the patterns transmitted by Asari were closer to the original Ittō-ryū tradition, that is, they had been better preserved against the "flowery training" and contained principles of handling the sword in actual combat. As the following discussion will show, however, even Asari's style did not avoid a degree of deviation from the original roots.

Shortly after Yamaoka met Asari, he concluded that there was no sense in the hasty and chaotic exchange of hits with the bamboo sword and that swordsmanship techniques should be precisely applied in a state of mental imperturbability. He also wrote that he had obtained the ability to judge instantly the technical level of his opponent just by observing his stance before the engagement began.[34] However, Yamaoka's quest for what he perceived as the authentic swordsmanship was not limited to the technical aspects of this art. He was simultaneously looking for the spiritual content that was supposed to play the role of "spokes" to the "wheel" of swordsmanship. Yamaoka did not find a spirit guide in Asari, and it was probably from this time that he started to practice the meditation of the Rinzai Zen sect under his first Zen teacher, Priest Gan'ō.[35] The choice of Rinzai Zen was not accidental; back in Takayama, Yamaoka's family had close ties with Sōyūji Temple belonging to this sect, and both Yamaoka's parents were buried there.[36] Henceforth, Yamaoka's daily routine consisted of training in swordsmanship during the day and meditation at night. In this period, he is said to have never gone to bed earlier than two o'clock in the morning.[37]

It should be stressed, however, that Yamaoka's absorption in Zen Buddhism was first of all rooted in his religious aspirations, not primarily in his quest for perfection in swordsmanship as all his biographers state. This is supported by the recollections of his live-in disciple, Ogura Tetsuju. Yamaoka once told Ogura that Zen Buddhism first caught his interest when he read the precept left by the famous monk of the Rinzai Zen sect of the Kamakura era, Daitō-kokushi (1282–1337).[38] The precept teaches the transience of time and the necessity of shaking off all worldly anxieties about food and clothes for the sake of realizing one's true nature.[39] Having a strong inclination to religion by birth, Yamaoka put this principle into practice and maintained it all his life, both before and after he began to study Zen seriously.

For Yamaoka, Zen Buddhism filled the spiritual vacuum left by the swordsmanship schools of the Bakumatsu period, which he felt had been completely stripped of deeper moral teachings, as in the case of Hokushin Ittō-ryū, or advocated empty theories of character perfection, as in the case of "flowery training." At the same time, like many of his contemporaries, Yamaoka also held on to the belief that the practice of Zen might elevate him to new heights of swordsmanship skill.[40] In his pursuit of what he believed to be the genuine warrior culture of the pre-Tokugawa ages, Yamaoka failed throughout his life to comprehend that it was esoteric Buddhism, not Zen, that had the most to do with the training and practical application of military skills among the *bushi* of the distant past.

Chapter 5

The Bloodless Surrender of Edo Castle

Finding the Right Messenger

With the exception of Yamaoka's joining the swordsmanship school of Asari Yoshiaki in 1864, the four-year period that followed his release from house arrest in December 1863 is a blank spot in his biography. It is clear that during this period Yamaoka quit the Bakufu Military Institute; however, neither the date nor the reason for Yamaoka's resignation are known.[1] House arrest and the resulting excess of spare time no doubt gave Yamaoka an opportunity to contemplate the events of the past few years. It would have been quite natural for him to come to realize how close he, as a swordsman pursuing the ideal of the "life-giving sword," had come to shedding blood during the Rōshigumi affair and that this was the direct outcome of his official service to the Bakufu, whose orders he had to obey. He most probably preferred to quit the official service in order to avoid the risk of further involvement in political violence and to devote himself entirely to his *musha shugyō* under Asari's guidance as well as his religious pursuits in Zen Buddhism.[2] However, even if Yamaoka had completely estranged himself from the political apparatus of the Bakufu, he never forgot about his warrior loyalty to the shogun and the Tokugawa family. The Meiji Restoration of 1868 put his loyalty to its most severe test.

January 3, 1868 witnessed the outbreak of the Boshin Civil War between the Bakufu and the new imperial government controlled by the powerful southern domains of Satsuma, Chōshū, and Hizen. The battles of Toba and Fushimi, in the vicinity of Kyoto, ended with the crushing defeat of the Bakufu and Shogun Tokugawa Yoshinobu's flight to Edo on January 12. The Bakufu's armed forces, particularly its navy, still posed a considerable threat to the imperial army, and for several weeks Yoshinobu vacillated between further war and surrender. Finally, he began to incline toward surrender; he dismissed the main advocates of continuing war among his entourage, and at the same time, advocates for peaceful reconciliation were put in charge of the most important affairs of the Bakufu. Among them were Katsu Kaishū, who became the commandant of the Bakufu army, and Ōkubo Ichiō, who was appointed the Bakufu finance minister.[3]

In order to break through the crisis, Yoshinobu and the top Bakufu officials made desperate efforts in two directions. One was the attempt to convey Yoshinobu's allegiance to the imperial government through sympathetic daimyos and connections in the imperial court; the other was the restructuring of the Bakufu apparatus, which led to a large-scale change of personnel and the promotion of a new system of government through public discussion. These efforts, however, did not produce any substantial results. By the end of January 1868 all the daimyos of Western Japan had sworn allegiance to the imperial government. On February 3 an imperial edict about the emperor's punitive expedition against the Bakufu was issued. On February 9 Arisugawanomiya, Imperial Prince Taruhito, was appointed to be commander-in-chief of the punitive expedition to the East, and a unified military chain of command that led the imperial army to Edo along Tōkaidō, Tōsandō, and Hokurikudō roads was established.[4] Under these circumstances, Yoshinobu officially announced his intention to surrender and secluded himself in Kan'eiji Temple in the Ueno District of Edo on February 12.[5]

After Yoshinobu's seclusion, the Bakufu repeatedly sent high-ranking messengers in order to convey his obedience and allegiance to the imperial government, but all were delayed or rejected. The situation was no better with members of the imperial government who sympathized with the Tokugawa family and appealed to stop the offensive on Edo. The imperial government either ignored their appeals or ordered them to contact the General Headquarters of the Imperial Army (hereafter referred to as General Headquarters). The latter was equal to a flat refusal because General Headquarters was moving the army to Edo and denied all appeals and petitions.[6] It is important to note a fact that has not received much attention among historians: the imperial government, for its part, never attempted to establish contact with the Bakufu to negotiate a peaceful surrender. This meant that the imperial government was firm in its determination to seize Edo with force even if it would have to exterminate Shogun Yoshinobu and the whole Tokugawa family.

Yoshinobu pinned his hopes most on Princess Kazunomiya, the widow of his predecessor, Shogun Iemochi. In the middle of February 1868, Princess Kazunomiya's messenger, Fuji, managed to obtain a reply from the imperial government that declared if it had evidence of the sincerity of Yoshinobu's wish to surrender, it would consider the possibility of letting the Tokugawa family survive. This was the first response of the imperial government that clearly stated its position. However, it was unofficial and conveyed secretly. Moreover, the basic policy of the imperial government remained unchanged.[7] It also should be mentioned that Princess Kazunomiya was not friendly to Yoshinobu, and her letter to the imperial government was prompted more by concern for her own well-being if Edo was attacked. She explicitly stated that she did not care about Yoshinobu's fate.[8]

On March 5, 1868 the commander in chief of the imperial army, Arisugawanomiya, arrived in the city of Sumpu, Suruga Province. The following day, General Headquarters held a military meeting during which the date of the all-out attack on Edo was scheduled for March 15.[9]

Yamaoka Tesshū as the Shogun's Emissary

Yamaoka Tesshū was suddenly vaulted into the center of events when the situation seemed absolutely hopeless for the Bakufu. As noted earlier, Yamaoka preferred to keep a low profile all his life, and his role in the bloodless surrender of Edo Castle, which had symbolized the political power of Tokugawa shoguns for several centuries, was no exception. Yet he left one writing on this event: "The writing about the negotiation with Saigō Takamori in the General Headquarters of the Imperial Army in Sumpu in March of the Boshin year of the Keiō era" (*Keiō Boshin sangatsu Sumpu Daisōtokufu ni oite Saigō Takamori-shi to dampan hikki*, 1882). This is usually abbreviated as *Boshin dampan hikki*; hereafter, it will be referred to as *BDH*.[10]

Yamaoka wrote *BDH* fifteen years after the bloodless surrender of Edo Castle. It was not intended for the public. The only thing that is known regarding its printing is that *BDH* started to circulate in print after Yamaoka's disciples published it without his permission.[11] Copies of this document can be found under slightly different titles in the archives of Japan's governmental institutions, such as the Imperial Household Archives. Its credibility is accepted by historians[12] and can be confirmed by the report of a retainer of the Kumamoto Domain, diaries of Katsu Kaishū and Ernest Satow, and a letter by Iwakura Tomosada, all of which will be mentioned later in this chapter. However, *BDH* has not received the attention it deserves; historians have overlooked some very important points of the text and made no attempt to compare it with other contemporary records.

First, it is necessary to address the question of how such a low-ranking retainer of the shogun as Yamaoka came to be chosen to go to Sumpu to convey Tokugawa Yoshinobu's assurance of his allegiance to the imperial government.[13] The threat to the shogun's life had become very real, to the degree that Yamaoka could not estrange himself anymore from the events of the time. In January 1868, he became an acting commander of Sei'eitai, a troop consisting of over three hundred Bakufu retainers who volunteered to guard Yoshinobu, and from February 12, the day when Yoshinobu secluded himself in Kan'eiji Temple in Ueno, guarded the outward perimeter of the shogun's new residence. The inner perimeter and interior were guarded by the Yūgekitai, whose commander was Takahashi Deishū, the brother of Yamaoka's wife.[14]

According to the chronological record of Yamaoka's life compiled by Murakami Yasumasa, it was Takahashi Deishū who recommended Yamaoka to the shogun.[15] Both Yoshinobu and the closest members of his entourage understood that the imperial government had refused to recognize the authority of all previous emissaries to represent the Tokugawa family, despite their high social standing.[16] Furthermore, this elite status made them excessively visible and often resulted in their detention en route by the imperial outposts. No doubt that is why it was decided to send a retainer whose low rank would make him less visible and more difficult to intercept. However, taking into consideration the difficulty of the task and the high risk of failure, the requirements for any such emissary were fearlessness, unstinting devotion to the shogun, and a readiness to sacrifice his life for him. Takahashi knew that Yamaoka possessed all these qualities, so it was quite natural that he recommended Yamaoka to the shogun.

Tokugawa Yoshinobu granted Yamaoka an audience on March 5.[17] As one committed to *musha shugyō*, Yamaoka absolutely insisted on sincerity, and despite his rank, he agreed to undertake this mission only after receiving Yoshinobu's personal commitment that he did not intend a double-dealing and that his intention to surrender was sincere. This is how Yamaoka recalled their dialogue in *BDH*:

> I asked my former lord, "Today, in this time of crisis, what is your intent behind the surrender?"

> My former lord replied in tears: "Although I revealed the utmost sincerity of my goodwill toward the Imperial Court by secluding myself, it seems there is no way I can live out my days since I have been labeled 'the enemy of the imperial court' by the imperial order. How sad that everyone hates me so much."

> I told my former lord: "Why are you whining and saying trifling things? You say you secluded yourself, but isn't there any deceit behind your seclusion? Aren't you plotting something else?"

> My former lord said: "I have no other intention. Whatever happens, I am absolutely sincere [in my resolution] not to oppose the Imperial Orders."

> I said: "If you have secluded yourself from true sincerity, your intent will reach the Imperial Court, and your anxiety will definitely be alleviated. I, Tetsutarō,[18] give my word, and I will exert myself to make sure that your sincerity is conveyed, at any cost."

In terms of the mental attitudes he demanded of a warrior, Yamaoka was ready to accept an order from the shogun and sacrifice himself only if that order was sincere. Yamaoka understood very well that when the country was on the brink of a large-scale civil war, any attempt on the part of the Bakufu to conceal hostile intentions behind a false surrender would make further war inevitable, and he did not want to promote an agenda that would guarantee large-scale loss of human life.

The dialogue between Yamaoka and Yoshinobu described in *BDH* demands our attention: a low-ranking retainer of the Bakufu not only dared to challenge the shogun's true intentions before accepting an order but even used language that treated Yoshinobu almost on equal terms. The usual assumption is that the warrior society of premodern Japan, as with any military structure, had a strict discipline that left no room for objections to seniors' orders. Nevertheless, the dialogue between Yamaoka and Yoshinobu suggests this was not always the case. Such attitudes did not mean a lack of discipline. They were similar to the *bushi* concept that warrior-writer Daidōji Yūzan expressed as "armor knows no etiquette."[19] This meant that, at war, the daily etiquette of peace should be replaced with a different kind of straightforward relationship that measured everything in terms of the effective and timely achievement of the final result. Although not on a daily basis, this was supposed to make *bushi* resort to a new level of self-assertiveness in extraordinary situations, even if it was at the risk of punishment by death.[20]

Both Yoshinobu and his entourage apparently greatly appreciated this attitude—at this crucial moment in history when, not only days, but every minute mattered, Japan and the Tokugawa family would have been doomed by a low-ranking Bakufu retainer who, although brave enough to break through the enemy positions and convey the shogun's wish to surrender, could only blindly accept orders from the imperial government. They required another quality of character: an independence of mind that could engage in negotiations and win its point regardless of the social standing of the opposing party. Yamaoka possessed this quality, even to the degree that, according to his own recollections in *BDH*, he had the "reputation of a rude man."[21] From personal experience, Takahashi Deishū no doubt knew of this, and it was probably another reason why he recommended Yamaoka to the shogun. This was an extremely important quality that was to prove decisive in the events of March 1868.

In *BDH*, Yamaoka described his state of mind after the audience with the shogun:

> I swore to Heaven and Earth that, determined to die and traveling alone, I would go to the general headquarters of the imperial army, appeal to its commander-in-chief about [the shogun's] sincerity, and ensure the safety of the country. I thought: "…Throwing my life away to save millions of human lives in the country is what I have been willing to do for a long time." My soul was clear as a cloudless blue sky with shining sun…

These words clearly reveal Yamaoka's pursuit of the "life-giving sword," which was the extension of the broader Buddhist principle of self-sacrifice. It was the kind of *musha shugyō* that aimed at achieving unparalleled mastery in the art of killing over decades, attached supreme importance to the ethical aspects of the application of the warrior's professional skill, and at the same time presumed a readiness to throw one's life away instantly for the sake of saving others.

The Yamaoka-Saigō Meeting in Sumpu

After the audience with Yoshinobu, Yamaoka was left to his own devices. He did not, however, rush into what was potentially a suicidal mission. According to *BDH*, the same day, he went to discuss his plan with several high-ranking officials of the Bakufu. However, none of them approved of the plan because they deemed it absolutely unrealizable. Finally, Yamaoka decided to go to the commandant of the Bakufu army, Katsu Kaishū. He had heard that Katsu was a man of "courage and ingenuity."[22] Katsu was suspicious; after several assassination attempts, he was afraid that Yamaoka intended to kill him because, like some of the other radical Bakufu retainers, Yamaoka might perceive Katsu's policy of allegiance to the imperial government as a betrayal of the Tokugawa family.[23] In his memoirs, Katsu recollected this episode:

I heard only the name of Yamaoka before, and it was the first time we met. And what I heard from Ōkubo Ichiō and others is that I should be wary of Yamaoka because he is going to kill me, so I never met him...[24]

The rumor about Yamaoka was no doubt exaggerated, but it can tell us a lot about the degree to which he was devoted to the Tokugawa family. Seeing that Katsu's wariness and reluctance to give a definite answer made him lose precious minutes, Yamaoka resorted to the same straightforwardness he had used in the conversation with Yoshinobu:

Now is not the time to cling to such trifling things as the imperial court or the Bakufu. We need to cope with the national crisis by national unity! Why are you hesitating?[25]

Katsu then asked Yamaoka about his plan, and in reply, Yamaoka explained:

> There are only two options for me after I reach the general headquarters of the imperial army: either I will be slashed to death or arrested. I will hand my long and short swords to them, and if they arrest me, I will obey; if they decide to slash me to death, I will try to convey [Yoshinobu's obedience and allegiance] in a few words to the commander-in-chief of the imperial army. If what I say does not suit them, they will cut off my head on the spot. If what I say suits them, I will only tell them that I will take care of the matter myself.[26] It cannot be that they indiscriminately and vainly kill people. What's so difficult about this [mission]?[27]

As Katsu wrote in his diary, he was impressed by Yamaoka's character during this meeting. He finally agreed and gave Yamaoka a letter addressed to Saigō Takamori, staff officer to the imperial army's commander in chief.[28]

Yamaoka left for Sumpu on March 5, the same day he met with Katsu.[29] He was accompanied by his old acquaintance from the Society of the Tiger's Tail, Masumitsu Kyūnosuke. Masumitsu was one of the leaders of a gang which, by the order of Saigō Takamori, engaged in provocations against the Bakufu in Eastern Japan. He had been detained by the Bakufu, under Katsu Kaishū's supervision, since the burning of the base of the gang located in the Satsuma residence in the Mita District of Edo in December 1867.[30] According to *BDH*, Masumitsu came (more likely, was brought by Bakufu troops) to Yamaoka's home shortly before his departure and requested to accompany him on the way to Sumpu. Katsu released Masumitsu into Yamaoka's care because he knew that Masumitsu's Satsuma dialect would make the task of Yamaoka's breaking through the enemy outposts much easier.

Yamaoka undoubtedly rode a horse,[31] but it took him several days to cover the distance that would normally take only a day or a day and a half.[32] The main reason for his slow pace lay in the fact that in the beginning, he had to move alone, most probably at night; the first outposts he had to pass through were occupied by Satsuma troops, among whom there might have been some of Masumitsu's acquaintances, and Yamaoka had to part with Masumitsu for a while. In spite of Yamaoka's wariness, a Satsuma outpost once spotted him, and to get out of the predicament, he resorted to a nonstandard tactic—he loudly proclaimed his true identity by saying: "Yamaoka Tetsutarō, the retainer of the enemy of the imperial court, Tokugawa Yoshinobu, is going to the headquarters of the imperial army!" No one dared to stop him.[33] This can be confirmed by the report of a retainer of the Kumamoto Domain who states that, when Yamaoka was halted by Satsuma troops, he told them: "The direct retainer of the Tokugawa family, Yamaoka, is going to meet with the staff of the imperial army headquarters Saigō on the business of his lord. He has no intention to fight. If you want to cut off his head, cut it off!"[34]

According to *BDH*, after passing through the Satsuma outposts, Masumitsu rejoined Yamaoka, and they proceeded easily to Sumpu through outposts held by other domains. On this leg of the journey, Yamaoka traveled behind Masumitsu, who identified both of them as Satsuma retainers, and the latter's Satsuma dialect seems to have worked better than any official pass.

Yamaoka reached Sumpu on March 9.[35] Katsu Kaishū's letter addressed to Saigō Takamori and Masumitsu's company seemed to have played their role; according to *BDH*, contrary to Yamaoka's expectations, he was immediately allowed to meet with Saigō. Their meeting in Sumpu became the basis for the realization of the bloodless surrender of Edo Castle and, consequently, brought about the ultimate outcome of the Meiji Restoration as we know it. Despite its importance, outside of *BDH* and the report of the aforementioned Kumamoto retainer appearing in Ishii Takashi's study of the Boshin Civil War,[36] there are no sources documenting the conversation. However, the two are generally in agreement on the content and the mood of the meeting. Furthermore, some entries in Katsu Kashū's and Ernest Satow's diaries regarding the results and consequences of this meeting serve as direct evidence supporting the credibility of Yamaoka's account. Given the significance of the Yamaoka-Saigō meeting, it is worth quoting the most important parts of the conversation from *BDH*.

Yamaoka: Is the purpose of your punitive expedition against the "enemy of the imperial court" an offensive that takes no consideration of the intentions of the opponent? Our Tokugawa family has many warriors too. Our lord Tokugawa Yoshinobu has secluded himself in Tōeizan Bodaiji Temple[37] [to express his wish] to surrender, and he did his best to persuade his retainers to do the same, but after all, he cannot control all of them. There are many Bakufu retainers who are going to resist the Will of the Imperial Court, or escape and plot a rebellion. This is the reason why you continue the offensive that ignores the intentions of the opponent. That is why, although our lord Tokugawa Yoshinobu respects the utmost sincerity of the goodwill and proper relationship between lord and retainer, his true intent has not reached the imperial court. I am deeply concerned with this state of affairs, and [that is why] I came to appeal to the commander-in-chief of the imperial army and to convey to you Yoshinobu's sincerity.

In the beginning, Saigō seemed to be unpersuaded by Yamaoka's appeal.

Saigō:　　We have already received a report about the beginning of [enemy] military operations in Kai Province. It is different from what you say.

Yamaoka:　This was done by runaway Bakufu retainers...

Saigō appeared to accept this but remained suspicious. Yamaoka also challenged Saigō, asking him:

Yamaoka:　Do you want to fight to the end of the world and engage exclusively in killing people? If so, [your army] can hardly be called the "army of the Emperor." The emperor is the parent of his people. It is said that it is the "army of the Emperor" that distinguishes between right and wrong.

Saigō's reply was conciliatory:

Saigō:　　It is not that I am fond of continuing the offensive. It is necessary merely to satisfy the conditions of surrender, and we will offer lenient treatment.

Yamaoka:　What are the conditions? Of course, Yoshinobu will not oppose the imperial order.

Saigō apparently began to show respect for Yamaoka, making a distinction between him and the shogun's previous envoys:

Saigō: The other day, the shogun's messengers from Seikan'in no Miya[38] and Tenshōin-dono[39] came. They spoke about his wish to surrender and seclusion, but they were so nervous that we could not understand anything. They had to go back without any result. Thanks to you who came to our place, I have understood the situation in Edo. It suits us very well. I will convey the contents of our talk to the commander-in-chief...

After a while, Saigō brought the following seven conditions.

1. In line with Yoshinobu's courageous decision to seclude himself and surrender, he should be deported to the Bizen Domain.
2. Surrender [Edo] Castle.
3. Surrender all warships.
4. Surrender all weapons.
5. Move all shogun retainers residing inside [Edo] Castle to Mukōjima and put them on their best behavior.
6. Supporters of Yoshinobu's thoughtless action[40] will be carefully scrutinized, and they assuredly will be given a chance for apology [and rehabilitation].
7. The Emperor has no intention to persecute either the guilty or the innocent. [His justness] paves the way for stabilization [in the country]. [However], anyone who will resort to uncontrollable violence will be suppressed by the imperial army.[41]

These conditions had been created in advance of Yamaoka's arrival, as the imperial government had considered the possibility of Yoshinobu's surrender.[42] However, it seemingly needed someone with the character of Yamaoka to convince Saigō that the shogun was genuinely ready to submit and make him show the conditions.

As historian Haraguchi Kiyoshi notes, in spite of the high social standing of all previous envoys from the Bakufu side, the imperial government did not recognize them as representing the Tokugawa family. The Yamaoka-Saigō meeting in Sumpu was not a formal negotiation between representatives of the Bakufu and the imperial government, and like previous messengers, Yamaoka's main task was to convince Saigō of the sincerity of Yoshinobu's intentions. Nevertheless, the meeting was of the utmost importance because it allowed the leaders of the two opposing sides to establish their first contact through Yamaoka, and the Bakufu side was for the first time informed of the surrender conditions.[43]

Contrary to the memoirs of Katsu Kaishū, there is no evidence that Katsu's letter, which Yamaoka had brought to Sumpu, influenced Saigō in any way beyond helping Yamaoka to see him.[44] On the other hand, as Saigō clearly stated during the meeting, and as Haraguchi Kiyoshi admits, Yamaoka convinced Saigō <u>for the first time</u> of the sincerity of Yoshinobu's wish to surrender.[45] While virtually every historian has overlooked this conversation, it can be argued that this was the most decisive moment in the entire surrender process.

Another major point is that, at a certain stage during the meeting, Yamaoka deviated from his initial role and entered into negotiations, dismissing social conventions between himself and Saigō and even the imperial court. In essence, he began performing a secondary mission, one that Yoshinobu and his entourage had considered a possibility when they sent him. In *BDH*, Yamaoka describes the part of the meeting after Saigō brought the surrender conditions:

Saigō: We will offer lenient treatment to the Tokugawa family if these [seven] conditions are fulfilled.

Yamaoka: I receive them humbly. However, there is one condition that I cannot accept under any circumstances.

Saigō: Which one?

Yamaoka: To deport my lord Yoshinobu alone to Bizen. This is absolutely impossible. Whatever happens, as a retainer indebted to the Tokugawa family, under no circumstances can I accept this. It will result in the start of war and senseless destruction of tens of thousands of lives. It is not something that the army of the Emperor should do. In this case, you will be just a murderer. That is why, under no circumstances can I accept this condition.

Saigō: It is the imperial order.

Yamaoka: Even if it is the imperial order, under no circumstances can I accept it.

Saigō: It is the imperial order!

Yamaoka: If so, let's trade places and talk for a while. Assume that your lord Shimazu[46] made a mistake and was stigmatized as the "enemy of the imperial court," and in the time when the punitive expedition of the imperial army has been launched and he decided to surrender and secluded himself, you are in my position. To render the best service to your lord, you humbly accept the Imperial Order similar to the one issued to my lord Yoshinobu, immediately give up your lord, and remain an indifferent and passive observer. What do you think about the bond between the lord and the retainer? Under no circumstances can I bear this!

What was so important about the first condition that Yamaoka flatly refused to accept it? The imperial government intended to detain Yoshinobu on the half of Japan's territory that was under its full control and that was close to the southern domains that stood behind the Meiji Restoration. At the same time, the Bizen daimyo, Ikeda Mochimasa, was Yoshinobu's brother, and the imperial government apparently expected that this fact would alleviate the anxiety of Bakufu retainers about the safety of their lord. However, for Yamaoka, it was clear that attempts to confine the shogun on enemy territory would outrage the Bakufu retainer corps and pro-Bakufu domains and provoke a large-scale civil war with consequent foreign intervention.

It is essential to remember that Yamaoka and Saigō were, first of all, enemies, and during this conversation, Yamaoka was constantly walking the line between life and death. Saigō could give the order to execute Yamaoka at any moment just for the manner in which he spoke to him. Both were mutually aware of the other's position, and Yamaoka's flat refusal to accept the first surrender condition was all the more convincing because Saigō, as a Satsuma warrior himself, could not fail to recognize Yamaoka's determination to die for his cause.

Here, Yamaoka repeatedly refers to the importance of saving human lives, and he again demonstrates a readiness to throw his own life away for the sake of saving others. However, Yamaoka's insistence on the sanctity of human life did not move Saigō. For Saigō, the fact that the order was issued by the emperor seems to have overridden all other considerations. Still, there was one thing that even Saigō, as a "man of exceptional fidelity,"[47] could not ignore—the paramount value of loyalty. Yamaoka, after all, placed Saigō in his shoes and, insisting on the value of loyalty between a *bushi* and his lord, convinced him to reconsider the imperial order.

> **Saigō:** You are absolutely right. As to Tokugawa Yoshinobu, I give my word and will arrange everything. You do not have to worry at all.

The report of a Kumamoto retainer mentions not only the fact that Yamaoka petitioned to stop the offensive on Edo, but also that Yamaoka warned about the difficulty of surrendering warships and weapons.[48] Still, it appears that the latter was not a point he insisted on. Instead, Yamaoka's principal concern was avoiding indefensible bloodshed, which was in line with his lifelong pursuit of the "life-giving sword."

Revisiting Yamaoka Tesshū's Role in the Bloodless Surrender of Edo Castle

So far, among the vast number of academic and nonacademic works on the Meiji Restoration and the Boshin Civil War, as well as Japanese history textbooks, plus encyclopedias of Japanese history and historical figures, there has been no established theory in regard to Yamaoka's role in the bloodless surrender of Edo Castle. The most common references to his role are merely along the lines of "he realized it" (but together with Katsu Kaishū and others), "opened the path to its realization," "laid the groundwork for it," or was merely "Katsu Kaishū's messenger."

When it comes to historical sites and monuments that commemorate the bloodless surrender of Edo Castle, Yamaoka's role is usually omitted. Instead, one can see only the two participants of the formal stage of the negotiations (March 13–14, 1868), Katsu Kaishū and Saigō Takamori, as, for example, on a big mosaic picture on the west exit wall of JR Tamachi Station in Tokyo. Another example is Yūki Somei's (1875–1957) famous painting *Edo kaijō dampan* (Edo Castle Surrender Negotiations), which is exhibited permanently at the Seitoku Kinen Kaigakan Museum in Tokyo and reprinted in numerous history textbooks and other widely published sources.

Japanese historians have also been dismissive of Yamaoka. Ishii Takashi and Iechika Yoshiki mention that Yamaoka returned to Edo after merely "protesting" against the deportation of Tokugawa Yoshinobu to Bizen.[49] Another historian, Matsuura Rei, wrote that Yamaoka did not have any authority to negotiate with the imperial army, suggesting that whatever Yamaoka said during the Sumpu meeting had no effect at all.[50] In the most comprehensive study of the bloodless surrender of Edo Castle, Haraguchi Kiyoshi wrote that the results of the Yamaoka-Saigō meeting only strengthened the possibility of a peaceful surrender of Edo Castle. Haraguchi emphasizes Yamaoka's role in conveying Yoshinobu's sincere wish to surrender to the imperial government. However, he does not even comment on Yamaoka's refusal to accept the first condition, which he calls just an "objection."[51] Thus, the whole negotiation process has been perceived as consisting of only one stage, that is, the formal negotiations between Katsu Kaishū and Saigō Takamori held on March 13–14, 1868 in Edo. Yamaoka came to be perceived simply as Katsu Kaishū's messenger, or at the very most, as the one who laid the groundwork for Katsu's subsequent "single-handed success."

However, historians have seriously underestimated the significance of Yamaoka's refusal to accept the very first of the surrender conditions, as well as overlooked several important facts appearing in *BDH* and other contemporary records. At the end of the meeting in Sumpu, Saigō gave Yamaoka the General Headquarters pass that allowed him to return to Edo quickly.[52] Yamaoka arrived in Edo the next day, on March 10[53] and immediately reported the surrender conditions and Saigō's commitment to Tokugawa Yoshinobu, Katsu Kaishū, Ōkubo Ichiō, and other top officials.[54] According to *BDH*, all the top officials were delighted at hearing that the imperial army had been properly informed of the situation in Edo, and Yoshinobu's joy "could not be expressed with words." This can be confirmed by Katsu's diary in which he wrote that all of the high-ranking envoys from the Bakufu had been rejected and that "only Yamaoka [managed] to reach the General Headquarters and obtain these formal written orders from the staff. When he returned to Edo, all Bakufu officials were aghast and had nothing to say."[55] Katsu further praised Yamaoka:

> Yamaoka…met and talked with Saigō in Sumpu. He conveyed the will of our lord and brought back the letter and surrender conditions from the general headquarters of the imperial army. Oh! Yamaoka is imperturbable and brave, he is very intelligent, he represented the great will of our lord so well, he did absolutely everything, [and there is nothing else to desire]. Indeed, he is worth admiration and respect.[56]

It goes without saying that if the Yamaoka-Saigō meeting had given only a slight hope for a peaceful reconciliation between the Bakufu and the imperial government or merely had become the first point of their contact, such prudent and cautious politicians as Tokugawa Yoshinobu, Katsu Kaishū, and others would not have been in a hurry to express their delight and praise Yamaoka so effusively.

Furthermore, the following passage from *BDH* implies that the Sumpu meeting had much more significance than has hitherto been thought. Yamaoka wrote the following regarding what happened after he reported to the Bakufu (emphasis added):

> [The Bakufu] immediately made an announcement throughout the city of Edo. Its summary is as follows. "The negotiations with the staff of the general headquarters of the imperial army Saigō Kichinosuke are finished; because [the imperial government] will offer lenient treatment [to the Tokugawa family] after the surrender conditions are satisfied, citizens should refrain from panic and engage in their family business." It was written on public notice boards erected throughout the city. This is when the citizens got some sense of security. After that, Saigō arrived in Edo, Katsu Awa[57] and I met with him in the Satsuma residence in Takanawa and pledged to fulfill the [six] surrender conditions[58] that we negotiated the other day. Saigō agreed and suspended the offensive.

This demonstrates that the Bakufu was confident of the successful completion of the surrender right after the Sumpu meeting, that is, even before holding formal negotiations with the imperial government. Otherwise, it could not have resorted to such an administrative act as calming the million population of Edo through the public notices about the result of the negotiations, which, according to Yamaoka, were "finished." The credibility of Yamaoka's words cited above can be confirmed through the diaries of Ernest Satow, the interpreter for the British envoy to Japan, Harry Parkes. This is what Satow wrote about the atmosphere in Edo two days after Yamaoka's return:

> On the 12th I went up again for a three days' stay, and found the city much quieter, owing to a feeling that the terms offered to Keiki[59] would be such as he could accept.[60]

What was the result of the Yamaoka-Saigō meeting? The most burning question for the Bakufu was the treatment of the Tokugawa family as a whole, and Tokugawa Yoshinobu in particular. The first surrender condition on deporting Yoshinobu to Bizen was directly related to this question, and it outweighed the other six conditions. These six conditions were minor, that is, quite natural demands on the surrendering side that undoubtedly had been expected by the Bakufu. Yamaoka secured a solution to the first and principal condition, which otherwise would have become the sticking point in the overall process of surrender. In other words, in Sumpu, he made Saigō guarantee lenient treatment of the Tokugawa family and Yoshinobu. That was the reason for the delight of the Bakufu officials upon Yamaoka's return, and that was what allowed them to calm the population of Edo. Judging from the Bakufu officials' reaction, what Yamaoka did went far beyond their expectations.

It is necessary to mention that there were three, not two main participants of the March 13–14 formal negotiations that followed the Yamaoka-Saigō meeting in Sumpu. Yamaoka also participated in them on equal terms together with Katsu Kaishū and Saigō Takamori. In *BDH*, Yamaoka clearly stated his participation,[61] and it can be confirmed by a letter of Iwakura Tomosada, who was the governor-general of the imperial army responsible for controlling the Tōsandō region. In this letter, dated March 15, 1868, Iwakura listed the names of three Bakufu negotiators: Katsu Kaishū, Ōkubo Ichiō, and Yamaoka Tesshū.[62] In spite of his low rank, already at this point, Yamaoka was regarded as an equal by the top officials of both the imperial government and the Bakufu.[63] This is another bit of evidence of the importance of the Yamaoka-Saigō meeting; otherwise, having Yamaoka present during the formal stage of the negotiations would not make any sense.

In the aftermath of the Yamaoka-Saigō meeting in Sumpu, representatives of both the Bakufu and General Headquarters were in no hurry to relieve pressure on each other—they were unsure of the imperial government's decision concerning the final form of the seven surrender conditions. Katsu Kaishū made preparations to burn down Edo if the imperial government attempted to seize it. And even though the March 13–14 formal negotiations ended with the suspension of the all-out attack on Edo, on March 14, Saigō Takamori issued a provisional order that formally meant only a postponement of the attack (the final order came from the General Headquarters on March 17).[64]

Against such a background, the content of the March 13–14 formal negotiations, which produced the suspension of the all-out attack and whose importance thus has been stressed more than anything by academic and popular authors alike, contrasts greatly with the gravity of the situation. On March 13, Yamaoka and Katsu merely gave Saigō a list of questions aimed at clarifying each of the surrender conditions brought by Yamaoka on March 10.[65] On March 14, Yamaoka and Katsu gave Saigō a petition in which the Bakufu formally requested permission for Yoshinobu to seclude himself in the Mito Domain and made a counterproposal aimed at amending the minor surrender conditions to its advantage. Saigō did not comment on the contents of the petition; he promised to pass it on to General Headquarters, saying that he did not have enough authority to determine every item of the surrender conditions on his own. He did, however, issue a provisional order to postpone the all-out attack on Edo for an indefinite time.[66]

Furthermore, even Katsu Kaishū, in his unusually self-serving memoirs, described these negotiations as just a "street-corner chat."[67] There is probably a great deal of exaggeration in such an account. Nonetheless, there is no evidence of violent discussion during these negotiations.[68] This was because the violent stage of the negotiations had been successfully navigated in the Bakufu's favor by Yamaoka alone in Sumpu in the most important part of the negotiation process. In other words, the March 13–14 meetings in Edo were just a formalization of what had already been agreed upon earlier between Yamaoka and Saigō.[69] The imperial government never moved Yoshinobu to Bizen or any other place close to the southern domains. It had to be very careful in the choice of Yoshinobu's residence, because it was necessary at all times to take into consideration the reaction of the Bakufu retainers. Thus, the bloodless surrender of Edo Castle was conditional and the overall negotiation process consisted of not one, but two stages. And it was the first stage, that is, the negotiations between Yamaoka Tesshū and Saigō Takamori in Sumpu that made the bloodless surrender possible and predetermined the outcome of the Meiji Restoration, not the formal negotiations held in Edo as it has been generally accepted.[70]

An Extraordinary Promotion

On the eve of the all-out attack on Edo, the atmosphere in the country was explosive.[71] Had Yamaoka blindly accepted the first surrender condition when less than a week remained until the scheduled all-out attack on Edo, Japan would have been doomed to a catastrophic civil war. However, Yamaoka was not guided by narrow political considerations or even primarily by internal and external conditions of the moment. His actions and statements throughout the whole negotiation process were rooted in his *musha shugyō*, and more than anything, his motivation was drawn from the "life-giving sword" philosophy, which aimed to avoid unnecessary loss of human life.[72] In a very real sense, the destiny of the Tokugawa family and of Japan was in Yamaoka's hands, and the Bakufu (and later, the Meiji government) recognized this. Shortly after the March 13–14 meetings in Edo, Yamaoka experienced a sudden and extraordinary promotion within the Bakufu.

In line with the custom in warrior society, according to which a lord granted a blade to a retainer who had performed a great exploit for him, on April 10, 1868, the day before the formal surrender of Edo Castle, Tokugawa Yoshinobu rewarded Yamaoka with a treasured dagger made by Rai Kunitoshi, a famous swordsmith of the Kamakura era.[73] In April(i) 1868, only a month after Edo Castle was surrendered to the imperial army, Yamaoka was appointed to be simultaneously the Bakufu great inspector and superintendent of finance.[74] In May 1868, Yamaoka became a Bakufu political leader along with Katsu Kaishū and Oda Izumi no Kami.[75] A member of the imperial government's Tōsandō

Vanguard Headquarters, Tani Kanjō, wrote about this period: "Among officials of the former Bakufu, those who attend to the most urgent affairs of state are Katsu Awa, Ōkubo Ichiō, and Yamaoka Tetsutarō."[76] As Yamaoka's later admirer Satō Hiroshi put it, if the Tokugawa Bakufu were to be likened to a big corporation, Yamaoka's promotion was, without exaggeration, similar to a mere clerk suddenly becoming one of the managing directors.[77]

Yamaoka was a *bushi* openly concerned about the moral and ethical issues of his profession. His lifelong pursuit of the "life-giving sword," rooted in what he perceived as immutable standards of the pre-Tokugawa warrior culture, eventually led him to play a central role in preventing a national disaster through the realization of the bloodless surrender of Edo Castle. To date, the enormity of his action in the events of March 1868 has been known only among his admirers, who have eulogized him as a "saint swordsman" (*kensei*)[78] or "great saint" (*taisei*).[79] However, they have not been able to provide a convincing argument in favor of Yamaoka's feat. For historians, he has been reduced to the status of a bit player.

Of course, it is important not to overstate the role of a single individual in a complex historical event. However, it is a fact that some individuals did play a crucial part in history: the generally accepted key role of Sakamoto Ryōma in the formation of the Satsuma-Chōshū alliance, which eventually resulted in the overthrow of the Tokugawa Bakufu, is just one example.[80] To underestimate Yamaoka's role in the bloodless surrender of Edo Castle is to distort our entire understanding of this epochal event. If we do not fully recognize it, we will be incapable of finding any logical explanation for the Bakufu's action in the wake of Yamaoka's meeting with Saigō, not least in promoting him so spectacularly. Finally, we will not be able to explain the development of his career from 1868 onward, both in the former Bakufu and in the Meiji government.[81]

Chapter 6

The Establishment of
Ittō Shōden Mutō-ryū

Yamaoka Tesshū's Career after the Bloodless Surrender of Edo Castle

The bloodless surrender of Edo Castle made it possible to avoid a nationwide civil war and prevent a large loss of civilian life in Edo. However, there were still thousands of radical and uncontrollable retainers of the Bakufu who fled to the northeast of Japan, and who continued to fight against the imperial army together with the northeastern domains. These events prolonged what is known as the Boshin Civil War until May 1869.

During this time, together with Katsu Kaishū and several other top Bakufu officials, Yamaoka Tesshū engaged in pacifying and preventing radical Bakufu retainers from sabotaging the realization of the surrender conditions. On April*(i)* 18, 1868, as a messenger from Tokugawa Yoshiyori, Yamaoka negotiated the disbandment of a mixed group of Bakufu deserters and Jōsai Domain retainers led by Iba Hachirō, Hitomi Katsutarō, and Hayashi Tadataka.[1] In April*(i)* through May, 1868 Yamaoka cooperated with Saigō Takamori and other members of the imperial government in an attempt to disband the rebellious Shōgitai group in Ueno, and for this purpose, he engaged in negotiations with the monk Kakuōin, the de facto leader of the Shōgitai, several times.[2]

In August 1868, the imperial government allotted a 700,000 *koku* Fuchū Domain (later renamed Shizuoka Domain) to the Tokugawa family. According to Katsu Kaishū's diary, Yoshinobu's relocation to Shizuoka was also made possible through Yamaoka's efforts; however, Katsu does not specify exactly what Yamaoka did.[3] From this point, Yamaoka, together with several other top Bakufu officials, was busy trying to find a way to support retainers of the Tokugawa family, who had moved to the new location and, in so doing, lost any means of making a living. One of these ways was to make land available for farming, and an interesting outcome of this is that, under Yamaoka's leadership, ex-retainers of the Bakufu started what became the famous green tea cultivation of Shizuoka.[4] In 1871, domains were replaced with prefectural governments, and Yamaoka held the position of deputy governor of Shizuoka Prefecture for some time. His feat in the bloodless surrender of Edo Castle was not forgotten by the Meiji government, and it consequently appointed him governor of Ibaraki and later the Imari (presently Saga) prefectures. Finally, in 1872, he was appointed to be a chamberlain of Emperor Meiji.

Thus, Yamaoka became one of several top officials of the former Bakufu who were employed in high posts in the Meiji government.[5] Still, Yamaoka's appointment as the chamberlain of Emperor Meiji can only be described as remarkable. First of all, a person from the enemy camp was chosen to be a member of the emperor's closest entourage. The popular story holds that the imperial government wanted to reform the education of Japanese emperors who, before the Meiji era, were traditionally surrounded by women; Emperor Meiji was surrounded by military men, and Yamaoka was recommended by Saigō Takamori.[6] However, the real situation appears to have been much more complicated. The Meiji government was still afraid of rebellion on the part of malcontent retainers of the former Bakufu and used Yamaoka to ease their frustration.[7] In other words, the goal of Yamaoka's appointment was to show retainers of the former Bakufu that a prominent figure from their side was also among the confidants of the emperor.

Indeed, retainers of the Bakufu had already expressed their wish to see someone from their side close to the emperor during the last stage of the Boshin Civil War, when the acting commander of the Bakufu navy, Enomoto Takeaki, attempted to establish a kind of autonomous republic in Hokkaido at the end of 1868 and the beginning of 1869. In a secret letter that Enomoto sent in December 1868 to the French envoy to Japan, Max Outrey, he says that one of the conditions for the peaceful reconciliation between his force and the imperial government should be placing someone from the Tokugawa family in the inner circle of the emperor. He suggested the former shogun Tokugawa Yoshinobu as a candidate.[8] Of course, neither Yoshinobu nor anyone else from the Tokugawa family was acceptable to the Meiji government. However, several years later, the main mediator of the bloodless surrender of Edo Castle, Yamaoka Tesshū, who had become one of the top figures on the side of the former Bakufu, fit this role perfectly. This fact illustrates the degree of Yamaoka's fame and influence among the retainers of the former Bakufu at the time.[9] In actuality, his service to Emperor Meiji also meant a simultaneous unofficial service to the Tokugawa family.

The Innermost Secret of "No-Opponent"

As a top official, Yamaoka never neglected his *musha shugyō*. However, it continued to be affected by unpredictable circumstances. In 1870, Asari Yoshiaki suddenly stopped teaching. The reasons are unclear, and the only thing that is known is that he "quit the art [of swordsmanship] and never took the sword again."[10] Lifelong training and teaching was customary among swordsmen of Asari's level, and the transmission of sword skills to the next generation was a matter of utmost importance for them. There was no way they could transmit their skill other than by taking the sword and demonstrating with their own example so that disciples could learn by imitation. That is why there had to be a grave reason for Asari's sudden withdrawal. The most probable explanation is that Asari had a serious health problem that prevented him from training and teaching and that this was concealed from the general public.

At this point, Asari appears to have been the only person whose skills Yamaoka recognized as superior to his own and closer to the original Ittō-ryū tradition. That is why Yamaoka revered him as his teacher and also considered him as one of the few partners worth training with. The following recollection by Yamaoka is probably related to the time when Asari stopped teaching:

> Once I resolved in my heart to master this Way,[11] I swore that even if swordsmanship is abolished in this world and there is not a single partner to train with, I will not stop until I comprehend fully the innermost secrets of this art...[12]

It seems that Yamaoka's frustration was heightened by the forthcoming abolishment of the warrior class, the ban on wearing the two swords (government decrees of 1871 and 1876),[13] and the beginning of the age of rapid Westernization and modernization, when many aspects of Japanese culture, including military arts, were regarded as anachronisms.

Yet the unfavorable circumstances of the 1870s only reinforced Yamaoka's resolve to preserve the traditional warrior culture and continue the quest for mastery in swordsmanship. From that time, Yamaoka started to practice sword techniques alone, imagining Asari in front of him.[14] This is how he described his experience:

> Every day I took the sword and, after the practice with other people, I used [to train] alone, imagining myself standing face to face with Asari. Asari would appear instantly before my sword and I felt like I was facing a mountain. Early in the morning of March 30, 1880, as usual I was [practicing sword techniques] against an imaginary Asari in the bedroom. However, I could not see his image. This is when I came to comprehend the innermost secret of "no-opponent" (*muteki no kyokusho*). After that I invited Asari and had him examine my art. Asari said: "You have comprehended the subtle principle very well." At this point, I established my own school and called it Mutō-ryū.[15]

Writing these lines only for himself, Yamaoka omitted many details, and the practice described by him above may produce an impression of a sort of "shadow sparring" against an imaginary opponent. However, such a practice was unlikely to be productive because Yamaoka would have been limited by the confines of his own imagination. In reality, what Yamaoka most likely did was similar to *musha shugyō* of the pre-Tokugawa ages when *bushi* secluded themselves on the grounds of Shintō shrines and Buddhist temples to concentrate on polishing their fighting skills. Yamaoka's practice was different only in that, serving in government, he trained at home over a much longer span of time.[16] What Yamaoka refers to as imagining Asari's outline was merely his effort to keep in mind Asari's level of mastery, which, in terms of the use of the wooden sword, was much higher than his own. By constantly keeping a high technical standard in his mind, Yamaoka felt he could prevent himself from going astray during his solitary training. In this, he set up a goal that he strove to achieve and surpass.[17]

It took Yamaoka about ten years of solitary training against what he described as the imaginary Asari Yoshiaki to comprehend the "innermost secret of 'no-opponent.'" An important point to note here is that Yamaoka did not develop a new swordsmanship technique. It was a mental attitude that he interpreted in his writings to be in line with Buddhist metaphysical principles. He later described his experience:

> After that,[18] when I thought of my ability to see the technical level of the opponent before the engagement, I realized that it had absolutely nothing to do with the opponent's skillfulness or unskillfulness, and that it was "I" which was creating "skillfulness" or "unskillfulness" in the opponent. If there is "I," there is the "opponent," and if there is no "I," there is no "opponent." If one truly comprehends this principle, there will be not even the slightest discrimination between "skillful" and "unskillful," "strong" and "weak," "big" and "small."[19]

The problem with this private writing (and actually several others) is that Yamaoka used the term *muteki*, which appears to have misled his admirers and biographers. The first semantic association this term brings up is "invincible" or "unbeatable," and this is why Yamaoka has come to be revered as an invincible "sword saint" (*kensei*) who, although he may not necessarily win, never loses.[20] However, this claim would have been rejected as arrogance by Yamaoka, who could not have failed to learn through his realistic approach to swordsmanship that no one is guaranteed to remain unharmed in actual combat. Yamaoka's quote above demonstrates that he actually used this term in the literal sense of the characters that compose it, that is, "no-opponent." He used it in the same way as he used the term *mutō* ("no-sword") in the name of his school Mutō-ryū (the School of No-Sword).

Yamaoka was not the first one who operated with the term *mutō*. A very early usage (the first half of the sixteenth century) can be found in a document written by the third headmaster of Tenshinshō-den Katori Shintō-ryū, Iizasa Wakasa no Kami Morinobu. However, it is not clear in what sense this term was used.[21] *Mutō* also appears in the list of techniques of Yagyū Shinkage-ryū.[22] In Yamaoka's notes on swordsmanship, we can find the meaning that he attributed to this term. He explained:

> The ultimate level in swordsmanship is when one reaches the [mental] state of "no-opponent." If one distinguishes between "skillful" and "unskillful," it is not "no-opponent." Such notions are the result of the workings of mind: when one faces an opponent who is more skillful, his mind "halts," he feels

unconfident and strained, and his swordsmanship performance does not go well; by creating the "opponent" in his mind, he "halts" it...If one faces an opponent who is less skillful, he feels confident and unconstrained, and he uses the sword with perfect freedom. This is because he thinks in his mind that [he can act] with perfect freedom. This is the evidence that there is not a single thing outside one's mind...In the name Mutō-ryū, which I apply to what I have contrived, I use *mutō*, that is, "there is no sword outside one's mind." "No-sword" is the same as "no-mind" (*mushin*). "No-mind" means not to "halt" one's mind. If one "halts" his mind, there is the "opponent"; if one does not "halt" his mind, there is no "opponent."[23]

In another writing, Yamaoka states that "the swordsmanship of Mutō-ryū is not concerned with victory or defeat. Its aim is gaining a natural victory through purifying one's heart and cultivating one's courage."[24] These passages may sound as if they derive from a Zen-based psychological theory of combat (*shimpō-ron*) removed from the realities of the battlefield and characteristic of the Tokugawa-era "flowery training," such as, for example, that upheld by the Sekiun-ryū school of swordsmanship.[25] However, if we accept that Yamaoka really comprehended something that brought him to an advanced level of swordsmanship skill, as he states in his writings, that would be a superficial impression. Some events in the aftermath of Yamaoka's revelation will show that he indeed comprehended something that gave him at least a deeper insight into how to handle the *bushi* traditional weapon in actual combat.

In terms of Yamaoka's interpretation of the highest level of mastery in swordsmanship, we need to consider what triggered Yamaoka's comprehension of the "innermost secret." So far, all of his biographies, without exception, have treated his breakthrough in swordsmanship as the natural extension of his reaching the final stage of Zen enlightenment. This version has also been uncritically accepted by scholars and swordsmanship historians.[26] They base their assertions on the fact that a famous Zen monk of the time, Tekisui, is said to have granted Yamaoka the certificate of achieving the final stage of enlightenment approximately at the same time as Yamaoka comprehended the "innermost secret." It is true that Yamaoka's Zen study intensified considerably after Asari Yoshiaki stopped teaching swordsmanship.[27] However, he never stated explicitly himself that he had reached the final stage of Zen enlightenment. Furthermore, as Shima Yoshitaka has demonstrated, according to the practice common in Zen circles, Tekisui granted Yamaoka a certificate that confirmed the latter's solving of only one of the numerous Rinzai Zen puzzles (*kōan*), and Yamaoka was very unlikely to receive a certificate proving his achievement of the final stage of Zen enlightenment[28] (neither an original nor a copy of such a certificate is to be found).

As noted earlier, Zen was irrelevant to the practical aspects of *bushi* martial skills as long as they remained martial. It appears that Yamaoka confused the suddenly elevated workings of his mind that brought him to an advanced level of understanding of swordsmanship principles with a kind of Zen-style religious revelation and, thus, came to describe his experience in his writings in Zen-Buddhist metaphysical terms. As far as swordsmanship is concerned, it cannot be denied that Yamaoka possessed an unusual mind whose workings were close to those of the founders of pre-Tokugawa military arts schools. Yamaoka's reconstruction of the Ittō-ryū predetermined patterns of movement, which will be discussed in the following section, will demonstrate this even more clearly. This mind allowed him to see fundamental problems in Japanese swordsmanship that few of his contemporaries had observed and made him the only one in the Bakumatsu period and early Meiji era to embark on the quest for and, finally, to undertake the task of revival of one of the pre-Tokugawa root lineages of Japanese swordsmanship. In the process of decades-long training, this mind continued to struggle with the problem of how to get rid of mannerisms and biases of contemporary swordsmanship and how to make the body work better in actual combat.

This body also had some unusual features. Yamaoka's physique was much bigger than that of the average Japanese man of the time. He was of massive stature, standing over six feet tall and weighing in at 231 pounds.[29] As his practice of the "all-day-long withstanding sparrings" demonstrate, this physique was driven by an extraordinary stamina and willpower.[30] Being a gifted swordsman by reputation, he undoubtedly possessed excellent reflexes and, of course, intuition. It was the reciprocal work of such an unusual mind and body that finally appears to have triggered Yamaoka's sudden comprehension of the "innermost secret" that he came to describe in Zen Buddhist terms. However, this arguably was a unique experience limited to the equally unique workings of his mind and body. None of

Yamaoka's disciples are known to have achieved a similar realization, even though he had a number of intensely devoted followers, such as Kagawa Zenjirō, who inherited his school.

In his *musha shugyō*, Yamaoka undoubtedly pursued a philosophical and ethical ideal of absolute and neutral truth that, in its neutrality, is raised over considerations of victory and defeat. At the same time, in his quest for the pre-Tokugawa warrior culture, he appears to have discovered that, as hereditary specialists, the pre-Tokugawa *bushi* developed mental attitudes that, as discussed in Chapter 1, allowed them to avoid duality in very practical matters. From Yamaoka's quotes above, it is clear that what he comprehended was transcendency over the duality of two opposites. The practical realization of the same notion was a natural part of the pre-Tokugawa *bushi* profession. This was not necessarily articulated as a "philosophy" adopted from Zen Buddhism or any other thought. If we take an example from Japanese archery, the emphasis upon posture, ritual, mental concentration, and character development was initially adopted by the Japanese from the Chinese nobility, and this adoption long predated any influence of Zen.[31] In this context, it is appropriate to cite the words of the shogun's regent in the Kamakura Bakufu, Hōjō Yasutoki (1183–1242), to the military commander Hōjō Tokiuji:

The only prerequisite for a [superior] archer is a skillful usage of his mind. This is why, in sleep or awake, he must not forget [the proper] inner attitude… Regardless of whether the target is far or close, big or small, whether he is surrounded by spectators, all of whom are women, or he is in a place where there is not a single person to watch him, he must maintain the state of mind as if he was standing in an arena of a palace watched by ten million people. Every time he releases an arrow, he must think that this very arrow is the last one and that, if it misses the target, in the absence of the second arrow, he will be shot by his enemy or torn to pieces by a [wild] animal.[32]

In this document, written seven centuries before Yamaoka lived, we see the same emphasis on transcendency over the duality of two opposites, as well as mention of the importance of ridding oneself of the "second chance" psychology. It is worth noting that Hōjō Yasutoki's writing is void of metaphysical terms and any reference to Buddhism or any other philosophy. This was nothing but warrior wisdom based on the simple, even crude, realism that underlay the daily life of the pre-Tokugawa *bushi* and that elevated them over such dual notions as "war" and "no war," "military" and "civil." These mental attitudes were cultivated through the realistic training methodologies of the hereditary warrior houses, not metaphysical philosophies. This is what Yamaoka finally arrived at years after he began his quest, although a skillful pre-Tokugawa *bushi* would find little remarkable about it. A point in passing here is that Yamaoka's mind and biology allowed him to achieve such a mental attitude without undergoing training according to the methodologies of the pre-Tokugawa *bushi*, which continued to look to him like pieces of a disassembled mosaic.

There is no evidence that Yamaoka ever tested his new achievement against anyone. It seems that he preferred to harbor it within himself. This may have been because he strove to master a skill that was practical in mortal combat, and its testing could result only in the death of one or both of the combatants. In the Bakumatsu period and Meiji era, most swordsmen seemed to him to be experienced and skillful only in sparring with the long bamboo sword. Any attempt to test a skill developed for actual combat against what he viewed as players of a game, accustomed to using only a toy weapon, would be unfair to the latter. It would also have misled him in regard to whether the outcome of the match was due to his achievement or merely the incompetence of his opponent. Finally, it would have undermined some of the basic ethical principles of his *musha shugyō*.

Back to the Past: Between Ittō-ryū and Mutō-ryū

What followed Yamaoka's comprehension of the "innermost secret" is full of contradictions. On the one hand, although he established his own school with a new name, he did not attempt to create a new technical system. As some of his writings will show, his intent was to preserve the heritage of Ittō-ryū in the form created by its sixteenth-century founder, Itō Ittōsai, without changing anything even slightly or adding anything new. On the other hand, he started to call himself "the reviver of the Way of the Sword" (*kendō chūkō*).[33] It appears that he perceived himself as the reviver of not only the Ittō-ryū tradition, but also Japanese swordsmanship as a whole—or more exactly, its quintessence.

One problem for our understanding of these events is that, probably far from the initial intention of the author, Yamaoka's writing on his solitary training and sudden revelation can give the impression that he achieved the highest level in Ittō-ryū (at least of the Nakanishi-ha lineage). However, this belief conflicts with the fact that, after Yamaoka comprehended the "innermost secret," he started to doubt the authenticity of the predetermined patterns of movement (*kata*) of Nakanishi-ha Ittō-ryū taught to him by Asari Yoshiaki. He felt that even these patterns had been distorted into a form of "flowery training"[34] (though, perhaps not as much as in other branches of Ittō-ryū). Yamaoka would say later to his disciples that even Asari "was not the real thing yet."[35] Naturally, the training of the pre-Tokugawa schools of military arts was structured so that their higher levels of skill and especially the innermost secrets could not be mastered and comprehended without first correctly mastering the lower levels of the art, all of which were based on the practice of predetermined patterns of movement. In short, without undergoing the practice of correct predetermined patterns of movement, one could not comprehend the innermost secrets. However, Yamaoka's writing suggests that he comprehended the "innermost secret" only to realize that what he was practicing under Asari's guidance was actually incorrect. This makes us wonder about what Yamaoka really comprehended. Besides the transcendency of duality, he appears to have achieved a unique vision that allowed him to sense the fundamental principles of handling the Japanese sword in actual combat and to use it better than others. However, this could not formally be described as the "innermost secret" of Ittō-ryū because, at this point, Yamaoka had not gone through the correct training of this school.

As we can see, up to this time, Yamaoka's lifelong quest for a swordsmanship school transmitting pre-Tokugawa skills had been unsuccessful. There is no evidence that he ever encountered any rare exceptions among military arts schools that managed to preserve pre-Tokugawa training methodologies through the Tokugawa era. This is not surprising, because, for whatever reason, he adhered to the Ittō-ryū lineage, and this limited his quest. Yamaoka was undoubtedly deeply frustrated upon realizing that even what he had learned from Asari showed signs of deviation from the original Ittō-ryū. His feeling of despair was probably heightened by the recognition that he was well into his forties, and after twenty-five years of restless searching, he was still far from his goal. In response, he chose the only remaining option. He embarked on an unprecedented attempt to revive one of the pre-Tokugawa swordsmanship lineages: he attempted to reconstruct the predetermined patterns of movement of Ittō-ryū and teach them to his disciples.[36]

In order to concentrate on the reconstruction and teaching of what he believed to be the genuine Ittō-ryū swordsmanship, Yamaoka resigned from his service in the Meiji government. The popular story holds that Yamaoka entered the service of Emperor Meiji on the condition that he would resign in exactly ten years.[37] Indeed, the dates of Yamaoka's entering and resigning from imperial service (June 1872 and June 1882 respectively) suggest deliberate calculation. However, Yamaoka was not the kind of a person who would quit while Emperor Meiji or the Tokugawa family still needed his service. He was not a careerist, and when he saw that both sides could do without him, he preferred to quit and devote all his time to his pursuits in swordsmanship. Still, even after his resignation, Yamaoka remained Emperor Meiji's chargè d'affaires, receiving the remuneration of a government official of the second grade.[38]

Obviously, Yamaoka was not absolutely sure of the correctness of his reconstructions, which were partly based on his experience as a swordsman and partly on his reading and analysis of the historical scrolls of Ittō-ryū and other schools,[39] but also partly on his intuitive understanding. This is probably one of the reasons why he used the new school name and did not claim to represent the genuine Ittō-ryū. His lack of confidence induced him to begin searching for the successor of the mainline Ittō-ryū from the Ono family, which he believed had transmitted the tradition for centuries directly and unchanged from Itō Ittōsai and who, he hoped, could confirm the correctness of his assumptions.[40]

Sometime in 1884, Yamaoka finally managed to find the headmaster of mainline Ittō-ryū in the ninth generation, Ono Nario (he was sixty-six years old at the time), who lived in retirement in a village in Chiba Prefecture. The only source that provides details of the encounter between Yamaoka and Nario is *Shumpūkan eizoku shu'isho* (Prospectus relating to the preservation of Shumpūkan training hall), collectively written by Yamaoka's disciples after his death, in 1890. This writing is not free from hagiographical traits; however, the fact that Yamaoka eventually became Nario's successor allows the assumption that its contents are generally correct and can be used for the purpose of this book, albeit with caution.

According to this document, on Yamaoka's invitation, in August of 1884, Nario, with a disciple, visited his Shumpūkan training hall and gave a demonstration of the Ittō-ryū predetermined patterns of movement as transmitted within the Ono family. Yamaoka is said to have been filled with admiration when he saw that there was no embellishment in the techniques, which seemed natural and practical in actual combat and, to him, to be truly the ones contrived by the founder of the school. Furthermore, it turned out that, in cardinal points, his reconstructions fully coincided with what he saw during the demonstration.[41] As Yoshida Tomoo notes, generations of headmasters of the Ono family consistently prohibited their disciples from sparring with the bamboo sword,[42] and we can assume that predetermined patterns of movement transmitted in the family had characteristics appropriate to pre-Tokugawa military arts schools—that is, speed, power, and precision.

The assertion that Yamaoka's reconstructions coincided with the techniques demonstrated by Ono Nario appears remarkable. It is difficult to say how Yamaoka could have reconstructed an intangible culture that had been born three hundred years before his time and was unknown in its original form outside the Ono family. Assuming that Yamaoka's reconstructions were accurate, it may simply have been the extraordinary byproduct of his exceptional natural gifts as a swordsman combined with his unique mental capacities, elevated and refined even more due to his ten-year solitary practice against the imagined figure of Asari Yoshiaki.

Ono Nario accepted Yamaoka's request to teach predetermined patterns of movement to the latter's disciples, and in September 1884, together with his family, he moved to a house in Tokyo provided by Yamaoka. Soon, Yamaoka and Ono Nario discovered that they were distant relatives, and because Ono Nario did not have heirs, the same month, he made Yamaoka the legitimate tenth headmaster of Ittō-ryū by granting him the heirloom sword Kamewaritō (the Barrel-Splitting Sword) and all secret traditional texts of the school transmitted in the Ono family.[43] In March 1885, Ono Nario further granted Yamaoka the license of full transmission,[44] and from that time, Yamaoka started to add Ittō Shōden (the Correct Transmission of Ittō[-ryū]) to the name of his school, so that the new version read Ittō Shōden Mutō-ryū.[45]

Here, it may be helpful to clarify what Yamaoka understood by the term "correct transmission" (shōden). He explains it in a document Ittō Shōden Mutō-ryū heihō jūni kajō mokuroku kōyakusho (The commentaries to the twelve-item list of Ittō Shōden Mutō-ryū military art):

> SHŌDEN is the "correct transmission" of what the founder Ittōsai Kagehisa transmitted to Ono Tadaaki and what has been transmitted to date through generations [of the Ono family] as it was, in its complete integrity, without adding anything alien.[46]

Yamaoka repeatedly stressed the need for full compliance with the teaching of the founder, Itō Ittōsai. He wrote:

> I have studied [swordsmanship] for almost forty years, and one day I suddenly came to comprehend [its innermost secret]. I established a new school, Mutō-ryū. However, it was possible only because I [strove] to find the standards of Ittōsai's tradition and not deviate from them even slightly; I felt the kindness and sympathy in the transmission of the innermost secrets [of swordsmanship], which Ittōsai developed by going through numerous mortal combats and extreme hardships in a span of many years. The old saying says: "The Way is born when the basis is firm." Regardless of your own understanding of what is good or not in combat, if you deviate from the ancient transmission of a school's founder, even if you practice swordsmanship all your life, you will not comprehend its innermost secrets.[47]

Another document, written by Yamaoka on January 27, 1885, shows that, at this stage, he was already confident that the "correct transmission" could not be found anywhere except in the root lineages of Japanese swordsmanship belonging to certain families. He states that people mistakenly think that Ittō-ryū is transmitted in its factions and branches. However, the true mainline of this school is the one that is transmitted only within the Ono family, through fifty predetermined patterns of movement accompanied by the main symbol of the school—the heirloom sword.[48] It remains unclear how Yamaoka could be so certain that Ittō-ryū was transmitted within the Ono family unchanged and fully in its original form. Yet a recent study by Yoshida Tomoo confirms Yamaoka's belief.[49]

Furthermore, Yamaoka pursued not only the predetermined patterns of movement that transmitted the technical skill of Ittō-ryū, but also what he believed were the characteristic mannerisms (*kuse*) of its sixteenth-century founder, Itō Ittōsai. In one of his writings, Yamaoka noted that the mannerisms of the founders of some pre-Tokugawa swordsmanship schools, including Ittō-ryū, were lost through generations of their disciples who went on to establish factions and branches. He pointed to the vital importance of an indissoluble continuity of teaching in military arts schools and stressed that there was a break, or a gap, in the process of transmission in most contemporary swordsmanship schools that was equal to the loss of a connection with the pre-Tokugawa tradition, that is, the loss of practicability in actual combat.[50]

Yet a question inevitably arises from the name of Yamaoka's school. On the one hand, he strove to do his best for the revival and preservation of the original Ittō-ryū; on the other hand, he did add something of his own and had no scruples in showing this through his school's name (the term *mutō*). In addressing this contradiction, first it is important not to confuse Yamaoka's stance with other branches of the root lineages of Japanese swordsmanship. More often than not, the creators of a branch of a root lineage placed their surnames before the name of a school for better public recognition; this was the case of Nakanishi-ha Ittō-ryū, Mizoguchi-ha Ittō-ryū, and so forth. These men deliberately tried to emphasize in the school name their difference from the root lineage, not their unity with it. Had Yamaoka done the same, his school name would have read as something like Yamaoka-ha Ittō-ryū.

An interesting fact giving a hint of the explanation of the contradiction is that, in the majority of secondary sources, Yamaoka's name follows the name of Asari Yoshiaki and concludes the genealogical tree of Nakanishi-ha Ittō-ryū, which was just a faction of Ittō-ryū.[51] Not only that: Yamaoka himself put his name after Asari's in his own swordsmanship scrolls that he issued to his disciples. In Yamaoka's writings, his name does not seem to have ever appeared after Ono Nario's, and it never concluded the genealogical tree of the original Ittō-ryū lineage, although this would have been a logical outcome of his encounter with Nario.

There appear to be several reasons for this. First, Yamaoka did not go as far as to get rid of training based on free sparring with the use of the bamboo sword and body protectors. As Yamaoka's writing of November 1884 clearly demonstrates, even after the encounter with Ono Nario he continued to believe that this kind of training was useful.[52] However, in reality, there was no such training in the time of the founder of Ittō-ryū, Itō Ittōsai. Furthermore, Yamaoka's emphasis on the psychological aspects of combat, which he felt he had acquired with the help of Zen Buddhism were not in line with the teaching of Ittō-ryū, which originally had no strong connection with Buddhism.[53]

There is no record of a discussion between Yamaoka and Ono Nario in regard to these points—or even whether there was such a discussion at all. The Ono family maintained the ban on sparring with the bamboo sword, and the only thing that can be said is that, admitting that Yamaoka managed to reconstruct the predetermined patterns of movement of Ittō-ryū, Nario probably discovered in Yamaoka an extraordinarily gifted swordsman. Being quite old and having no worthy successors at the time, he preferred to recognize Yamaoka as his legitimate successor and ignore some points in his practice that were not in accord with mainline Ittō-ryū. When it comes to Yamaoka, he appears to have found a compromise to the two mutually exclusive methods of training in swordsmanship. One possibility is that he did not want to get rid of sparring with the bamboo sword because he continued to consider it as one of the ways to train breath and stamina among his disciples.[54] Whatever the case, after the encounter with Ono Nario, Yamaoka understood clearly that his Zen-style psychological interpretations and training based on sparring with the bamboo sword were foreign to the original Ittō-ryū. Honest admission of his own deviation was the most probable reason why he put his name after Asari's in his swordsmanship scrolls, as well as why he used his own school name.

Thus, it can be said that, although the *bushi* intangible culture of the pre-Tokugawa ages was something that Yamaoka longed for all his life, he never achieved a complete understanding of this culture historically. This is evident from the fact that he does not appear to have ever clearly distinguished between armored and unarmored modes of combat. Also, with the exception of his boyhood in Takayama and a short-term study of spearmanship under Yamaoka Seizan, there is no evidence that Yamaoka ever attempted to acquire skills in handling multiple kinds of weapons. The narrow specialization of a "swordsman" was unknown in the pre-Tokugawa ages, when one of the main factors dividing life from death in actual combat was the ability to understand and handle all manner of arms.

Conclusion

Yamaoka Tesshū taught Ittō Shōden Mutō-ryū until his death in July 1888. His death was widely covered in the Meiji press. For ten days, newspapers published articles praising his feat in the bloodless surrender of Edo Castle and other accomplishments. His writings related to the events of March–May 1868, such as *BDH*, were also reprinted in a series of newspaper articles.[1] Several thousand people attended his funeral, and it is said that Emperor Meiji watched the procession from a tower of the imperial palace.[2]

Yamaoka's name is associated with the creation of an unparalleled number of calligraphy works,[3] reconstruction of Buddhist temples in the "age of Buddhism persecution" in Japan, laying the foundations for the production of the famous green tea in Shizuoka Prefecture, devoted service to the Tokugawa family and Emperor Meiji, and many other accomplishments. However, the field where he invested his energy most was *musha shugyō* through the practice of swordsmanship and the quest for the intangible culture of the *bushi* of the "distant past." Yamaoka was the one who, to date, made the last attempt in Japanese history to establish a swordsmanship school deeply rooted in the pre-Tokugawa tradition.[4] In the era of Japan's Westernization and industrialization, when the Meiji government was building a mass conscript army, he attempted to revive Japanese swordsmanship, both technically and spiritually, according to the standards of the pre-Tokugawa ages. In the broader sense, it was an uncompromising striving for the preservation of what he believed was the genuine warrior culture, inseparably linked with the warrior's body.

As Sugie Masatoshi notes, Yamaoka's school of swordsmanship, Ittō Shōden Mutō-ryū, did not spread in the Meiji era because it urged its practitioners to return to the ancient form of the practice of swordsmanship (i.e., as the art of handling the real sword in actual combat), which was unsuitable for the sportive *kendō* swordsmanship of the time. Still, the school's emphasis on the "ideal of character formation through the practice of swordsmanship" did influence greatly educational aspects of

Japanese swordsmanship of the time.[5] However, as Yamaoka's writings discussed in this book show, he was not interested in changing what he perceived as the ancient and immutable canons of swordsmanship for the sake of easy consumption by his contemporaries. The fact that only the educational aspect of Yamaoka's school was positively received by contemporary *kendō* points once again to the dissonance between means and goals inherited by contemporary versions of Japanese military arts from the Tokugawa era.

Yamaoka's school has survived to our days through six generations of informal successors. He never made anyone his formal successor by issuing a license of full transmission (*menkyo kaiden*) and granting the heirloom Kamewaritō sword of Ittō-ryū.[6] As a famous figure of the early Meiji era, by the end of his life, Yamaoka had to attend to too many matters simultaneously, and this probably distracted him from nurturing the next generation of Mutō-ryū swordsmen. Remaining chargè d'affaires of Emperor Meiji, he exerted himself in helping the poor and the reconstruction of Buddhist temples. To gather money for various social projects, Yamaoka, being the fifty-second headmaster of the Jubokudō style of calligraphy, wrote and sold tens of thousands of calligraphy pieces. Of course, not all of them were masterpieces, but it was his famous name (signature), which people bought. Being an ardent follower of Buddhism, Yamaoka also spent a great deal of time copying Buddhist sutras.[7]

Another possibility is that Yamaoka could not find a worthy candidate among his disciples because they lacked innate physical and mental qualities comparable to his own. Because there were no formal successors, Yamaoka's death actually meant the extinction of the mainline Ittō-ryū, one of the three root lineages of Japanese swordsmanship, since Ono Nario also died seven months before Yamaoka.[8]

Yamaoka's emphasis on the importance of being consistent in achieving one's goal in any undertaking at whatever cost did sometimes overshadow his philosophy of the "life-giving sword."[9] It is likely to be the reason why this philosophy does not seem to have been inherited by his disciples. Kusaka Ryūnosuke, one of the main architects of Japan's attack on Pearl Harbor and later battles in the Pacific Ocean, trained in Ittō Shōden Mutō-ryū. He is said to have applied the most advanced theoretical teachings of this swordsmanship school to the naval warfare of that time[10] (eventually, he became the fourth headmaster of the school). Such an application of the school's heritage contrasted sharply with the "life-giving sword" philosophy of its founder, who, according to the available sources, is known not to have killed a single person in his life and who was central to the bloodless surrender of Edo Castle.

Notes

Introduction

1. Ushiyama 1937, pp. 67–84; 1967, pp. 81–96; 1976, pp. 221–241. Ōmori Sōgen 1970, pp. 160–162. Satō Hiroshi 2002, pp. 229–233.
2. Many of these figures studied swordsmanship under Yamaoka. They also consulted with him about the practice of Zen Buddhism or achieving success in their respective professions (Maruyama 1918b, pp. 28–31, 37, 47–52, 71–72. Ushiyama 1937, pp. 183–222, 238–239, 325–337, 339–342, 358–364. Maekawa 1977, pp. 250–260. Yano 1999, pp. 54–73).
3. Yamaoka's indifference to money, social status, and fame is also noted by Iechika Yoshiki (Iechika 2005, p. 125). See also Ōmori Sōgen 1970, p. 115.
4. Tesshū means "Iron Boat," Deishū "Muddy Boat," and Kaishū "Sea Boat."
5. Recent newspaper examples include *Yomiuri Shimbun* (2008/5/15; 2009/1/6), *Mainichi Shimbun* (2007/12/9; 2008/8/3; 2008/9/6; 2008/10/24), and *Sankei Shimbun* (2008/10/17). Fictionalized accounts include the multivolume novel *Yamaoka Tesshū* by Iwasaki Sakae (Iwasaki 1945a-b, 1968) and a novel by the same title by Nanjō Norio (Nanjō 1978). Yamaoka appears in a Kabuki play *Keiki inochigoi* (Pleading for Keiki's life) written by Mayama Seika (Mayama 1940–1942).
6. See *Daisekai* no. 9(2) (1954/2); *Shin Bummei* no. 5(12) (1955/12); *Jitsugyō No Nihon* no. 59(12) (1956/5); *Shūkan Asahi* no. 103(13) (1998/3/27), 103(35) (1998/8/10); *Sapio* no. 12(18) (2000/10/25); *Nihon Oyobi Nihonjin* no. 1650 (2004); *Verdad* no. 122–198 (2005/6–2011/10). See also Ōmori Sōgen 1970, p. 212; Harazono 1990; Satō Hiroshi 2002, pp. 235–238.
7. http://www.ndl.go.jp/portrait/e/datas/207.html?c=0 (accessed on October 20, 2011).
8. On the "Meiji bias," see Totman 1980, pp. 558–565.
9. The document appears in Ōmori Sōgen 1970, p. 254.
10. The memoir appears in Ishizu 1933, pp. 94–95.
11. The memoir appears in Ushiyama 1937, pp. 1–2.
12. Although only from the artistic viewpoint, Yamaoka's calligraphy was thoroughly studied by Terayama Katsujō. See Terayama 1977, 1982, 1997, 2003.

13. Murakami Yasumasa, the sixth headmaster of the Ittō Shōden Mutō-ryū school of swordsmanship established by Yamaoka late in his life, privately published only a few dozen copies of this chronological record of Yamaoka's life. One photocopy of this handwritten work can be found in the National Diet Library of Japan (Tokyo).

14. Furuta 1971. Imamura 1971, pp. 228–232. Watatani 1971, pp. 255–258. Tominaga 1972, pp. 374–377. Watatani and Yamada 1978, pp. 69–70. Ishioka et al. 1980, pp. 183–188. Kōdansha 1983, pp. 205–207. Terayama 1997. Kodama and Ōtsubo 2001. Takemura 2002, 2005. Maebayashi 2006, pp. 171–173.

15. Some minor and not very informative English works on Yamaoka are Bennet and Moate 2008, and Zenshōan 2009. The latter, titled *Yamaoka Tesshū: Zen and Swordsmanship from the Yamaoka Tesshū Archives*, is a translation of a semi-biographical work published in 1918 by Maruyama Bokuden, the third priest of Zenshōan Temple (Maruyama 1918b). It should be treated with caution as the translation appears to have been done without much editing of the original text. The original presents a fragmentary assemblage of anecdotes and stories about Yamaoka, recollections of his relatives, friends, and acquaintances, as well as some of his writings. All these are listed without particular chronological order and more often than not are undated. Maruyama did not conduct any research into Yamaoka's life and the data in his book is not cross-checked with other sources. It contains many inaccuracies in regard to Yamaoka's life in particular and Japanese history in general. That being said, a small portion of information in Maruyama's book can be used for research on Yamaoka, but only by an informed and careful scholar of the field.

16. King 1993, Hurst 1998. Oleg Benesch gives his own short outline of Yamaoka's biography in his doctoral dissertation (2011), however, it is superficial and extremely inaccurate. Benesch's treatment of both Abe Masato's counterfeits of Yamaoka's discourse on Bushidō and of my argument in regard to their fraudulent nature is a groundless speculation that should not appear in a defended PhD thesis.

17. Shima 2000, 2007a-b, 2008a-c.

18. Shima 2007a.

19. To be discussed in Chapter 6.

20. Anshin 2006, 2007a-c, 2008.

21. Abe 1902, 1903a-e, 1907. Also, Abe 1934, 1940.

22. Anshin 2006. Shima Yoshitaka also questioned the content of Abe Masato's works, but he only suggested the possibility that they did not correspond to reality (Shima 2000, pp. 201–202).

23. Abe 1997, 1999, 2001. See also Abe 1990. *Tesshū zuihitsu* is reprinted nowadays under several different titles, such as *Tesshū zuikan roku* (Records of Tesshū's thoughts and feelings) and *Eiketsu kyojin o kataru* (Stories about a great hero and titan).
24. Anshin 2007c.
25. Besides Ogura Tetsuju, Yamaoka's disciples Yanagida Genjirō and Kagawa Zenjirō also left some memoirs, but they are fragmentary, deal mostly with their own training at Yamaoka's swordsmanship training hall, Shumpūkan, and offer very little information about Yamaoka (see Asano 1970 and Morikawa 1983).
26. Anshin 2009.
27. Maruyama 1918b, p. 51.
28. The text of the scroll appears in Ushiyama 1937, pp. 281–288.

Chapter 1   Prior to His Time

1. Anshin (2012).
2. Ibid.
3. Ibid.
4. Ibid.
5. Chakrabarty 1998, p. 295.
6. Anshin 2009, p. 10.
7. Ibid., pp. 35–84.
8. *Rokuhara-dono go-kakun* (The house rules of His Highness Rokuhara, according to Kakei 1967 [pp. 6–9] and Ozawa 2003 [p. 457], written sometime between 1237 and 1247) and *Gokurakuji-dono go-shōsoku* (A letter from His Highness Gokurakuji, according to Kakei 1967 [pp. 9–10] and Ozawa 2003 [p. 460], written sometime between 1256 and 1261) by Hōjō Shigetoki; *Chikubashō* (Selected precepts for young generations, ca. 1383) supposedly by Shiba Yoshimasa; *Sōunji-dono nijū ikkajō* (Twenty-one rules of His Highness Sōunji, end of the fifteenth – beginning of the sixteenth century) by Hōjō Sōun; *Tako Tokitaka kakun* (Tako Tokitaka's house rules, ca. 1544) by Tako Tokitaka; *Kikkawa Motoharu shisoku Hiro'ie e no kunkai shojō* (Kikkawa Motoharu's letter with admonishments to his son Hiro'ie, late sixteenth century) by Kikkawa Motoharu; *Honda Heihachirō Tadakatsu kakun* (House rules of Honda Heihachirō Tadakatsu, creation date unknown) by Honda Tadakatsu (1548–1610). According to Kuwata Tadachika (2003, p. 11), *Rokuhara-dono go-kakun* and *Gokurakuji-dono go-shōsoku* are the oldest surviving warrior precepts in Japan.

9. Anshin 2009, pp. 35–42.

10. *Yoshisada-ki* appearing in Saeki et al. 1942, vol. 1, p. 320.

11. Anshin 2009, pp. 43–50.

12. Ibid., pp. 49–50.

13. Examples of practical knowledge of the hereditary warrior houses can be found in *Gokurakuji-dono go-shōsoku* (written sometime between 1256 and 1261) by Hōjō Shigetoki; *Yoshisada-ki* (first half of the fourteenth century); *Sōunji-dono nijū ikkajō* (end of the fifteenth – beginning of the sixteenth century) by Hōjō Sōun; *Tako Tokitaka kakun* (ca. 1544) by Tako Tokitaka; *Asakura Sōteki waki* (Records of Asakura Sōteki's discourse, early 1550s) by Asakura Norikage; *Hosokawa Yūsai oboegaki* (Records of Hosokawa Yūsai, late sixteenth or early seventeenth century) by Hosokawa Yūsai. A late and rare example (the beginning of the nineteenth century), whose content is close to pre-Tokugawa texts, is *Bugaku keimō* (Education in military science) by Rikimaru Tōzan.

14. Anshin 2009, pp. 47–49.

15. According to probably one of the best summarizations of the culture of death of pre–Tokugawa *bushi* appearing in Daidōji Yūzan's *Budō shoshinshū* (*A collection of precepts for young warriors*, early eighteenth century). Warrior precepts of the Tokugawa era are characterized by academic moralizing, an emphasis on the theoretical study of military strategy, and virtually a complete neglect of physical training. An important exception to the norm is Daidōji Yūzan's *Budō shoshinshū*. This work of Daidōji, a man who lived during the Great Tokugawa Peace, paradoxically may be regarded as the quintessence of the pre-Tokugawa *bushi* culture. The majority of points he makes can be seen in pre-Tokugawa texts, and sometimes he appears to cite them but without referring to the source. However, it was his ability to bring together, in a written form, the various aspects of the *bushi* culture, dispersed or mentioned unsystematically in pre-Tokugawa texts, to the extent necessary for the reader to grasp its foundations that makes *Budō shoshinshū* an extremely valuable source. The version of *Budō shoshinshū* closest to the original was edited by Yoshida Yutaka and reprinted in 1971 by Tokuma Shoten. For details, see Anshin 2009, pp. 25–28, 37–39, 50–56. Interesting studies of the distant origins of the warrior culture of death, centered on the custom of belly-cutting (*seppuku*), can be found in Ōkuma 1973 and Tokuji 1972, 1994.

16. Fukunaga 1987, p. 9. Hurst 1998, pp. 105–109. Fujiki 2005. Sakai 2005, pp. 6, 27–28, 67, 96–97, 128, 130, 136–141, 146–159, 194–195, 369. Anshin 2009, pp. 52–55. The double-edged sword has been given great symbolic importance both in Japan and her continental neighbors, not the single-edged sword. The reason why the double-edged sword has been so revered

lies in its tridimensional symbolism: two cutting edges of the blade and tip, two flat surfaces, and the unity of two equal longitudinal parts, each having one cutting edge (Anshin 2009, pp. 53–54).

17. Appears in Saeki et al. 1942, vol. 1, pp. 231–232. Ise Sadachika (1417–1473), at one point the de facto ruler of Japan, admonished his son that the study of fields other than military arts is secondary to the study of the two Ways of archery and horsemanship, in which he should train every morning and night without rest (*Gusoku no tame kyōkun issatsu* [A letter with precepts for my son, written between 1457 and 1460] by Ise Sadachika, appears in Ozawa 2003, p. 82). "The two Ways of archery and horsemanship" (*kyūba*) in this context might be used as a synecdoche for "military arts" in general. A military commander of the late sixteenth century, Kuroda Josui, called training in military arts such as spearmanship, swordsmanship, archery, and horsemanship "the most fundamental aspect of the warrior's life" (*Kuroda Josui kyōyu* [Kuroda Josui's precepts], early 1600s) by Kuroda Josui (appears in Saeki et al. 1944, *bekkan*, p. 354).

18. The idea is explicitly stated in, for example, the letter of Hōjō Yasutoki (1183–1242), the shogun's regent in the Kamakura Bakufu, to a military commander Hōjō Tokiuji (appears in Saeki et al. 1942, vol. 1, p. 232); *Kuroda Josui kyōyu* (early 1600s) by Kuroda Josui and *Kuroda Nagamasa kahō* (The house law of Kuroda Nagamasa, 1622) by Kuroda Nagamasa (both appear in Saeki et al. 1944, *bekkan*, pp. 353–354, 361–362). A more general mention that a military commander must be an example for his retainers in all aspects of life can be found in *Yoshisada-ki* (first half of the fourteenth century) appearing in Saeki et al. 1942, vol. 1, p. 310. See also Uozumi 2008, p. 56.

19. Anshin 2009, pp. 55–56, 71.

20. Farris 1992, pp. 172–174.

21. Anshin 2009, pp. 57–59.

22. Ibid., pp. 57–58.

23. Farris 1992, p. 172. Friday 1997, p. 13.

24. A very rare example of a written document that mentions the practices and know-how of a hereditary warrior house is *Yoshisada-ki* of the first half of the fourteenth century (a detailed study of this document can be found in Tokuda 1991, 1992, 1993).

25. Friday 1997, p. 13. Hurst 1998, pp. 45, 112.

26. Hinatsu 1716, p. 52. Shiga 1767, p. 121. Tamon 1841. Minamoto 1843, p. 209. Yatagawa and Koike 1906, p. 70. Hori 1934, pp. 33–34, 38, 153–155. Yamada 1960, p. 18. Imamura et al. 1966, vol. 2, pp. 235–237; 1982, vol. 3, p. 5. Imamura 1971, pp. 14–15, 18. Watatani and Yamada 1978, pp. 208,

437–438. Tominaga 1972, pp. 31–33. Ishioka et al. 1980, pp. 15, 26–27, 53–54. Tsumoto 1983, p. 204. Kensei Tsukahara Bokuden Seitan Gohyakunen-sai Kinen Jigyō Jikkō Iinkai 1989, pp. 16–17, 48. Maebayashi 1992, p. 52. Shinjimbutsu Ōraisha 1994, pp. 50, 53. Friday 1997, pp. 19–24. Hurst 1998, p. 47. Yokose 2000, pp. 12–13, 26–27. Asakura 2005, p. 128. Gakushū Kenkyūsha 2005, pp. 17–18; 2006, p. 21; 2008, p. 6. Nippon Budōkan 2008, p. 105. Hinatsu Shigetaka (1716, p. 11) and Shiga Yoshinobu (1767, p. 113) also mention "the divine warriors of Kashima and Katori [grand shrines]" in regard to the origins of Japanese military strategy (Shiga apparently cites Hinatsu's words related to the Kashima swordsmanship and strategy).

27. Ōtake 2007, pp. 27, 30.

28. Hinatsu 1716, p. 52. Tamon 1841. Minamoto 1843, pp. 192, 201–203. Shimokawa 1925, p. 157. Hori 1934, pp. 38, 55. Yamada 1960, p. 16. Tominaga 1972, pp. 31–33, 41–43. Watatani and Yamada 1978, pp. 213, 228. Ishioka et al. 1980, pp. 15–16. Kensei Tsukahara Bokuden Seitan Gohyakunen-sai Kinen Jigyō Jikkō Iinkai 1989, p. 17. Shinjimbutsu Ōraisha 1994, p. 50. Yokose 2000, pp. 12–13. Asakura 2005, p. 128.

29. Hinatsu 1716, p. 63. Shiga 1767, p. 123. Hori 1934, p. 54. Yamada 1960, pp. 25–26. Watanabe 1967, p. 41. Imamura 1971, p. 138. Watatani 1971, pp. 16–17. Tominaga 1972, pp. 31, 35. Watatani and Yamada 1978, pp. 683–685. Ishioka et al. 1980, pp. 89–90. Kōdansha 1983, p. 162. Waterhouse 1996, pp. 28–30. Yokose 2000, pp. 38–39.

30. Hinatsu 1716, pp. 63–66. Shiga 1767, p. 123. Hatori et al. 1843, pp. 159–160. Minamoto 1843, pp. 212–213. Shimokawa 1925, pp. 158, 203–204. Hori 1934, pp. 38–39, 54, 177. Yamada 1960, pp. 23, 25–27. Watatani 1971, p. 18. Tominaga 1972, pp. 31, 38–39. Watatani and Yamada 1978, p. 574. Ishioka et al. 1980, pp. 16, 46–47, 90. Kōdansha 1983, pp. 145, 161–162. Shinjimbutsu Ōraisha 1994, pp. 58–61. Waterhouse 1996, p. 30. Hurst 1998, p. 50. Yokose 2000, p. 69. It is also possible to see accounts of a certain Oda-ryū allegedly established by a military commander Oda Takatomo (1337–1414), who studied swordsmanship under either Chūjō Nagahide's grandfather Yorihira or Nagahide himself (Hatori et al. 1843, p. 161. Hori 1934, pp. 39, 177. Yamada 1960, pp. 24–25. Watatani 1971, p. 18. Tominaga 1972, p. 38, Watatani and Yamada 1978, pp. 157–158. Ishioka et al. 1980, pp. 15–16). However, regardless of the source, Oda-ryū's description is always limited to just a few lines of vague information, and it is unclear whether this school existed or it was just a kind of "style" that was claimed by the Oda family but that was not taught to outsiders.

31. Watatani 1971, pp. 16–18. Tominaga 1972, pp. 35–37. Watatani and Yamada 1978, pp. 573–574, 683–685. Kōdansha 1983, p. 145. Waterhouse 1996, p. 28.

32. Tominaga 1972, p. 36. See also Ishioka et al. 1980, p. 89.
33. Imamura 1982, p. 12. Hurst 1998, p. 46. Anshin 2009, pp. 11, 29–31, 62. It should be noted that sometimes Ogasawara-ryū (archery, the beginning of the thirteenth century) and Ōtsubo-ryū (horsemanship, from the end of the fourteenth to the beginning of the fifteenth century) are mentioned as the first "schools" of military arts (Imamura 1982, p. 12, Nakabayashi 1983, p. 16, note 2). However, there is no established theory with regard to the period of their birth, and the above dates may well reflect the time when they were not formalized yet as "schools." What is more important, they were not military but ceremonial. See the discussion of their character in Nishiyama 1982, pp. 261–262.
34. Tominaga 1972, p. 31. Ishioka et al. 1980, p. 14. Hurst 1998, p. 51.
35. Waterhouse 1996, p. 30. Friday 1997, pp. 14–15, 37.
36. In actuality, the practice of sealing a nondisclosure pledge in blood upon entrance (*keppan*) was not limited to military arts schools; it was common in many other areas as well. This was often a simultaneous oath to the god-protectors of an art, such as Marishiten in the case of military arts.
37. It is unclear how this was achieved in the pre-Tokugawa ages, but it may be that they used techniques similar to the training halls (*dōjō*) of the Tokugawa era, which, for example, placed very narrow windows close to the ceiling (Tominaga 1972, p. 272).
38. Examples of such methods in Tenshinshō-den Katori Shintō-ryū can be found in Gakushū Kenkyūsha 2005, pp. 14–16; 2008, pp. 11–33; Ōtake 2007, pp. 109, 155. Examples in the mainline Daitō-ryū Aikijūjutsu can be found at http://daito-ryu.org/en/kondo-katsuyuki.html (accessed on October 20, 2011).
39. Hori 1934, p. 44. Ōtake 1977, vol. 2, p. 23; 1985b, pp. 40–41; 2007, pp. 46, 109; 2009a, pp. 51–52. Reid and Croucher 1983, pp. 131–133, 141. Sasama 1985, pp. 31–32. Farris 1992. Iizasa 2000, pp. 19–21. Yokose 2000, p. 15. Nihon Kobudō Kyōkai 2002, p. 38. Gakushū Kenkyūsha 2005, pp. 9, 12; 2008, pp. 11–12. Anshin 2009, pp. 47–48, 114. An example of an old warrior document explaining, both in text and graphically, techniques designed for targeting openings in the opponent's armor can be found in Hori 1934, pp. 51–54.
40. Anshin 2009, pp. 67–68, 72–73, 91–92. Many esoteric practices of the *bushi* employed sword symbolism, such as the usage of the "nine magical lines" (*kuji*) and the "tenth magical sign" (*jūji*). In regard to *kuji* and *jūji* used by Japanese warriors, see Ōtake 1975; 1978 (vol. 3), pp. 14–19; 2007, pp. 246–255.
41. Anshin 2009, pp. 68, 72. Here, it is necessary to mention the recent tendency in academic works to negate the practical value and historical relevance of close-combat skills transmitted in pre-Tokugawa schools of military arts (see, for example, Nakamura Toshio 1981, Nishiyama 1982, Ōtsuka 1995,

Suzuki Masaya 2000, Yuasa Akira 2000, Friday 2005). Their assertions can be summed up in two major points: pre-Tokugawa *bushi* did not receive any systematic martial training as all their time was consumed by war; battlefield tactics in medieval Japan gradually changed from individual to group combat, and individual close-combat skills taught by the formalized schools of military arts were irrelevant to what was expected from fighting men who had to act as an organized force. The primary evidence for this is battlefield wound statistics from various historical periods that show that wounds inflicted by the bladed weapons were few compared to those inflicted by projectile weapons. Some scholars also cite Ko'idegiri Ichiun's words appearing in *Sekiun-ryū kenjutsu sho* (A writing on the swordsmanship of Sekiun-ryū, 1686) that *bushi* did not engage in military arts training before the dawning of the Great Tokugawa Peace simply because they were too busy at war. These assertions are untenable because, as mentioned earlier, the formalized schools of military arts were only the tip of the iceberg of military skills and training methodologies transmitted in the hereditary warrior houses. Professional warriors received an extensive and systematic instruction from their childhood because, without such systematic training, the hereditary warrior lineages as such simply could not survive for generations. When it comes to battlefield wound statistics, one should be cautious about taking them at face value without due attention to the peculiarities of *bushi* bodily practices. Scholars also ignore such primary materials as pre-Tokugawa warrior house rules and precepts, in which military commanders and daimyos consistently call upon their subordinates to train earnestly in all kinds of individual close-combat skills. These skills were as important as the capability to act as an organized force. Finally, in the case of Ko'idegiri Ichiun, his swordsmanship school, Sekiun-ryū, presents an extreme example of the Tokugawa-era "flowery training" completely removed from the realities of actual combat (this is confirmed by the study of Maebayashi Kiyokazu [1992, 1999]). Ko'idegiri's writings should not be consulted with regard to the training of pre-Tokugawa *bushi*. A detailed discussion of these issues can be found in Anshin 2009, pp. 68–73.

42. Anshin, pp. 66, 87.
43. Waterhouse 1996, p. 28.
44. Yuasa Yasuo 1986, pp. 28–29.
45. Waterhouse 1996.
46. In times of unrest preceding the Tokugawa era, spy activities could sometimes be conducted by wandering the country under the pretext of *musha shugyō*.
47. An emphasis on the importance of wandering the country makes our understanding of *musha shugyō* quite narrow and limited. Such a viewpoint

overlooks the fact that not many *bushi* engaged in this kind of practice. Needless to say, should all the *bushi* have practiced *musha shugyō* in the form of wandering the country, lords would have remained without retainers and Japan's society would have fallen into chaos.

48. Tominaga 1972, Hurst 1998.

49. There are no records indicating *musha shugyō* in the form of wandering the country by Iizasa Chōisai, the fifteenth-century founder of Tenshinshō-den Katori Shintō-ryū, the oldest attested military arts school in Japan. Instead, they point to his austere training in the grounds of the Katori Jingū Grand Shrine (Hinatsu 1716, p. 52. Hatori et al. 1843, p. 158. Minamoto 1843, p. 204. Seimiya 1877, the reverse side of page 15. Shimokawa 1925, pp. 198–199. Hori 1934, pp. 167–168. Yamada 1960, pp. 27–29. Imamura et al. 1966, vol. 2, pp. 238–239; 1982, vol. 3, pp. 8–9. Tominaga 1972, pp. 33–34. Ōtake 1977, vol. 1, p. 16; 1979, p. 26; 1981, p. 22; 2007, pp. 8–11. Ishioka et al. 1980, p. 28. Chiba Sōgo Ginkō 1981, p. 104. Kendō Nihon 1981, p. 49. Reid and Croucher 1983, pp. 120–121. Kōdansha 1983, p. 144. Tsumoto 1983, p. 204. Akita Shoten 1987, p. 159. Ōmori Nobumasa 1991, p. 227. Shinjimbutsu Ōraisha 1994, pp. 50–52. Nihon Kobudō Kyōkai 1997, p 83. Iizasa 2000, p. 19. Yokose 2000, p. 13. Asakura 2005, pp. 128–129. Gakushū Kenkyūsha 2005, pp. 8–9; 2008, pp. 6–7. Nippon Budōkan 2008, p. 170. Anshin 2009, pp. 43–44). This book also provides examples of the *musha shugyō* of Yamaoka Seizan and Yamaoka Tesshū in the Bakumatsu, period who never wandered the country.

50. It should be noted that the phrase *musha shugyō* does not appear in Yamaoka's surviving records in regard to his own training. However, insofar as his entire life is consistent with the meaning of this term as described here, I consider it legitimate to use this phrase when analyzing his conduct.

51. Anshin 2009, pp. 65–66, 79–80. A point to bear in mind is that this philosophy was not unique to *bushi*. The combination of the art of killing with intense spiritual self-cultivation is actually a concept that can be found in Chinese military treatises written two thousand years ago, such as *Sun Tzu*.

52. According to this myth, the attempts of the goddess Amaterasu Ōkami to rule the Izumo Land (Japan) were disrupted by violent gods of the land who obeyed the supreme god Ōkuninushi no Kami. After two unsuccessful attempts to persuade Ōkuninushi no Kami to relinquish the Izumo Land, Amaterasu Ōkami held a council with countless other gods who recommended in chorus Futsunushi no Ōkami as the most appropriate god for subduing the Izumo Land. At the same time, the god Takemikazuchi no Ōkami volunteered to join this mission, and both gods were sent to the Izumo Land. The god Ōkuninushi no Kami agreed to obey the order of Amaterasu Ōkami as soon

as the gods Futsunushi and Takemikazuchi descended on the Izumo Land and demonstrated their martial might by sticking the hilts of their unsheathed swords into the ground (some variations of this myth maintain that the gods Futsunushi and Takemikazuchi not only stuck the hilts of their unsheathed swords into the ground, but also sat cross-legged on their tips).

53. The legend says that, in the land of Kumano, Emperor Jimmu and his subordinates were exposed to the poisonous breath of the wild gods of the Kumanozan mountain, and they lost consciousness. A native of Kumano by the name of Takakuraji presented Emperor Jimmu with a sword whose divine power helped the emperor to recover his senses, and all the wild gods were destroyed magically by the sword, which was not even swung.

54. Ōtake 1981, p. 23; 2007, pp. 14–15, 290–291.

55. Uozumi 2008, p. iii.

56. Uncritical academic and nonacademic writers have revered Musashi as a "great master of swordsmanship" or even a "saint swordsman" without attaching any importance to the fact that he did not choose the means to engage in what he perceived as the process of self-perfection. David Waterhouse even maintains that the Japanese cultural phenomenon of *musha shugyō* reached its apogee in the life and career of Musashi (Waterhouse 1996, p. 28). Even though its authenticity is questioned, scholars and popular writers have been preoccupied with Musashi's *Gorin no sho* (*The book of five rings*, ca. 1644) as well as his personality, when considering *bushi* moral values, including Bushidō (Satō Kenji 1950; Shitō 1967; Murakami Ichirō 1975; Taniguchi Katsuomi 1988; Sakurai 1989; Maebayashi 1992; Tanaka 2001–2007; Jugen 2003; Kubo 2003; Moriyasu 2003; Shimura 2003a-b; Tateno 2003; Terabayashi 2003; Uozumi 2002, 2005, 2008). Uozumi Takashi argued that Musashi embodies the "Way of the Japanese people," while Suzuki Kunio goes as far as to maintain that *Gorin no sho*, which is actually a treatise on the art of killing human beings, contains an image of a man who should serve as a model for people of the twenty-first century (Uozumi 2002, Suzuki Kunio 2006).

57. Uozumi 2008, pp. 70, 84.

58. Uozumi Takashi (2008, p. 84) mentions the fact that such low social appraisal is used by some authors to denigrate Musashi. At the same time, Uozumi attempts to embellish Musashi by recalculating his stipend to a higher figure according to different criteria. However, it is not convincing because Uozumi does not apply the same criteria to the other swordsmen's stipends. Uozumi also tries to explain Musashi's failure to receive any treatment from the Tokugawa Bakufu by the fact that his "thinking advanced beyond his times" (2008, p. 70), but this is an uncritical idealization of Musashi.

Notes

Chapter 1   Prior to His Time

59. For example, in regard to Yamaoka Tesshū, John Stevens (1984, p. ix) states that "perhaps the only comparable figure in Japan is the sixteenth-century swordsman Miyamoto Musashi." The impetus for the Musashi boom in Japan, and later overseas, was Yoshikawa Eiji's novel *Miyamoto Musashi*, which was published as a newspaper serialization from 1935 to 1939. This serialization became a book in 1939, and it was also used for numerous theater and radio plays, TV and cinema films. The fictionalized image of Musashi has, through the process of repetition, become a historical reality in its own right, but as Yoshikawa himself admitted, "There are almost no records about Musashi that could be trusted as true historical facts. [If we are to summarize the truth about Musashi], it will take no more than sixty to seventy lines of printed text" (cited from Uozumi 2008, pp. i-ii. One line of printed text to which Yoshikawa refers had forty-two characters [Uozumi 2008, p. ii]). Apparently, few people know this, and Musashi continues to be one of the most recognizable warrior figures in popular culture. His treatise on the art of killing has even become a manual for doing successful business among modern businessmen. Musashi has also been an object of reverence and commemoration in one of his supposed homelands in Mimasaka City, Okayama Prefecture, where one can find a major training center bearing his name. In Japan, modern *kendō* tournaments are sometimes held in commemoration of Musashi.
60. Hurst 1998, p. 55.
61. Nihon Kobudō Kyōkai 2002, p. 11. Reliable data does not exist for the early Tokugawa era.
62. This text by Matsushita Gunkō appears in Kōdansha 1983, p. 127.
63. Kōdansha 1983, p. 132. In the time of the third Tokugawa shogun, Iemitsu, the number of warriors who had lost their lords after the "daimyo purge" reached five hundred thousand (Hirakawa 2006, p. 124). See also Vaporis 1994, p. 103.
64. See, for example, Matsushita Gunkō's detailed criticism in Kōdansha 1983, p. 127. Another military scholar of the first half of the eighteenth century, Arisawa Munesada (1689–1752), wrote that the practice of military arts for the sake of outward appearance and entertainment should be strictly prohibited (*Shoshi kokoroe* [What all warriors must know, written late in the author's life] appearing in Saeki et al. 1944, *bekkan*, p. 100). Examples of other contemporary criticisms of training in the military arts can be found in Shimokawa 1925, pp. 224–226.
65. Isoda 2003, pp. 27–66, 363–372. Fuse 2006, pp. 37–38.
66. Hurst 1998, pp. 92–94. Fuse 2006, pp. 37–38.
67. Kōdansha 1983, pp. 139–140. Hurst 1998, p. 65. The Bakufu edict (*buke shohatto*) of 1615 exalted the "unity of literary and military arts" (*bumbu*

ryōdō) as the cornerstone of the *bushi* education. In the case of the latter, the practice of swordsmanship was particularly emphasized. The Tokugawa Bakufu's policy was later adopted by the majority of domains (Ōmori Nobumasa 1976a, p. 102).

68. Ishikawa 1960; Watanabe 1967; Imamura 1989; Fuse 2006. The connection between subclasses and particular kinds of military arts resulted in strong specialization within a *bushi* subclass. Naturally, the ranks of teachers of military arts schools were also in direct correlation with the social order. Low-ranking teachers of military arts could not teach *bushi* from higher subclasses of warrior society (Fuse 2006).

69. Watanabe 1967, pp. 1, 3–4. Ōmori Nobumasa 1974, pp. 67, 69. Kōdansha 1983, pp. 121–122, 125, 127. Ishioka et al. 1980, p. 21. Maebayashi and Watanabe 1988, p. 178. Maebayashi 1992, pp. 51, 55. Hurst 1998, pp. 66, 69–70.

70. One of the rare exceptions is William Bodiford, who quite convincingly showed that there was practically no connection between Japanese swordsmanship and Zen before the peaceful Tokugawa era (Bodiford 2005). See also Hall 1990, p. 1.

71. Suzuki Daisetsu 1938, 1959.

72. Herrigel 1953.

73. Friday 1997, p. 201, note 9.

74. This last name is sometimes read as Kamiizumi.

75. Yagyū 1957, p. 14. Yamada 1960, pp. 38–50. Imamura 1971, pp. 30–31, 38. Yokose 2000, p. 55. Kōizumi Ise no Kami is also said to have studied Tenshinshō-den Katori Shintō-ryū and Nen-ryū (Yagyū 1957, p. 14; Yokose 2000, p. 55; Ōtake 2007, pp. 28, 30).

76. Yagyū 1957, p. 13. Imamura 1971, p. 34.

77. Ōmori Nobumasa 1974, pp. 68, 70, 72.

78. Ibid., p. 72. Maebayashi 1995, p. 62. Bodiford 2005, p. 156.

79. Ōmori Nobumasa 1976a, p. 110. Yokose 2000, pp. 54–55.

80. Ōmori Nobumasa 1976a, pp. 102, 107, 110; p. 112, notes 17, 18. Ishioka et al. 1980, p. 19. Kōdansha 1983, pp. 121–122. Yuasa Yasuo 1986, p. 56–57. Maebayashi and Watanabe 1988, pp. 176–177, 182–184. Maebayashi 1992, pp. 53–55; 1995, p. 51. Hurst 1998, p. 192–193. Monk Takuan was also a teacher of Zen to the third Tokugawa shogun Iemitsu.

81. Hurst 1998, p. 192.

82. Ōmori Nobumasa 1974, p. 67. Maebayashi 1992, p. 63, note 17. Hurst 1998, pp. 92, 177–179.

83. *Tako Tokitaka kakun* appearing in Ozawa 2003, p. 164; *Shingen kahō* appearing in Saeki et al. 1942, vol. 1, p. 335; *Kuroda Nagamasa chakushi Tadayuki kunkai shojō* appearing in Ozawa 2003, p. 407.

84. Taniguchi Shinko 2005, pp. 90–93.
85. Tominaga 1972, p. 277. Ōtsuka 1995, p. 6. Nakamura Tamio 1999, p. 60; 2001a.
86. Yagyū 1957, p. 214. Imamura 1971, p. 152. Tominaga 1972, pp. 276, 448–449. Kōdansha 1983, p. 123. Sasama 1985, p. 33. Friday 1997, p. 119. Hurst 1998, p. 84. Yokose 2000, p. 57. Gakushū Kenkyūsha 2005, pp. 28, 31.
87. Anshin 2009, pp. 111–115.
88. Imamura 1971, p. 30. Yokose 2000, p. 55.
89. Some legendary stories state that Kōizumi used his bamboo sword for the first time in duels in order not to hurt his opponents (Watatani 1971, pp. 52–53. Tominaga 1972, p. 448. Hurst 1998, pp. 61–62). This is undoubtedly fiction unless we accept that Kōizumi was not as skillful as he is praised for being.
90. Strictly speaking, what has been communicated to the general public by the Yagyū family as "Shinkage-ryū" seems to have little in common with the original Shinkage-ryū established by Kōizumi Ise no Kami, and the name "Yagyū-ryū" is more appropriate to the school. Komagawa Kaishin-ryū, which traces its origins to Kōizumi's direct disciple Komagawa Tarōzaemon and is presently transmitted by Kuroda Tetsuzan, appears to have retained far more of the elements of the original Shinkage-ryū (see Kuroda 1992, pp. 19–20, 24, 26–27, 32, 77, 391; 1997, p. 112). The predetermined patterns of movement of Komagawa Kaishin-ryū are characterized by the use of the wooden sword at blinding speed appropriate to the school that traces its origins to the pre-Tokugawa ages. Still, there is a possibility that the Yagyū family separated the less practical skill taught to shoguns and disciples from outside the family from the real skill, which was transmitted in secrecy.
91. Hori 1934, p. 88. Watanabe 1967, p. 46. Imamura 1971, p. 152. Tominaga 1972, pp. 324–325. Watatani and Yamada 1978, pp. 328–329. Kōdansha 1983, p. 123. Nakamura Tamio 1999, pp. 59–60; 2001a.
92. Watanabe 1967, p. 46. Imamura 1971, pp. 152–155. Tominaga 1972, pp. 277, 324–326. Watatani and Yamada 1978, pp. 328–329. Kōdansha 1983, pp. 123–124. Hurst 1998, p. 84. Nakamura Tamio 1999, p. 60; 2001a.
93. Hori 1934, p. 91. Watanabe 1967, pp. 6–7. Imamura 1971, p. 153. Tominaga 1972, pp. 277, 337. Watatani and Yamada 1978, p. 653. Kōdansha 1983, p. 124. Ōtsuka 1995, pp. 6–9, 8–12. Hurst 1998, p. 84. Nakamura Tamio 1999, p. 70; 2001b. Nakanishi Tsugutake further improved training equipment for free sparring (Ōtsuka 1995, p. 6).
94. Enomoto 1978, p. 265. Kōdansha 1983, p. 125. Ōtsuka 1995, p. 6.
95. Hurst 1998, p. 87.
96. Ibid., p. 92. Fuse 2006, pp. 28, 56–57.
97. Hurst 1998, pp. 67, 88, 178–179. Fuse 2006, pp. 195–196, 204–205.

98. Fuse 2006, p. 195.
99. Enomoto 1988, p. 348. Ōtsuka 1995, pp. 10–12. Fuse 2006, p. 196.
100. Enomoto 1978, pp. 266–267.
101. Fuse 2006, pp. 57, 195–196, 204–205, 211. See also Hurst 1998, pp. 92–93.
102. Watanabe 1967, pp. 2–3, 20–22. Enomoto 1978, p. 265.
103. Enomoto 1978, pp. 265–266. Ōtsuka 1995, p. 14. Nakamura Tamio 2001b. Fuse 2006, p. 199.
104. Hori 1934, pp. 94–95. Imamura 1971, p. 213. Sasama 1985, p. 33. Kōdansha 1983, p. 196. Enomoto 1988, pp. 346, 354. Nakamura Tamio 2001b.
105. Naruse 1940, pp. 51–52, 55–57, 71–74. Tsumoto 1983, p. 203. Ōtsuka 1995, p. 27.
106. Oimatsu 1968, pp. 3–4.
107. Friday 1997, p. 202, note 19. Hurst 1998, pp. 67–68.
108. See Taniguchi Shinko 2005 on the regulation of violence among the *bushi* by Tokugawa law.
109. Ōkuma 1973, pp. 129, 131–132.

Chapter 2   Boyhood and Youth

1. Murakami Yasumasa 1999, p. 140.
2. In many sources, the forename of Tesshū's father is read as Takayoshi. I use the reading given in Ushiyama 1967 (p. 9) and Murakami Yasumasa 1999 (p. 14).
3. One *koku* is equal to 4.96 bushels of rice.
4. Ushiyama 1976, p. 9. Kōdansha 1983, p. 205. Murakami Yasumasa 1999, pp. 1–7, 14, 17, 19. The salary that Ono Takatomi received for his service was expressed in *hyō* units (200 *hyō*), but since these units were exempted from taxation, they were equal to 200 *koku*.
5. At the time in question, only three Shintō shrines in Japan had the highest rank of "grand shrine" (*jingū*)—Ise Jingū, Katori Jingū, and Kashima Jingū.
6. Imamura 1971, p. 229. Watatani 1971, p. 255. Tominaga 1972, p. 374. Ushiyama 1976, p. 11. Ishioka et al. 1980, p. 183. Murakami Yasumasa 1999, pp. 19, 23. There are no records indicating what branch or faction of Shinkage-ryū Tesshū practiced. Sometimes the name of the school that Yamaoka studied under Kusumi Kantekisai, may appear as Jikishinkage-ryū. As mentioned earlier, the training of small children in warrior arts was a characteristic feature of the training methodologies of pre-Tokugawa hereditary warrior houses. Although these methodologies were practically lost during the Great Tokugawa Peace, the custom of beginning training in swordsmanship at a very young age had been retained until the end of this era, and Tesshū was no exception. Other examples include Ōishi Susumu,

who was the first one to use the extralong bamboo sword for interschool matches in the Bakumatsu period. He is said to have begun training in spearmanship and swordsmanship at the age of four or five (Watatani 1971, p. 226). A ten-year-old son of Chiba Shūsaku, the founder of Hokushin Ittō-ryū, is said to have participated in an interschool match before the daimyo of the Mito Domain, Tokugawa Nariaki (Hoshi 1993, p. 31). Studies of the Hikone Domain show that sons of the daimyos of this domain began their training in swordsmanship, spearmanship, and archery between the ages of ten and eleven (Mori 2005, pp. 60–61).

7. Ushiyama 1976, pp. 12–13. Ishioka et al. 1980, p. 183. Murakami Yasumasa 1999, pp. 23–26, 31. The fact that the former intendant of Hida Province was Kusumi Kantekisai's younger brother (Murakami Yasumasa 1999, pp. 23–25) hints at some relationship between the Ono and Kusumi families, and Tesshū's entrance into Kusumi Kantekisai's swordsmanship school, as well as his father's new appointment, do not seem to have been accidental.

8. Murakami Yasumasa 1999, pp. 29–30, 35, 40, 42–43, 54–57.

9. Kōdansha 1983, p. 206. Murakami Yasumasa 1999, p. 42. According to the Japanese encyclopedia *Kōjien* (5th edition by Iwanami Shoten), *kirigami* (also *kirigami menkyo*) was given to those who reached one of the highest ranks in Japanese traditional arts, which usually preceded the final level of "full transmission" (*menkyo kaiden*, etc.). It was a piece of paper containing a description of what the disciple had learned.

10. Imamura 1971, p. 229. Watatani 1971, p. 255. Tominaga 1972, p. 374. Watatani and Yamada 1978, p. 69. Kōdansha 1983, p. 206. Iwasa 1987, p. 178. Ishioka et al. 1980, p. 183. Murakami Yasumasa 1999, pp. 48–53.

11. Ema 1935, pp. 16–18. Imamura 1971, p. 229. Watatani 1971, pp. 255–256. Watatani and Yamada 1978, p. 69. Ishioka et al. 1980, p. 183. Kōdansha 1983, p. 205. Murakami Yasumasa 1999, pp. 28–29, 31, 33–35, 38, 41. The document certifying the grant of the pseudonym appears in Iwasa 1987, p. 77.

12. Iwasa 1987, pp. 162–163.

13. Ushiyama 1976, p. 23.

14. Iwasa 1987, p. 108.

15. Ushiyama 1976, pp. 27–28. Murakami Yasumasa 1999, pp. 39–40.

16. Sakura 1893, pp. 7–8. Ushiyama 1976, p. 28.

17. Sakura 1893, pp. 7, 10–11. Maruyama 1918b, p. 4. Imamura 1971, p. 229. Watatani 1971, p. 255.

18. Iwasa 1987, p. 18.

19. These letters appear in Iwasa 1987, pp. 86, 90.

20. Maruyama 1918b, pp. 4–5. Ushiyama 1937, pp. 11–12. Watatani 1971, p. 256. Murakami Yasumasa 1999, pp. 44, 58–59, 85–86.

21. According to Tesshū's letter addressed to Iwasa Ittei appearing in Iwasa 1987, p. 91.
22. Iwasa 1987, p. 178.
23. Murakami Yasumasa 1999, p. 58.
24. Ibid., pp. 89–90. See also Watatani 1971, pp. 256–257; Ishioka et al. 1980, p. 184.
25. Yasumasa 1999, p. 88.
26. The letter is dated June 1853 and appears in Iwasa 1987, pp. 95, 97–98. Even after his return to Edo Tesshū and Iwasa were in correspondence until the death of the latter in November of 1858 (Ema 1935, pp. 56–63).
27. Jansen 1961, pp. 82–83. Inoue et al. 1996, vol. 12, pp. 4–8. Nakamura Tamio 2001b.
28. Jansen 1961, p. 81.
29. The draft of this writing appears in Maruyama 1918b, pp. 8–9.
30. Watatani 1971, p. 256. Tominaga 1972, p. 374. Watatani and Yamada 1978, p. 69. Ishioka et al. 1980, p. 184. Murakami Yasumasa 1999, pp. 94, 105. See also Enomoto 1979, p. 253.
31. Yamada 1960, p. 339. Imamura 1971, pp. 218–219. Tominaga 1972, pp. 353–356. Enomoto 1979, pp. 258–259. Ishioka et al. 1980, pp. 173, 175–176. Kōdansha 1983, p. 193. Nakabayashi 1983, p. 16, note 13. Hurst 1998, pp. 88–90. Ōtsuka 1995, p. 14. Maebayashi 2006, pp. 316–319. See also Miyachi 2009, pp. 6–7.
32. Shimokawa 1925, p. 287. Yamada 1960, p. 340. Watanabe 1967, pp. 34–35. Tominaga 1972, p. 355. Watatani and Yamada 1978, p. 760.
33. Fujishima 1957, p. 103. Yamada 1960, p. 342. Oyamatsu 1974, pp. 62, 65, 93–94. Ishioka et al. 1980, p. 175. Gakushū Kenkyūsha 2005, p. 118. For spiritual, philosophical, and esoteric aspects of Ittō-ryū, see Sasamori 1965 and Ōmori Nobumasa 1976b.
34. Fujishima 1957, p. 103. Yamada 1960, p. 343. Watanabe 1967, p. 35. Imamura 1971, pp. 220–221. Watatani 1971, p. 209. Tominaga 1972, pp. 353, 355. Ishioka et al. 1980, pp. 173–174. Kōdansha 1983, pp. 194–195. Hurst 1998, p. 89. Gakushū Kenkyūsha 2005, p. 118. "Gembukan" is a generic name for a number of training facilities located in a very wide area. Together with other similar training halls, such as Rempeikan (Gekkenkan) of Shintō Munen-ryū, Shigakkan of Kyōshin Meichi-ryū, and the training hall of Shingyōtō-ryū, Gembukan was also counted as one of the "four largest swordsmanship training halls in Edo" of the Bakumatsu period.
35. From an untitled original document written by Yamaoka on January 8, 1882. Preserved in Shumpūkan Bunko, Tamagawa Library, Kanazawa City (item number 30-1-107 *Yamaoka Tetsutarō jikihitsu kendō sho, dai issatsu*).

Yamaoka writes about his abilities at the age of "about twenty." However, Murakami Yasumasa points to the exact age of nineteen (Murakami Yasumasa 1999, p. 92).

36. Sakura 1893, pp. 10–12. Imamura 1971, pp. 229–230. Tominaga 1972, p. 374. Ishioka et al. 1980, p. 184. Kōdansha 1983, p. 206. Murakami Yasumasa 1999, pp. 92, 127–128.

37. Sakura 1893, pp. 10–12. Murakami Yasumasa 1999, pp. 92, 127–128.

38. Murakami Yasumasa 1999, pp. 90–91, 93. The name of the spearmanship school transmitted in the Yamaoka family is not clear.

39. The biography of Yamaoka Seizan by Nakamura Masanao in Fukuda 1879, p. 27. Ushiyama 1937, p. 20. Watatani 1971, p. 256. Tominaga 1972, p. 374. Watatani and Yamada 1978, p. 69. Murakami Yasumasa 1999, pp. 93–94.

40. This biography is not dated, but it was already published in Fukuda 1879.

41. The shrine dedicated to the worship of Tokugawa Ieyasu, the founder of the Tokugawa Bakufu.

42. The biography of Yamaoka Seizan by Nakamura Masanao in Fukuda 1879, pp. 28–30.

43. Referring to Yamaoka Seizan.

44. The biography of Yamaoka Seizan by Nakamura Masanao in Fukuda 1879, p. 28.

45. Ibid., p. 29.

46. Ushiyama 1937, p. 21; 1976, p. 47. Murakami Yasumasa 1999, pp. 94–95.

47. Murakami Yasumasa 1999, pp. 93–95.

48. Ushiyama 1942b, pp. 26–30, 33. Imamura 1971, p. 229. Watatani 1971, p. 256. Tominaga 1972, p. 374. Watatani and Yamada 1978, p. 69. Ishioka et al. 1980, p. 184. Kōdansha 1983, p. 206. Murakami Yasumasa 1999, pp. 95–97.

49. Inoue et al. 1996, vol. 12, pp. 57–58. Nakamura Tamio 2001b.

50. Andō 1930. Enomoto 1978, p. 266. Inoue et al. 1996, vol. 12, p. 57.

51. Enomoto 1979, p. 244.

52. Ibid., p. 244. See also Inoue et al. 1996, vol. 12, pp. 57–58. Much later, in May 1864, the Bakufu also established the Literary and Military Arts Training Hall (Bumbu Keikojō) in Kyoto for its retainers who resided in the old capital. In February 1866, it was reopened as a more advanced institution that received the name Bumbujō, or the Literary and Military Arts Hall, and was a smaller version of the Bakufu Military Institute in Edo. The Bumbujō curriculum included training in swordsmanship, spearmanship, and general scholarship. Only Bakufu retainers were allowed to attend the Bumbujō (Kikuchi 2005, pp. 83–85).

53. Andō 1930. Enomoto 1978, pp. 266, 281. Izumi 1988, pp. 6–9. Inoue et al. 1996, vol. 12, p. 58.

54. Andō 1930.

55. Ibid.

56. Ibid. Enomoto 1978, pp. 245, 266–267; 1979, p. 262. Nakamura Tamio 2001b.

57. Watatani 1971, p. 256. Tominaga 1972, p. 374. Watatani and Yamada 1978, p. 69. Ishioka et al. 1980, p. 184. Murakami Yasumasa 1999, p. 105. See also Enomoto 1979, p. 253.

58. Murakami Yasumasa 1999, pp. 105–106. In the *Gembukan shusseki daigai* (General list of Gembukan attendees), listing people who trained at the Gembukan training hall in 1857–1858, Tesshū's name (Ono Tetsutarō) appears along with his title as the assistant of the Bakufu Military Institute. Although by that time, Tesshū had already become the heir of the Yamaoka family, for some reason, he appears in the list as Ono Tetsutarō and a dependant of his elder brother Takakata. Presently, there are no historical materials that could shed light on the reason for this discrepancy. It is also worth mentioning that besides Tesshū, at least five other young men in this list also worked as assistants of swordsmanship instruction at the Military Institute (Oyamatsu 1974, pp. 224–225).

59. Andō 1930, pp. 55–57. Here, again, Yamaoka appears in the list of participants as "Ono Tetsutarō" and a dependant of his elder brother Takakata.

60. Andō 1930, pp. 62, 68.

61. Andō 1930.

62. In 1857, Yamaoka submitted two petitions (Murakami Yasumasa 1999, pp. 107–108). However, the contents of only one have survived.

63. The draft of this writing appears in Maruyama 1918b, pp. 8–9. See also Imamura 1971, pp. 230–231.

64. Andō 1930.

65. Ansart 2007.

66. Daidōji [early XVIII c.], pp. 159–163. See my earlier note on the nature of Daidōji Yūzan's precepts.

67. A detailed analysis of the developments of the Boshin Civil War can be found in Ōyama 1988, Kikuchi and Itō 1998, Hōya 2007.

68. Izumi 1988, pp. 6–9. Part of the reason lies with the behind-the-scenes activity of the Ogasawara-ryū school of archery, which aimed at including its instructors in the personnel of the Bakufu Military Institute. Nevertheless, the main reasons for the introduction of archery were political (ibid.).

Chapter 3   Expel the Foreigners, Protect the Shogun

1. Jansen 1961, pp. 81, 85–86, 105. Still, it is necessary to bear in mind that the teaching or general atmosphere of private swordsmanship training halls

did not necessarily have to be nationalistic, nor did their heads publicly call for the "reverence of the emperor and expulsion of the barbarians," although they could advocate this ideology personally.

2. Oyamatsu 1974, p. 93. Murakami Yasumasa 1999, p. 108.
3. Oyamatsu 1974, p. 93.
4. Ibid., pp. 26–30, 33, 35–40, 60, 62, 70–74, 83–85, 92–96, 105, 241.
5. Oyamatsu 1974.
6. Inoue et al. 1996, vol. 12, p. 106.
7. Restoration activists frequently used the term "ugly barbarians" when referring to foreigners in their correspondence.
8. Oyamatsu 1974, p. 125.
9. Inoue et al. 1996, vol. 12, p. 105.
10. Oyamatsu 1974, pp. 101–102, 124. Takano 2004, p. 145. Additionally, the Japanese language has a figurative expression for doing something dangerous: "as if to step on a tiger's tail, or to walk on spring ice" (Maekawa 1977, p. 42).
11. Maekawa 1977, p. 112.
12. Oyamatsu 1974, pp. 102, 110, 123–124. Maekawa 1977, p. 114.
13. Maekawa 1977, p. 114.
14. Andō 1930, p. 110. Murakami Yasumasa 1999, pp. 108–110. Odaka 2004a, p. 13.
15. The writing appears in Yamaji 1913, p. 130. The wording in Japanese is (emphasis added): "*Ware-ra no dōshi ni hi-shitaru Yamaoka Tetsutarō…*"
16. See Maruyama 1918b, pp. 11–14.
17. Maekawa 1977, pp. 116–121.
18. This is evident from Yamaoka's role in the bloodless surrender of Edo Castle, discussed in Chapter 5, as well as the development of his career after 1868, discussed in Chapter 5 and Chapter 6.
19. Oyamatsu 1974, pp. 110–111, 123–124.
20. Inoue et al. 1996, vol. 12, pp. 105–106.
21. Oyamatsu 1974, pp. 124–125.
22. Murakami Yasumasa 1999, pp. 113–114.
23. Ogura Tetsuju's recollection appearing in Ushiyama 1937, pp. 109–110.
24. Jansen 1961, pp. 94, 106.
25. Oyamatsu 1974, pp. 110–111, 123–124.
26. Jansen 1961, pp. 99–100.
27. Oyamatsu 1974, pp. 123–125. Maekawa 1977, pp. 46–47.
28. Oyamatsu 1974, p. 126.
29. Such informers were used not only for information gathering, but also for catching thieves, arsonists, and other criminals.

30. Oyamatsu 1974, pp. 124–125. Maekawa 1977, pp. 47–48.
31. Oyamatsu 1974, pp. 125–129, 130–131, 133. Maekawa 1977, pp. 49–51.
32. Oyamatsu 1974, p. 123.
33. Maekawa 1977, p. 58.
34. Copies of these documents were preserved by the Yamaoka family and published for the first time in Kuzuu 1929 (pp. 218, 222–224).
35. Jansen 1961, p. 96.
36. Murakami Yasumasa 1999, pp. 117– 123.
37. Inoue et al. 1996, vol. 12, pp. 140–141, 144–145.
38. Anshin 2009, pp. 201–206.
39. Odaka 2004a, p. 34. At the beginning of September 1862, the Bakufu resolved to take a crucial step to achieve the final realization of unity with the imperial court: it was decided that Shogun Tokugawa Iemochi should pay a visit to the imperial court in Kyoto, an event that had not happened for the past 230 years, since the third shogun Tokugawa Iemitsu's visit in 1634. However, the Bakufu still owed a debt to the imperial court, which, unless paid off, was a great obstacle to this unity; back in October 1861, as a step toward unity with the Bakufu, the imperial court approved the marriage between Shogun Tokugawa Iemochi and Princess Kazunomiya and the moving of the latter to Edo in exchange for the Bakufu's promise to "expel the barbarians." The top officials of the Bakufu knew that during their visit to Kyoto, they themselves and the shogun would have to demonstrate clearly whether they were going to keep their promise or arbitrarily open the country to the foreign powers (Inoue et al. 1996, vol. 12, pp. 107, 143–144). In spite of the fact that the Bakufu had not determined or stated clearly its position yet in regard to the "expulsion of the barbarians," for many radicals, including Kiyokawa Hachirō, the shogun's visit to Kyoto appeared to be a sign that the Bakufu was conceding more and more to the pressure of the imperial court and was becoming inclined to the implementation of the "expulsion of the barbarians" (Odaka 2004b, pp. 163–164). As Kiyokawa wrote in the letter to his father dated September 21, 1862, after the unsuccessful attempt to raise a rebellion in Kyoto, he returned to Edo in August 1862 (Oyamatsu 1974, p. 180) with an initial aim to try again to burn down foreign settlements in Yokohama together with Mito radicals, and he even prepared a big sum of money and obtained the consent of the radicals for the realization of his plan. However, Kiyokawa saw that the Bakufu had started to "move in the right direction" (i.e., take a subordinate position to the imperial court and incline to the decisive "expulsion of the barbarians"). Kiyokawa's friends, such as, for example, Masaki Tetsuma from Tosa, whom Kiyokawa called "the most prominent retainer of the Tosa lord" (Kiyokawa Hachirō's letter to his father

dated October 28, 1862; appears in Yamaji 1913, p. 453), also advised him that he should avoid any radical action for the time being and do his best to support the Bakufu, which seemed to be inclined to the "expulsion of the barbarians," that the whole country should act as one through the unity of the imperial court and the Bakufu to protect itself against the barbarians' defilement, and that the most urgent task for Kiyokawa was amnesty (Masaki Tetsuma's letter to Kiyokawa Hachirō, dated September 4, 1862; appears in Odaka 2004a, pp. 12–13). Kiyokawa realized that the situation in the country was becoming favorable and the timing was ripe for rehabilitating himself and those associates who were still alive and imprisoned in Edo and his terrorist activity would only spoil everything. He decided to abandon his scheme temporarily, watch the Bakufu's policy as it unfolded, and make efforts to seek amnesty for himself and his associates (Odaka 2004a, p. 11; 2004b, pp. 163–164). This is how Kiyokawa Hachirō came to cooperate with the Bakufu and became the behind-the-scenes architect of the Rōshigumi recruitment (Oyamatsu 1974, p. 196. Maekawa 1977, p. 70. Odaka 2004a, p. 50).

40. Maekawa 1977, p. 78.
41. Kiyokawa declined the Bakufu's offer to become the official leader of the Rōshigumi (*rōshi tōdori*). This is why Kiyokawa's name does not appear on any of the Rōshigumi member lists. Still, he continued to exert a great influence, controlling the majority of the *rōshi* from behind the scenes, and the Bakufu treated Kiyokawa as an adviser who was allowed to accompany *rōshi* on the way to Kyoto (Maekawa 1977, pp. 83–86. Odaka 2004a, pp. 229–230).
42. Kiyokawa's wish to return to Edo suited the Bakufu; seeing that the Rōshigumi failed to perform its duties, the Bakufu sought to withdraw the group of troublesome *rōshi* from Kyoto on the threshold of the shogun's visit to the old capital, and any excuse for this would do, such as the possibility of war with Great Britain, which at the time sent warships to Yokohama to demand retribution for the Namamugi Incident (August 21, 1862). One of the *rōshi* superintendents, Takahashi Deishū, and an Aizu *bushi*, Shiba Ta'ichirō, recollected that the possibility of war with Great Britain was merely an excuse for returning the *rōshi* to Edo (Maekawa 1977, pp. 81–82).
43. Maekawa 1977, p. 95.
44. Oyamatsu 1974, pp. 112, 212–218, 221. Maekawa 1977, pp. 100–101. Kikuchi 2005, pp. 139–144.
45. Oyamatsu 1974, p. 221. Maekawa 1977, p. 107. Murakami Yasumasa 1999, p. 123.
46. See Takahashi's argument with the Bakufu supreme councilor, Matsudaira Shungaku, over the formation of the Rōshigumi in Maekawa 1977, p. 70.

47. From *Shidankai sokkiroku* (The stenographic interviews of the Society for Historical Recollections), 101st collection (1901/4/12), pp. 18–20.
48. Maekawa 1977, pp. 79–80. Maekawa Shūji maintains that the imperial edict addressed to the Bakufu and exhorting the "expulsion of the barbarians" is confused in many Kiyokawa Hachirō-related sources with the imperial edict that Kiyokawa received from the imperial court through the Peers School (Gakushūin) in Kyoto. Maekawa also doubts that a separate notice on the "expulsion of the barbarians" issued by the imperial regent and attached to the edict to the Rōshigumi ever existed (Maekawa 1977, pp. 78–79).
49. Murakami Yasumasa 1999, p. 124.

Chapter 4   "The Truth of the Ancient Ways"—
The Beginning of the Quest

1. The writing is dated November 1884 and appears in Ōmori Sōgen 1970, p. 250.
2. Over five feet long.
3. Meaning that Chiba used a big barrel lid as an impromptu shield against Ōishi's long bamboo sword. Yamaoka's original writing mentions the volume of the barrel as four *to*, which is equal to approximately nineteen gallons.
4. This document appears in Maruyama 1918a, pp. 118–119. The version published in Maruyama 1918a does not have a date, but an identical writing appearing in Ōmori Sōgen 1970 (p. 241) has the date of September 14, 1883. Enomoto Shōji argues that Chiba Shūsaku's use of the barrel lid is not a fictitious story (Enomoto 1988, pp. 360–361).
5. According to the Japanese encyclopedia *Kōjien* (fifth edition by Iwanami Shoten), "ten fists," or *totsuka*, means the length of ten grips and, depending on the size of one's hands, is equal to approximately 2.6 to 3.3 feet. It is necessary to note that "ten fists" is the total length of a straight line drawn between the tip of the unsheathed blade and the pommel. If the Japanese long sword is gripped along its curvature, its length may exceed slightly the length of "ten fists."
6. Yamaoka writes "the bamboo sword," but this is apparently a mistake quite characteristic of his sloppy literary style. "The sword training substitues" is more suitable here as there were no bamboo swords in the "ancient times," to which Yamaoka refers. Yamaoka's another writing demonstrates that he was aware that "in the distant past (*chūko*), all swordsmanship schools [adhered to the practice] only with the wooden swords, without body

protectors (*sumen*)" (dated November 1884; appears in Ōmori Sōgen 1970, pp. 250–251).

7. This document appears in Maruyama 1918a, pp. 118–119. The version published in Maruyama 1918a does not have a date but an identical writing appearing in Ōmori Sōgen 1970 (p. 241) has the date of September 14, 1883. Another writing by Yamaoka (dated March 30, 1883), which stresses the importance of the "ten fists" length, appears in Ōmori Sōgen 1970, pp. 238–241.

8. This writing, dated September 1883, appears in Ōmori Sōgen 1970, p. 242.

9. The "nine-fists-long sword" (*kokonotsuka no tsurugi*) and the "eight-fists-long sword" (*yatsuka no tsurugi*) also appear in Japanese mythology but not as often as the "ten-fists-long sword." Yamaoka's quote above also mentions usage of the lesser length.

10. Sakai 2005, p. 127.

11. Kendō Nihon 1981, p. 49. Ōtake 1985a, p. 34; 1985b, pp. 37–38; 2007, pp. 50–59; 2009a, p. 46; 2009b, p. 53. Ogasawara 1995, pp. 55–56. Yokose 2000, p. 18. A military commander of the late sixteenth century Hosokawa Yūsai stressed the importance of the "standard length" (*nishaku ni sun, san sun* in his terms) and pointed to the fact that longer swords get easily stuck in the enemy's armor (*Hosokawa Yūsai oboegaki* [late sixteenth or early seventeenth century] appearing in Saeki et al. 1943, vol. 8, p. 234). Some exceptions should be mentioned. Longer swords could sometimes be used for mounted combat. The short Nambokuchō era (1336–1392) is characterized by the appearance of giant swords of five to seven feet long (*ōdachi* or *nodachi*) that were used in armored combat (Imamura 1971, p. 235; Hiroi 1971, pp. 93–94; Kōdansha 1983, pp. 111–112, 114; Sasama 1985, p. 32). However, it was a temporary phenomenon, and many of these giant swords were shortened (*suriage*) in the following Muromachi era (Hiroi 1971, p. 94; Ogasawara 1995, p. 55). It goes without saying that the handling of such swords required enormous physical strength, which not many men possessed. Some scholars and swordsmanship historians correlate the enlargement of the long sword and the progress in swordsmanship skills from the late Heian to the Muromachi eras (Shimokawa 1925; Kōdansha 1983) or maintain that lighter and shorter swords were of little use during battles where heavy armor was used (Imamura 1971). This viewpoint is based on depictions of warriors in famous war tales, such as *Hōgen monogatari* (*Tale of the disorder in the Hōgen years*, the early thirteenth century), *Heike monogatari* (*Tale of the Heike*, the early thirteenth century), *Heiji monogatari* (*Tale of the Heiji rebellion*, the second half of the thirteenth century), *Taiheiki* (*Chronicle of the grand pacification*, the second half of the fourteenth century), and many

others. However, it ignores the tendencies toward drama and exaggeration in these heroic epics. Furthermore, this viewpoint also completely ignores the realities of actual combat. The standard Japanese sword can inflict a deep wound even with a slight touch of its cutting edge (Ōtsuka 1995, p. 7), i.e., it is possible to cut merely by pulling the blade without using much power. That is why, when it comes to pre-Tokugawa close-quarters engagement with the use of cold steel, victory was gained prior to contact with the opponent's body, and speed of action was the decisive factor. As a general rule, long heavy weapons and speed are incompatible.

12. Naruse 1940, pp. 55–57. Naruse Kanji participated in this war and was in charge of sword repair. His book contains valuable summarizations of the types of damage to the Japanese sword (the so-called *guntō*, which in many cases were pre-Meiji blades with new guards, sheaths, and other accessories corresponding to the standards of the post-Meiji Japanese army). Naruse also provides numerous testimonies of Japanese soldiers and officers in regard to the usage of the Japanese sword in action. In this particular case, the summarized testimony is that "in the combat with real blades, the distance to the enemy seems much closer than in usual life." It is obvious that the distortion of the sense of distance was mistakenly perceived as a result of a changed psychological state in actual combat. At the time in question, the majority of Japanese men used to train in *kendō* with long bamboo swords, and other testimonies in Naruse's book repeatedly state that *kendō* training was absolutely useless for actual combat. The testimony about distancing shows clearly that most Japanese were not aware of the fundamental problem that comes from the discrepancy between the length of the real sword and its training substitute.

13. One of the rare exceptions is Ōtsuka 1995. However, this work is not consistent in its criticism of the practicability of *kendō* in actual combat, and it takes at face value attempts to turn *kendō* into "practical swordsmanship" in the first half of the twentieth century in order to make it usable on the battlefield. Although taken seriously by many, the very idea of turning *kendō* into a practical skill was absurd because the Japanese had almost never faced enemies with swords during their wars of expansion in the first half of the twentieth century.

14. Ittō Shōden Mutō-ryū, a swordsmanship school that Yamaoka Tesshū established early in the Meiji era, has been preserved to the present, and it inherited the length of Yamaoka's bamboo sword measured as *san shaku ni sun*, which is equal to "ten fists" (Sasama 1985, p. 33; Shiina 2008, p. 84). Still, it is not clear in which period of his life Yamaoka started to use this length.

15. Hori 1934, p. 95. Enomoto 1978, pp. 266–267; 1979, pp. 260–262; 1988, p. 362. Kōdansha 1983, pp. 136–138. Nakamura Tamio 2001b.

16. The *san shaku hassun* length established by the Bakufu remains the official length of the bamboo sword in modern *kendō* (Hurst 1998, p. 152). Similar attempts to shorten the bamboo sword were made in the first half of the twentieth century as part of the tendency to return *kendō* to its practical meaning in the time of Japan's wars of expansion (Ōtsuka 1995, p. 122). However, the length of the bamboo sword appears to have never decreased to the length of the real sword.

17. Enomoto 1978, pp. 271–282.

18. The document is dated July 1882. Appears in Ōmori Sōgen 1970, pp. 236–237.

19. Although not Yamaoka's contemporary, another renowned swordsman, Shirai Tooru (1783–1843), also spent many years of his life in sparring-based swordsmanship and eventually came to criticize not only interschool matches but sparring itself (Kōdansha 1983, p. 191. Enomoto 1988, pp. 359; 369, note 8).

20. This is clear from Yamaoka's writing dated November 1884 and appearing in Ōmori Sōgen 1970, pp. 250–251.

21. Enomoto 1978, 1979.

22. Rather rarely, the same idea of the immutability of the standards of the *bushi* culture can be found in some other Tokugawa-era writings: *Budō shoshinshū* (*A collection of precepts for young warriors*, the early eighteenth century) by Daidōji Yūzan or *Bugaku keimō* (Education in military science, the beginning of the nineteenth century) by Rikimaru Tōzan (appears in Saeki et al. 1942, vol. 5, p. 238).

23. From Yamaoka's writing, which he wrote as an admonishment to his disciples after he opened his Shumpūkan training hall (appears in Maruyama 1918b, pp. 35–36).

24. Appears in Maruyama 1918b, pp. 35–36. See also Kuzuu 1929, pp. 54–55; Murakami Yasumasa 1999, pp. 109–110.

25. Maruyama 1918b, p. 10. Kuzuu 1929, p. 53. Here, the term *shiai* in *bokken jiai* is used in the sense of "training," not "match."

26. Murakami Yasumasa 1999, pp. 111–112.

27. This writing by Ogyū Sorai appears in Ishioka et al. 1980, p. 21.

28. Imamura 1971, p. 231. Watatani 1971, p. 257. Tominaga 1972, p. 374. Watatani and Yamada 1978, p. 69. Ishioka et al. 1980, p. 184. Kōdansha 1983, p. 206. Murakami Yasumasa 1999, pp. 115, 125–126.

29. Murakami Yasumasa 1999, pp. 125, 164–166.

30. Another forename of Asari Yoshiaki.

31. From Yamaoka's writing appearing in Ushiyama 1937, pp. 90–91.

32. Murakami Yasumasa 1999, pp. 127–133.

33. Anshin 2009, pp. 113–114.

34. From an untitled original document written by Yamaoka on January 8, 1882. Preserved in Shumpūkan Bunko, Tamagawa Library, Kanazawa City (item number 30-1-107 *Yamaoka Tetsutarō jikihitsu kendō sho, dai issatsu*). See also Murakami Yasumasa 1999, pp. 137, 139.

35. Ogino and Obata 1890, jō, p. 115. Watatani 1971, p. 257. Murakami Yasumasa 1999, p. 137. In a short autobiography allegedly ascribed to Yamaoka (appearing for example in Ushiyama 1937, pp. 7–8), it is stated that Yamaoka, upon hearing from his father that their distant ancestor had performed great military exploits on battlefields after mastering Zen, understood that Zen was the only means to maintain the proper state of mind when facing life-and-death situations and practiced it devotedly from then. Practically identical parts of this autobiography appear in classical Chinese in the first biography of Yamaoka, *Yamaoka Tesshū koji den* (A biography of layman Yamaoka Tesshū) published by one of his Zen teachers Ogino Dokuon in 1889, a year after Yamaoka's death. The location of the original of the autobiography is unknown, and it is highly likely that it was written by someone else. Yamaoka's biographer, Ushiyama Eiji, questioned the authenticity of this document by pointing to a mistake in Yamaoka's title of the "fifty-third headmaster" of the Jubokudō style of calligraphy, whereas in reality Yamaoka was the fifty-second (Ushiyama 1937, p. 8). Also, the autobiography states that Yamaoka became absorbed in Zen-Buddhism at the age of thirteen; however, this happened only after he turned twenty-eight.

36. Ema 1935.

37. From the recollections of Ogura Tetsuju in Ushiyama 1937, p. 36.

38. Ibid., p. 35.

39. See the precept of Daitō-kokushi in Umezu 1991, pp. 97–99.

40. Maruyama 1918b, pp. 38–40, 50–51. The same mistaken belief can be found, for example, in the memoirs of another of the Three Boats of the Bakumatsu Period, Katsu Kaishū (Katsu 1892–1896, pp. 292–295, 297).

Chapter 5   The Bloodless Surrender of Edo Castle

1. The Bakufu Military Institute has not been investigated thoroughly so far and presents one of the "blank spots" in Japanese history. The only works on the institute are Enomoto 1979, 2008. However, Enomoto considers this institution only from the point of view of the history of Japanese swordsmanship and does not provide any broad political or military analysis. The most comprehensive source of factual data on the Military Institute is Andō 1930, which also includes lists of staff for various years. Yamaoka's

name does not appear in the lists of staff of the Military Institute following his release from house arrest. It is possible that Yamaoka's involvement in the Rōshigumi affair became a direct or indirect reason for his resignation from the Military Institute.

2. In this case, Yamaoka would not have been unique in his dissociation from official service for the sake of avoiding involvement in violence and bloodshed. Such military arts schools as Tenshinshō-den Katori Shintō-ryū, Takenouchi-ryū Jūjutsu, and Maniwa Nen-ryū, all established before the Tokugawa era, for centuries maintained bans that prohibited their headmasters from official service for the same purpose. See Anshin 2009, pp. 73–77, 195.

3. Haraguchi 1971, pp. 91–92, 103, 106. The only work that deals exclusively with the overall course of the bloodless surrender of Edo Castle was written by historian Haraguchi Kiyoshi (1971, 1972). This obviously is the most comprehensive study and, unlike the majority of other Japanese scholars who tend to emphasize the role of senior individuals such as the commandant of the Bakufu army, Katsu Kaishū, Princess Kazunomiya, or the British envoy to Japan, Harry Parkes, Haraguchi gives a more balanced view of the developments of March–April of 1868. Haraguchi's work is cited extensively in this chapter for the dates of events and other background information, but it will be shown that, similarly to the rest of scholars, he also seriously underestimated Yamaoka Tesshū's role.

4. The real power was in the hands of staff from the Satsuma and Chōshū domains, particularly Saigō Takamori.

5. Haraguchi 1971, pp. 104–105, 113.

6. Ibid., pp. 119–121, 125. Iechika 2005, pp. 18–20.

7. Haraguchi 1971, pp. 103, 105–106, 119. Later on March 8, Tokugawa Yoshinobu was informed by Princess Kazunomiya's messenger Fuji that, depending on how the Bakufu fulfilled the surrender conditions, the imperial government would consider offering lenient treatment to the Tokugawa family. However, the surrender conditions were not specified, and there was no one yet to mediate negotiations between Yoshinobu and the imperial government (Haraguchi 1972, p. 56).

8. Iechika 2005, pp. 18–19.

9. One of the main reasons for scheduling the exact day of the all-out attack was a military provocation against the imperial army organized on March 6 in the Katsunuma area of Kai Province by the leader of the Shinsengumi group, Kondō Isami. The group was utterly defeated in this battle (Haraguchi 1971, pp. 126–127; Kikuchi and Itō 1998, jō, pp. 65, 82). At the time, the Shinsengumi was temporarily renamed the Kōyō Chimbutai (Kai Province Suppression Unit).

10. Original preserved in Zenshōan Temple, Tokyo.

11. See a detailed discussion of the circumstances behind the creation of this writing in Anshin 2007b.

12. Haraguchi Kiyoshi uses it in Haraguchi 1971, 1972. Iechika Yoshiki (2005, p. 25) cites from the version of *BDH* appearing in one of Tokugawa Yoshinobu's biographies.

13. Although born in the noble and wealthy family of a high-ranking Bakufu official, Yamaoka was not a careerist, and furthermore, he deliberately lowered his social status by marrying Yamaoka Fusako and becoming the heir of the Yamaoka family, which stood much lower within the Bakufu hierarchy than the Ono family (Ushiyama 1937, p. 21; 1942b, pp. 26–30, 33; 1976, p. 47. Imamura 1971, p. 229. Watatani 1971, p. 256. Tominaga 1972, p. 374. Watatani and Yamada 1978, p. 69. Ishioka et al. 1980, p. 184. Kōdansha 1983, p. 206. Murakami Yasumasa 1999, pp. 93–97). This act again reveals Yamaoka's indifference to worldly matters.

14. Murakami Yasumasa 1999, pp. 145, 147–148. Iechika 2005, p. 20.

15. Murakami Yasumasa 1999, pp. 149–150. See also Haraguchi 1971, p. 129, note 69.

16. Haraguchi 1971, p. 133.

17. Murakami Yasumasa 1999, pp. 149–150.

18. Yamaoka referring to himself by his formal forename.

19. Daidōji [early XVIII c.], p. 45.

20. The same kind of straightforwardness can be found in Takahashi Deishū's argument with the Bakufu supreme councilor, Matsudaira Shungaku, and senior councilor, Itakura Katsukiyo, over the Rōshigumi (appears in *Shidankai sokkiroku* [The stenographic interviews of the Society for Historical Recollections], 101st collection [1901/4/12], pp. 18–20).

21. Yamaoka's straightforwardness, which recognized no social convention-alities, is also revealed in a famous anecdote about the time, long after the Boshin Civil War, when he served as chamberlain to young Emperor Meiji. It is said that once Emperor Meiji got drunk and challenged Yamaoka to a sumo match. Yamaoka refused flatly, but Emperor Meiji forcefully drew him into grappling. Yamaoka is said to have thrown the emperor, shouting "Foolish prince!" The emperor was slightly injured, but he never punished or even reproached Yamaoka (Ishii Sōkichi 1951. Ushiyama 1937, pp. 185–188; 1967, pp. 197–200; 1974, pp. 238–241; 1976, pp. 179–180. Satō Hiroshi 2002, pp. 198–200).

22. *BDH*.

23. Ibid. *KKZ*, vol. 1, pp. 32, 322. Matsuura 1968, p. 157. The atmosphere in Edo on the eve of the all-out attack was extremely explosive, and high-ranking

Chapter 5   The Bloodless Surrender of Edo Castle

Bakufu retainers who advocated peaceful surrender were in danger of being targeted by radical retainers of the Bakufu opposing the surrender (Haraguchi 1972, pp. 56–57).

24. Katsu 1892–1896, p. 374.
25. From the memoir of Ogura Tetsuju, to whom Yamaoka retold the content of his conversation with Katsu many years later (appears in Ushiyama 1937, pp. 135–137).
26. Meaning the further negotiation process.
27. *BDH*.
28. Haraguchi 1971, p. 129. *KKZ*, vol. 1, p. 31. *KKZ2*, vol. 19, pp. 27–28. *KN*, vol. 3, p. 69.
29. *KKZ2*, vol. 19, pp. 27–28. *KN*, vol. 3, p. 69.
30. Haraguchi 1971, p. 129. Kikuchi and Itō 1998, jō, p. 23. Sasaki 1977, p. 21.
31. The majority of popular sources maintain that Yamaoka started on foot, which is unrealistic in a situation when the shogun's life and the destiny of Japan were at stake. The most probable reason for such a misconception can be found in the end of *BDH*. A Satsuma retainer, Murata Shimpachi, tried to catch and kill Yamaoka on the way to Sumpu but failed because Yamaoka moved faster. Long after the Sumpu negotiations, Murata called Yamaoka and half in jest told him that he had wanted to kill him but had failed. Yamaoka, also joking, replied, "I am a native of Edo. [Our] legs are the fastest." It goes without saying that Yamaoka used "legs" figuratively in this case.
32. After the Yamaoka-Saigō meeting in Sumpu, General Headquarters ordered Saigō Takamori to leave for Edo early on the morning of March 11. Saigō arrived in the Satsuma residence in the Takanawa area of Edo on March 13 (Haraguchi 1972, p. 56). Taking into consideration the fact that Saigō negotiated with Yamaoka and Katsu Kaishū the same day, it took him about a day and a half to reach Edo without excessive haste. As we shall see, it took Yamaoka one day to get from Sumpu to Edo using the General Headquarters pass that Saigō gave him after their meeting.
33. *BDH*.
34. The report appears in Ishii Takashi 1968, p. 68.
35. Haraguchi 1971, p. 129.
36. Ishii Takashi 1968.
37. Kan'eiji Temple in Ueno.
38. The nun name of Princess Kazunomiya, the widow of the fourteenth shogun, Tokugawa Iemochi.
39. The nun name of Atsuhime, the widow of the thirteenth shogun, Tokugawa Iesada.

40. "Yoshinobu's thoughtless action": the Toba and Fushimi battles in the vicinity of Kyoto.

41. Haraguchi 1971, 131–132. *KKZ*, vol. 1, 32–33, 307–308. *KKZ2*, vol. 19, 29–30. Saigō Takamori Zenshū Henshū Iinkai 1977, vol. 2, 430. Only five conditions are mentioned in *BDH*, but this was one place where Yamaoka's memory failed him.

42. Haraguchi 1971, pp. 120–128, 132.

43. Ibid., p. 133.

44. In the late period of his life, Katsu bragged that he easily made Saigō come to Edo with just one letter. He also said that Saigō "trusted just one word of mine and came to Edo all alone" (*KKZ*, vol. 1, p. 350. Katsu 1892–1896, pp. 70, 72). In this, Katsu does not mention the Yamaoka-Saigō meeting at all and refers only to a short notice that he sent to the imperial army after this meeting to determine the time and place for the following formalization process (Katsu also brags in his memoirs about his "single-handed" success in the negotiations over the bloodless surrender of Edo Castle [*KKZ*, vol. 1, pp. 310–312, 349, 362–364, 384–385]). Thus, he gives the impression that it was his "one word" or "one letter" that made Saigō trust him and come to Edo. Haraguchi Kiyoshi supposed that, although there is no supporting evidence, Saigō should have taken into consideration the assertions in Katsu's letter that Yamaoka delivered to Saigō (the letter can be found in *KKZ*, vol. 1, pp. 31–32; *KKZ* vol. 2, pp. 297–298; *KKZ2*, vol. 19, pp. 27–28). However, Katsu's earlier letters to the imperial government (dated January 18, February 5, and February 15 of 1868) show that his petitions alone had little value (appear in *KKZ*, vol. 2, pp. 290–291, 294–296; Tōkyō-to Edo Tōkyō Hakubutsukan Toshi Rekishi Kenkyūshitsu 2001, pp. 77–82). From the fact that the imperial army moved decisively toward Edo, we can conclude that Katsu's earlier letters were ignored in the same way as the petitions of all previous messengers of the Bakufu had been; Katsu's letter to Saigō was no exception.

45. Haraguchi 1971, p. 133.

46. Shimazu Tadayoshi, the last daimyo of the Satsuma Domain.

47. Ravina 2004.

48. Ishii Takashi 1968, p. 68.

49. Ishii Takashi 1968, p. 68. Iechika 2005, p. 21.

50. Matsuura 1968, pp. 170–171.

51. Haraguchi 1972, p. 79.

52. *BDH*.

53. According to the record in Katsu Kaishū's diary (*KKZ*, vol. 1, p. 32. *KKZ2*, vol. 19, p. 29).

Chapter 5   The Bloodless Surrender of Edo Castle

54. *BDH.*
55. *KKZ*, vol. 1, p. 33.
56. Ibid., vol. 1, p. 32. *KKZ2*, vol. 19, p. 29. See also Katsu's memoir in *KKZ*, vol. 1, pp. 307–308.
57. Awa no Kami was Katsu Kaishū's title at the time.
58. Yamaoka writes "four." However, this is the kind of detail where his memory lapses again.
59. The Chinese reading of the characters of Tokugawa Yoshinobu's first name.
60. Satow 1921, p. 365.
61. In *BDH*, Yamaoka also mentions that, besides the negotiation of the surrender conditions on March 13–14, he was also in charge of protecting Saigō from radical Bakufu retainers on the latter's route to and from the negotiation.
62. The letter appears in Tada 1927, chū, p. 374. Yamaoka's forename in Iwakura's letter appears as Tetsutarō.
63. Historian Iechika Yoshiki also states that Yamaoka participated in the March 13–14 negotiations (Iechika 2005, pp. 21–22). Haraguchi Kiyoshi noted that besides Katsu Kaishū, there was another representative of the Bakufu who negotiated with Saigō Takamori on both days, most likely Yamaoka (Haraguchi 1972, pp. 57–61). In the list of questions given to Saigō during the March 13 meeting in Edo, Yamaoka appears as "one more person" after the names of the other two negotiators, Katsu Kaishū and Saigō Takamori. Haraguchi argues that Yamaoka's presence during the March 13 negotiation might have been necessary merely to confirm Saigō's oral commitments that he made in Sumpu (Haraguchi 1972, p. 61). However, such a viewpoint greatly underestimates Yamaoka's role. Haraguchi also assumes that "one more person" could be not a negotiator but a witness, and in this case, it was not Yamaoka, but most likely inspector Sakurai Shōbee (Haraguchi 1972, pp. 58–60). This view is mistaken because if the two sides had needed witnesses, there would have been witnesses from both sides, not only the Bakufu. Secondly, the name and title of the witnesses should have been recorded accurately and not appeared as "one more person"; otherwise there would be no sense in having witnesses present during the negotiations. Yamaoka was put as "one more person" in the list of the three negotiators because of his low rank. Katsu Kaishū apparently deemed it inappropriate to record the name of a participant of low rank in documents related to an event of the utmost gravity for the country.
64. Haraguchi 1972, pp. 64–65, 104. *KKZ*, vol. 1, pp. 33, 312–313, 362, 385. *KKZ2*, vol. 19, p. 30. *KN*, vol. 3, pp. 69–70.
65. Haraguchi 1972, pp. 56–59.
66. Ibid., pp. 61–64. *KN*, vol. 3, pp. 69–70.

67. Katsu recollected: "The surrender of Edo Castle was completed during that street-corner chat" and also "…Saigō trusted point by point everything I said and did not show disbelief even once" (Katsu 1892–1896, pp. 70, 73). He does not mention Yamaoka's name in this context at all.

68. Haraguchi 1972, pp. 56–57.

69. Other factors that Saigō had to take into consideration when suspending the all-out attack on Edo were peasant uprisings that had been occurring in Eastern Japan since the end of February 1868, as well as the protest of the British envoy to Japan, Harry Parkes, who is believed to have exerted some limited influence on Saigō on the eve of the March 14 negotiations (Haraguchi 1972, pp. 66–70). He was also likely to give some consideration to the promise of Princess Kazunomiya, the widow of the fourteenth shogun Iemochi, to commit suicide if the imperial army launched an attack on Edo and extinguished the Tokugawa family (Iechika 2005, p. 19).

70. A more detailed reconsideration of historiographical issues related to the bloodless surrender of Edo Castle and Yamaoka Tesshū's role in it can be found in Anshin 2009, pp. 164–188.

71. This atmosphere is well depicted in Yamaoka's *BDH* and Katsu Kaishū's diary and memoirs (*KKZ*, vol. 1, pp. 32, 305, 311–312, 359, 383–384. *KKZ2*, vol. 19, p. 29). See also Haraguchi 1972, pp. 56–57.

72. As we could see, the swordsman Yamaoka Tesshū was not Katsu Kaishū's messenger. After Yamaoka received the directive of Tokugawa Yoshinobu, he acted fully on his own both before visiting Katsu on March 5 and after that. Yamaoka had Katsu's letter on him as he headed to Sumpu, but Katsu neither guided Yamaoka beforehand nor later. Katsu appears to have never stated explicitly that he sent Yamaoka to Sumpu as his messenger. Besides his diary mentioned earlier, Katsu also recollected in his later oral memoirs that Yamaoka came to his place himself and suggested he go to Sumpu (Katsu 1892–1896, p. 374). It seems that the fact that Yamaoka had Katsu's letter on him as he went to Sumpu made him look like Katsu's messenger in the eyes of later generations.

73. This fact is mentioned by Yamaoka in a curriculum vitae that he wrote in June of 1887, a year before his death. This curriculum vitae is preserved in Zenshōan Temple, Tokyo. It has been unknown to the general public, and that is why the fact that Yamaoka received the dagger by Rai Kunitoshi from Tokugawa Yoshinobu does not appear in any published source. It is necessary to mention that the same day Tokugawa Yoshinobu also rewarded Katsu Kaishū with a sword (*KKZ*, vol. 1, p. 41. *KKZ2*, vol. 19, pp. 43–44).

74. *Kōshi Zappō*, 1868/i4/7, column title "Yamaoka Tetsutarō-ra no nimmen."

75. *Kōko shimbun*, 1868/5/22, column title "Katsu, Yamaoka-ra kanjiyaku to naru."

76. Shimauchi 1912, jō, pp. 90–91.
77. Satō Hiroshi 2002, p. 159. The Bakufu retainer Shirato Ishisuke provides another example of an unusual promotion similar to Yamaoka's. On February 27, 1868, Shirato was promoted from a troop commander to the acting deputy commandant of the Bakufu army. On March 18, he became the commandant of the Bakufu army, and on April 28, he finally became the great inspector. As Haraguchi Kiyoshi notes, even for a time of unrest in the country, it was extraordinary career progress (Haraguchi 1972, p. 83). It is strange that Haraguchi as well as other historians did not pay attention to the same extraordinary rise in the life of Yamaoka Tesshū shortly after the bloodless surrender of Edo Castle; if they had, it would have told them a lot about the importance of the Yamaoka-Saigō meeting in Sumpu and Yamaoka's overall role in the negotiation process.
78. Ushiyama 1942a, 1976. Murakami Yasumasa 1999. Satō Hiroshi 2002.
79. Akiyama 1991a-b, Nabekura 1991. See also Kamikawa 1997.
80. For the discussion of Sakamoto Ryōma, see, for example, Jansen 1961.
81. It is helpful also to consider Tokugawa Yoshinobu's assessment of the three main participants from the Bakufu side in the political events of March–April of 1868: Yamaoka Tesshū, Katsu Kaishū, and Ōkubo Ichiō. Yoshinobu's assessment was candid because he conveyed it to his biographer, Shibusawa Ei'ichi, years after the deaths of the three men. While not a single word of criticism is said about Yamaoka, the other two are quietly chastised for their attitudes and actions in the 1860s (Iechika 2005, pp. 126–127). About Katsu's role after Yoshinobu's flight to Edo in January 1868, Yoshinobu said that "Katsu's attitude [and deeds] in this period were somewhat different from what is widely known in the world. What is known in the world is fully based on Katsu's narrative, and it is not free from some exaggeration" (memoirs of Tokugawa Yoshinobu appearing in Shibusawa 1966). What Yoshinobu refers to as "Katsu's narrative" is Katsu's self-serving memoirs of the 1890s, which remained largely unchallenged by his contemporaries only because Katsu outlived the majority of the other participants of the events of March–April 1868. The discrepancy between what Katsu wrote in his diaries about Yamaoka and his exaggerated memoirs is not difficult to understand. There is no doubt that the former was more candid because Katsu did not intend it to be published.

Chapter 6   The Establishment of Ittō Shōden Mutō-ryū

1. Kikuchi and Itō 1998, jō, p. 51. See also an entry (dated April(i) 16, 1868) in Katsu Kaishū's diary (*KKZ*, vol. 1, p. 240).

2. *KRK*.
3. *KKZ*, vol. 1, p. 240. *KN*, vol. 3, p. 123.
4. Ushiyama 1937, pp. 179–182; 1942a, pp. 115–119; 1967, pp. 191–195; 1976, pp. 158–163. Satō Hiroshi 2002, pp. 161–174.
5. Among others were Katsu Kaishū, Ōkubo Ichiō, Enomoto Takeaki, Ōtori Keisuke.
6. Maruyama 1918b, p. 28. Ushiyama 1937, p. 183; 1942a, p. 121; 1967, pp. 196–197; 1974, pp. 232–233; 1976. pp. 169–171. Satō Hiroshi 2002, pp. 192–196. Maruyama Bokuden (1918b, p. 28) maintained that Yamaoka was recommended not only by Saigō, but also the prominent Meiji statesman Iwakura Tomomi.
7. I am indebted to Professor Shima Yoshitaka of Waseda University for calling my attention to this fact.
8. Ishii Takashi 1973, vol. 3, p. 957.
9. Ōmori Hōkō, the publisher of what appears to be the first published version of Yamaoka's *BDH*, wrote in its afterword that "of course, everybody knows how great was the service which [Yamaoka] rendered for the Realm but its details [as depicted in Yamaoka's writing] are still unknown to the public" (Yamaoka 1882). In 1889, a year after Yamaoka's death, Ichihara Rokubee, a resident of Takayama in Hida Province where Yamaoka spent his childhood, wrote a prospectus relating to building a monument in commemoration of Yamaoka. Ichihara states: "I will omit here [the description of Yamaoka's] utmost loyalty and duty revealed by him during the Restoration as all people know it" (Ema 1935, p. 45). It appears that during his life and shortly after his death, Yamaoka's role in the bloodless surrender of Edo Castle was common knowledge among many Japanese.
10. Murakami Yasumasa 1999, pp. 167–168.
11. Referring to swordsmanship.
12. From an untitled original document written by Yamaoka on January 8, 1882. Preserved in Shumpūkan Bunko, Tamagawa Library, Kanazawa City (item number 30-1-107 *Yamaoka Tetsutarō jikihitsu kendō sho, dai issatsu*).
13. In 1871, the Japanese warrior class was officially abolished by government decree (Sampatsu Dattō Rei). Yet, the decree left the questions of retaining the *bushi* hairstyle and wearing the two swords in daily life to the warriors' discretion. It can be said that this class was abolished once and for all in 1876 by another decree (Haitō Rei) that prohibited the wearing of blades to anyone except persons in military and police service, as well as government officials who were required to wear special attire on the occasion of important official events.
14. Murakami Yasumasa 1999, pp. 168–171.

15. From Yamaoka's writing dated June 1880 (appears in Ōmori Sōgen 1970, p. 233).

16. As noted earlier, Yamaoka's teacher of spearmanship, Yamaoka Seizan, also engaged in austere training regularly on the grounds of his residence.

17. It should be noted that Yamaoka did not imagine opposing Asari while practicing Zen meditation. Zen Buddhism negates imaginary techniques during this kind of practice (Maebayashi 2006, p. 159). This is one of the pieces of evidence that a document titled *Kempō to zenri* (Swordsmanship and the principles of Zen), which is attributed to Yamaoka (dated April 1880) and appears, for example, in Ōmori Sōgen 1970 (pp. 229–232), is a counterfeit, most likely also produced by Abe Masato as discussed in the introduction to this book. In this document, Yamaoka allegedly describes his imaginary training with Asari while practicing Zen meditation. This counterfeit is apparently based on a much shorter but genuine writing by Yamaoka, dated June 1883 (also appears in Ōmori Sōgen 1970, p. 233). Other reasons to believe *Kempō to zenri* is a counterfeit are as follows: the document is excessively verbose, which is unusual for Yamaoka's writings; it contains literary expressions that cannot be found in any other authentic writing by Yamaoka; the style is ornate and is different from Yamaoka's style, which is plain and straightforward; the document contains a description of how Yamaoka's disciple and Asari Yoshiaki were filled with admiration on seeing the unusual powers that Yamaoka gained after his comprehension of the "innermost secret"—Yamaoka, as a person who all his life avoided fame and preferred to stay in the shadows, never wrote about himself in this way; and the description of how Asari examined Yamaoka's revelation is unrealistic because it depicts a kind of sparring in which the wooden sword and body protectors, including the helmet, are used simultaneously—only a person lacking the very basic understanding of Japanese swordsmanship could write in this way. On counterfeits of Yamaoka's writings and the features of his literary style, see Anshin 2006, 2007b.

18. After Yamaoka's comprehension of the "innermost secret."

19. From an untitled original document written by Yamaoka on January 8, 1882. Preserved in Shumpūkan Bunko, Tamagawa Library, Kanazawa City (item number 30-1-107 *Yamaoka Tetsutarō jikihitsu kendō sho, dai issatsu*).

20. Murakami Yasumasa 1999.

21. Appears in Imamura et al. 1966, vol. 2, p. 260; 1982, vol. 3, p. 22.

22. Yokose 2000, p. 62.

23. From Yamaoka's writing dated April 10, 1884 (appears in Ōmori Sōgen 1970, p. 248). There are at least two other writings in which Yamaoka explains in

similar terms the meaning of his school's name (appearing in Ōmori Sōgen 1970, pp. 251–252).

24. From an undated writing (appears in Ōmori Sōgen 1970, p. 252).
25. Maebayashi 1992, 1999.
26. Yamada 1960, pp. 362–366. Imamura 1971, p. 231. Tominaga 1972, p. 374. Ishioka et al. 1980, pp. 183–186. Kōdansha 1983, pp. 206–207. Hurst 1998, pp. 74–75. Maebayashi 2006, pp. 171–173.
27. Murakami Yasumasa 1999, pp. 168–170, 192, 217–218.
28. Shima 2007a.
29. Tominaga 1972, p. 374. Kōdansha 1983, p. 206. Murakami Yasumasa 1999, p. 128. Zenshōan 2009, p. 135. The largeness of Yamaoka's stature is also clear from the size of his training wear, which is preserved in Zenshōan Temple, Tokyo.
30. Several years after Yamaoka's death, his disciples wrote a document, *Shumpūkan eizoku shu'isho* (1890), which states that, until about a month before Yamaoka's death, when his health deteriorated as he was in the last stages of stomach cancer, he is said to have trained often with his disciples in his training hall and his performance did not differ even slightly from the time when he was healthy (appears in Ōmori Sōgen 1970, p. 254). Yamaoka's teacher of spearmanship, Seizan, also trained on his own and taught his disciples when he had serious health problems, and his performance is said to have not been influenced even slightly (the biography of Yamaoka Seizan by Nakamura Masanao in Fukuda 1879, p. 28).
31. Hurst 1998, p. 109.
32. Hōjō Yasutoki's letter appearing in Saeki et al. 1942, vol. 1, pp. 231–232.
33. This title is seen in Yamaoka's writing dated July 1882 (appears in Ōmori Sōgen 1970, p. 237). See also Murakami Yasumasa 1999, pp. 171–172, 232.
34. Murakami Yasumasa 1999, pp. 233.
35. From the recollections of Yamaoka's live-in disciple Ogura Tetsuju appearing in Ushiyama 1937, p. 19.
36. Murakami Yasumasa 1999, p. 233.
37. Maruyama 1918b, p. 28. Ushiyama 1937, pp. 183–184; 1942a, pp. 121, 136–137; 1974, pp. 232–233. Satō Hiroshi 2002, pp. 192–196.
38. Murakami Yasumasa 1999, pp. 252–253.
39. Pursuing the "ancient truth" in this period of his life, Yamaoka copied a large number of the swordsmanship texts of Ittō-ryū and other schools (Murakami Yasumasa 1999, pp. 240, 242–245, 253–254, 263–265, 269–271, 279–280, 283–285).
40. Murakami Yasumasa 1999, pp. 233–234.
41. *Shumpūkan eizoku shu'isho* (appearing in Ōmori Sōgen 1970, p. 254). See also Murakami Yasumasa 1999, pp. 186–187, 275–277.
42. Yoshida 2007, p. 130.

43. Imamura 1971, p. 232. Watatani 1971, p. 257. Tominaga 1972, p. 376. Watatani and Yamada 1978, p. 69. Ishioka et al. 1980, p. 185. Kōdansha 1983, p. 206. Murakami Yasumasa 1999, pp. 277–278, 280. Yoshida 2007, p. 160.
44. The license is preserved in Zenshōan Temple, Tokyo. Because Nario made Yamaoka his successor earlier, the grant of this license was probably intended not for Yamaoka himself but rather to make society aware of the fact that Yamaoka had become a legitimate successor.
45. Murakami Yasumasa 1999, pp. 285–286. See also Ōmori Sōgen 1970, pp. 113–114.
46. The document appears in Ōmori Sōgen 1970, p. 114. Ōmori Sōgen suggests that this document was written in 1885.
47. This writing, dated September 1883, appears in Ōmori Sōgen 1970, p. 242. In another document, dated June 1885, Yamaoka wrote again that "the school like my Mutō-ryū has not lost the teaching principles of the founder" (appears in Ōmori Sōgen 1970, p. 253).
48. The document appears in Ōmori Sōgen 1970, pp. 114–115.
49. Yoshida 2007, pp. 160–157. According to the recent study by Yoshida Tomoo (2007, p. 137), out of the fifty predetermined patterns of movement of the mainline Ittō-ryū, only twenty-five were transmitted from the founder Itō Ittōsai. The other twenty-five were created by the second headmaster of the Ono family, Tadatsune. Of course, Yamaoka did not know this at the time. However, it does not contradict his quest for what he perceived as the genuine Ittō-ryū tradition as long as the other twenty-five forms were based on the same technical principles and mannerisms and remained practical. Judging from Yamaoka's reaction to Ono Nario's demonstration, he did not feel that even one form deviated from the Ittō-ryū tradition.
50. From a scroll that Yamaoka issued to his disciples when they reached the first level of swordsmanship skill in his school (*Ittō-ryū heihō jūni kajō mokuroku* [The twelve-item list of Ittō-ryū military art]). The text of the scroll appears in Ushiyama 1937, pp. 281–288. There is no date in the published version of this scroll, but presumably, it was written after Yamaoka's encounter with the ninth headmaster of the mainline Ittō-ryū, Ono Nario. Otherwise, it would have been impossible for him to know what the mannerisms of Itō Ittōsai were.
51. Sometimes, Yamaoka's name can be simultaneously linked to the names of both Asari Yoshiaki and Ono Nario (see, for example, Shimokawa 1925, p. 287. Watatani 1971, p. 258; Ishioka et al. 1980, p. 188. Yoshida 2007, p. 159). However, it is evident that Yamaoka completely switched to the mainline Ittō-ryū transmitted in the Ono family.
52. This writing appears in Ōmori Sōgen 1970, pp. 250–251.
53. Ōmori Nobumasa 1976b, pp. 46, 52.

54. In the Bakumatsu period, we can find another example of such a compromise. Kubota Sugane of Tamiya-ryū, like Yamaoka, criticized all contemporary swordsmen for losing touch with the realities of actual combat and introduced an eclectic mix of training methodologies, that is, training in predetermined patterns of movement with the bamboo sword (Enomoto 1978, pp. 276–280, 282–283; 1979, p. 262). However, Yamaoka would undoubtedly have been very skeptical of such eclecticism.

Conclusion

1. *Chōya Shimbun*, 1888/7/20, "Shikyo: Katsu Kaishū no chōshi." *Tōkyō Nichinichi Shimbun*, 1888/07/21–22, 24–28, "Kōseki idan (1–7)." *Tōkyō Nichinichi Shimbun*, 1888/07/29, "Tokugawa-ke zōyo no Musashi no katana o Iwakura Tomomi ni kenjō."
2. Ushiyama 1937, pp. 466–470; 1942a, pp. 310–316; 1967, pp. 217–219, 441–445; 1974, pp. 257–258; 1976, pp. 270–272. Maruyama 1918b, pp. 82–83.
3. Yamaoka is estimated to have created about one million calligraphy works during his life (Terayama 1977, p. 63. Ōmori Sōgen 1970, pp. 61–62, 68).
4. The post-1868 era witnessed the establishment of *iai* schools, such as Shintō-ryū by Hibino Raifū and Musō Shinden-ryū by Nakayama Hakudō. However, they inherited distinctive features of the "flowery training" of the Tokugawa era, such as extremely slow movement, performing techniques from the *seiza* position, and incorrect positioning of the long sword (see Anshin 2009, pp. 219–228).
5. Sugie 1974, 1984.
6. Yamaoka did issue the license of full transmission to his disciple Hasegawa Umpachirō shortly before the death of the latter. However, it was a gesture of solace in Hasegawa's last moments rather than formal recognition of the school's transmission (Ushiyama 1937, pp. 239–240).
7. Ushiyama 1937, pp. 385–387, 390–392; 1967, pp. 105–112; 1976, pp. 253–256, 258, 265. Ōmori Sōgen 1970, pp. 61–62, 68, 75–80, 160–162. Satō Hiroshi 2002, pp. 229–235.
8. Ono Nario died in December 1887 (Murakami Yasumasa 1999, p. 304).
9. Yamaoka is known for having adhered strictly to this principle from his childhood (Maruyama 1918b, pp. 3, 7–8. Kuzuu 1929, pp. 18–20. Ogura Tetusju's recollections in Ushiyama 1937, pp. 85–89). He taught this principle to Usui Rokurō, who committed the "last revenge killing (*katakiuchi*) of the Meiji era" (Ushiyama 1937, pp. 257–262. See also a series of articles dedicated to this incident in *Tōkyō Nichinichi Shimbun*, 1881/9/24, 26–27).
10. Tobe 1992, pp. 203–204.

Selected Bibliography

Abbreviations

BDH   Yamaoka Tesshū (Tetsutarō). 1882. *Keiō Boshin sangatsu Sumpu Daisōtokufu ni oite Saigō Takamori-shi to dampan hikki* (usually abbreviated as *Boshin dampan hikki*). Original preserved in Zenshōan Temple, Tokyo.

KKZ   Katsu Kaishū Zenshū Kankōkai, ed. 1972–1973. *Katsu Kaishū zenshū*. 23 vols. Tokyo: Kōdansha.

KKZ2   Katsube Mitake et al., eds. 1972–1973. *Katsu Kaishū zenshū*. 23 vols. Tokyo: Keisō Shobō.

KN   Tōkyō-to Edo Tōkyō Hakubutsukan Toshi Rekishi Kenkyūshitsu, ed. 2002–2006. *Katsu Kaishū kankei shiryō: Kaishū nikki*. 4 vols. Tokyo: Tōkyō-to and other publishers.

KRK   Yamaoka Tesshū (Tetsutarō). 1883. *Keiō Boshin shigatsu Tōeizan ni tonshū suru Shōgitai oyobi shotai o kaisan seshimubeki jōshi toshite Yamaoka Tetsutarō kore ni omomuki, Kakuōin to rongi no ki* (usually abbreviated as *Kakuōin rongi ki*). Draft preserved in Zenshōan Temple, Tokyo.

Abe Masato, ed. 1902. *Bushidō*. Tokyo: Kōyūkan.

———, ed. 1903a. *Joshidō: Tesshū fujin Fusako danwa*. Tokyo: Daigakkan.

———, ed. 1903b. *Sanshū hiketsu: Tesshū, Kaishū, Deishū*. Tokyo: Yūhikaku.

———, ed. 1903c. *Tesshū zuihitsu*. Tokyo: Kōyūkan.

———, ed. 1903d. *Tokugawa seidō: Ieyasu ikun, Sanshū hojutsu*. Tokyo: Yūhikaku.

———, ed. 1903e. *Deishū ikō*. Tokyo: Kokkōsha.

———, ed. 1907. *Tesshū genkō roku*. Tokyo: Kōyūkan (reprint of Abe 1903c under a different title).

———, ed. [1903] 1934. *Tesshū genkō roku*. Published by Kawai Tokutarō in Ichikawa-machi (reprint of Abe 1903c under a different title).

———, ed. 1940. *Bushidō*. Revised edition. Tokyo: Daitō Shuppansha.

———, ed. [1903] 1990. *Eiketsu kyojin o kataru*. Tokyo: Nihon Shuppan Hōsō Kikaku (reprint of Abe 1903c under a different title).

———, ed. [1940?] 1997. *Bushidō: bumbu ryōdō no shisō*. Reprint. Tokyo: Daitō Shuppansha (Abe Masato's work edited by Katsube Mitake and published under a different title).

———, ed. [1940?] 1999. *Yamaoka Tesshū no Bushidō*. Reprint. Tokyo: Kadokawa Shoten (Abe Masato's work edited by Katsube Mitake and published under a different title).

———, ed. [1903] 2001. *Tesshū zuikan roku*. Tokyo: Kokusho Kankōkai (reprint of Abe 1903c under a different title).

Akita Shoten, ed. 1987. "Kobudō nijū ryūha Katori ni kaisu! Katori Shintō-ryū shiso Iizasa Chōisai no seitan roppyaku nen o kinen suru daiembukai." *Rekishi To Tabi* no. 14 (12).

Akiyama Kōki. 1991a. *Ishin no taisei Yamaoka Tesshū* (chi no maki). Tokyo: Nihon Shuppan Hōsō Kikaku.

———. 1991b. *Ishin no taisei Yamaoka Tesshū* (jin no maki). Tokyo: Nihon Shuppan Hōsō Kikaku.

Andō Naokata. [1930] 1988. *Kōbusho*. Reprint. Tokyo: Jukai Shorin.

Ansart, Olivier. 2007. "Loyalty in seventeenth and eighteenth century samurai discourse." *Japanese Studies* no. 27(2).

Anshin, Anatoliy. 2006. "Yamaoka Tesshū no zuihitsu to kōwa kiroku ni tsuite." *Chiba Daigaku Nihon Bunka Ronsō* no. 7 (can be viewed online at www. tesshu.info).

———. 2007a. "Yamaoka Tesshū no kōseki o tataeta *Masamune tantō ki* no kōshō." *Nihon Kambungaku Kenkyū* no. 2 (can be viewed online at www.tesshu.info).

———. 2007b. "Yamaoka Tesshū ga kaita Edo muketsu kaijō no shimatsusho." *Nihon Rekishi* no. 708 (can be viewed online at www.tesshu.info).

————. 2007c. "Ushiyama Eiji ga hensan shita Yamaoka Tesshū no denki ni tsuite." *Chiba Daigaku Nihon Bunka Ronsō* no. 8 (can be viewed online at www.tesshu.info).

————. 2008. "Yamaoka Tesshū to meitō 'Musashi Masamune.'" *Nihon Rekishi* no. 722.

————. 2009. *The Intangible Warrior Culture of Japan: Bodily Practices, Mental Attitudes, and Values of the Two-sworded Men from the Fifteenth to the Twenty-first Centuries.* PhD diss., University of New South Wales.

————. (2012). "Samurai" (in-press). *Cultural Sociology of the Middle East, Asia, and Africa: An Encyclopedia.* SAGE Publications.

Asakura Kazuyoshi. 2005. "Kengō monogatari 1: Iizasa Chōisai." *Kendō Nihon* no. 350.

Asano Satako. 1970. *Shidan Mutō-ryū: Yamaoka Tesshū to deshi Genjirō.* Tokyo: Hōbunkan.

Benesch, Oleg 2011. *Bushidō: The Creation of a Martial Ethic in Late Meiji Japan.* PhD diss., the University of British Columbia, Vancouver.

Bennett, Alexander, and Sarah Moate, eds. 2008. *Ken Zen Sho: The Zen Calligraphy and Painting of Yamaoka Tesshu.* Tokyo: Bunkasha International Corporation.

Bodiford, William. 2005. "Zen to Nihon no kenjutsu no saikō." A translation from English in *Nihon no kyōiku ni "budō" o: 21 seiki ni shin-gi-tai o kitaeru.* Edited by Yamada Shōji and Alexander Bennett. Tokyo: Meiji Tosho Shuppan.

Chakrabarty, Dipesh. 1998. "Revisiting the tradition/modernity binary." In *Mirror of Modernity: Invented Traditions of Modern Japan.* Edited by Stephen Vlastos. Berkeley: University of California Press.

Chiba Tokuji. 1972. *Seppuku no hanashi: nihonjin wa naze hara o kiru ka.* Tokyo: Kōdansha.

————. 1994. *Nihonjin wa naze seppuku suru no ka.* Tokyo: Tōkyōdō Shuppan.

Chiba Sōgo Ginkō, ed. 1981. "Tenshin Shōden Katori Shintō-ryū." In *Chiba ni ikiru: kyōdo ga unda meishō, meikō, meijin.* Chiba-shi: Chiba Sōgo Ginkō Gyōmu-bu Gyōmu-ka.

Daidōji Yūzan. [early XVIII c.] 1971. *Budō shoshinshū.* Edited by Yoshida Yutaka. Tokyo: Tokuma Shoten.

Ema Nakashi, ed. 1935. *Hida ni okeru Yamaoka Tesshū.* Takayama-machi: Takayama Kankō Kyōkai.

Enomoto Shōji. 1978. "Bakumatsu kenjutsu no henshitsu katei ni kansuru kenkyū: toku ni Tamiya-ryū Kubota Sugane no kenjutsu-kan o chūshin toshite." *Akademia: Jimbun Shizen Kagaku Hen/Hoken Tai'iku Hen* no. 28.

————. 1979. "Bakumatsu kenjutsu no henshitsu katei ni kansuru kenkyū 2: Kōbusho no kenjutsu kyōiku to soko ni okeru kenjutsuka no kenjutsu riron o chūshin toshite." *Akademia: Jimbun Shizen Kagaku Hen/Hoken Tai'iku Hen* no. 29.

————. 1988. "Bakumatsu kendō ni okeru nijūteki seikaku no keisei katei." In *Nihon budōgaku kenkyū: Watanabe Ichirō kyōju taikan kinen ronshū*. Edited by Watanabe Ichirō Kyōju Taikan Kinen Kai. Tokyo: Shimazu Shobō.

Farris, William. 1992. *Heavenly Warriors: The Evolution of Japan's Military, 500–1300*. Cambridge, MA: Council on East Asian Studies, Harvard University.

Friday, Karl. 1997. *Legacies of the Sword: The Kashima-Shinryu and Samurai Martial Culture*. Honolulu: University of Hawai'i Press.

————. 2005. "Bu no michi to ryūha bugei to kassen bujutsu no ichi kōsatsu." A translation from English in *Nihon no kyōiku ni "budō" o: 21 seiki ni shin-gi-tai o kitaeru*. Edited by Yamada Shōji and Alexander Bennett. Tokyo: Meiji Tosho Shuppan.

Fujiki Hisashi. 2005. *Katanagari: buki o fūin shita minshū*. Tokyo: Iwanami Shoten.

Fujishima Ikko. 1957. *Hokushin Ittō-ryū*. Tokyo: Wadō Shuppansha.

Fukuda Uchū, ed. 1879. *Meika kibun: kinko shiden*. Published by Manabe Busuke in Osaka.

Fukunaga Mitsuji. 1987. *Dōkyō shisō-shi kenkyū*. Tokyo: Iwanami Shoten.

Furuta Shōkin. 1971. "Yamaoka Tesshū." *Nihon Daigaku Seishin Bunka Kenkyūjo Kyōiku Seido Kenkyūjo Kiyō* no. 5.

Fuse Kenji. 2006. *Kakyū bushi to Bakumatsu Meiji: Kawagoe, Maebashi-han no bujutsu ryūha to shizoku jusan*. Tokyo: Iwata Shoin.

Gakushū Kenkyūsha, ed. 2005. *Nihon no kenjutsu*. Tokyo: Gakushū Kenkyūsha.

————, ed. 2006. *Nihon no kenjutsu 2*. Tokyo: Gakushū Kenkyūsha.

————, ed. 2008. *Nihon no kenjutsu: DVD serekushon*. Tokyo: Gakushū Kenkyūsha.

Hall, David. 1990. *Marishiten: Buddhism and the Warrior Goddess*. PhD diss., University of California, Berkeley.

Haraguchi Kiyoshi. 1971. "Edojō akewatashi no ichikōsatsu 1." *Meijō Shōgaku* no. 21(2).

————. 1972. "Edojō akewatashi no ichikōsatsu 2, kan." *Meijō Shōgaku* no. 21(3).

Harazono Mitsunori. 1990. *Shiden Saigō Takamori to Yamaoka Tesshū: nihonjin no Bushidō*. Tokyo: Nihon Shuppan Hōsō Kikaku.

Hatori Yōsei et al., ed. [1843] 1995. *Shinsen bujutsu ryūso roku*. In *Shimpen bujutsu sōsho*. Enlarged edition by Budōsho Kankōkai. Tokyo: Shinjimbutsu Ōraisha.

Herrigel, Eugen. 1953. *Zen in the Art of Archery*. Translated by R. F. C. Hull. New York: Vintage Books.

Hinatsu Shigetaka. [1716] 1995. *Honchō bugei shōden*. In *Shimpen bujutsu sōsho*. Enlarged edition by Budōsho Kankōkai. Tokyo: Shinjimbutsu Ōraisha.

Hirakawa Arata. 2006. "Ishin henkaku-ki chiiki shakai to rīdā: chūkansō-ron kara miru Rōshigumi to Shinsengumi." In *Chiiki shakai to rīdā tachi*. Edited by Hirakawa Arata and Taniyama Masamichi. Tokyo: Yoshikawa Kōbunkan.

Hiroi Yūichi. 1971. *Tōken no mikata: gijutsu to ryūha*. Tokyo: Dai'ichi Hōki Shuppan.

Hori Shōhei. [1934] 1986. *Dai Nihon kendō-shi*. In *Kindai kendō meicho taikei*, Vol. 10. Edited by Imamura Yoshio et al. Kyoto: Dōhōsha Shuppan.

Hoshi Kōji. 1993. *Yomigaeru Hokuto no ken: jitsuroku Hokushin Ittō-ryū*. Tokyo: Kawade Shobō Shinsha.

Hōya Tooru. 2007. *Boshin sensō*. Tokyo: Yoshikawa Kōbunkan.

Hurst, Cameron. 1998. *Armed Martial Arts of Japan: Swordsmanship and Archery*. New Haven, CT: Yale University Press.

Iechika Yoshiki. 2005. *Sono go no Yoshinobu: Taishō made ikita shōgun*. Tokyo: Kōdansha.

Iizasa Yasusada. 2000. "'Heihō wa heihō nari'—issei o fūbi shita sōgō bujutsu: Tenshinshō-den Katori Shintō-ryū." In *Rekishi gunzō shirīzu 63: Miyamoto Musashi*. Edited and published by Gakushū Kenkyūsha in Tokyo.

Imamura Yoshio. 1971. *Zusetsu Nihon kengō-shi*. Tokyo: Shinjimbutsu Ōraisha.

———. 1982. "Budō-shi gaisetsu." In *Nihon budō taikei*, Vol. 10. Edited by Imamura Yoshio et al. Kyoto: Dōhōsha Shuppan.

———. 1989. *Shūtei 19 seiki ni okeru Nihon tai'iku no kenkyū*. Tokyo: Dai'ichi Shobō.

Imamura Yoshio et al., eds. 1966–1967. *Nihon budō zenshū*. 7 vols. Tokyo: Jimbutsu Ōraisha.

——— et al., eds. 1982. *Nihon budō taikei*. 10 vols. Kyoto: Dōhōsha Shuppan.

Inoue Mitsusada et al., eds. 1996. *Nihon rekishi taikei*. 18 vols. Tokyo: Yamakawa Shuppansha.

Ishii Sōkichi. 1951. "Meiji kyūtei hishi: Yamaoka Tesshū sumō kangen no shinsō." *Keizai Ōrai* no. 3(6).

Ishii Takashi. 1968. *Ishin no nairan*. Tokyo: Shiseidō.

———. 1973. *Meiji ishin no kokusaiteki kankyō*. 3 vols. Enlarged and revised edition. Tokyo: Yoshikawa Kōbunkan.

Ishikawa Ken. 1960. *Nihon gakkō-shi no kenkyū*. Tokyo: Shōgakkan.

Ishioka Hisao et al. 1980. *Nihon no kobujutsu*. Tokyo: Shinjimbutsu Ōraisha.

Ishizu Hiroshi. 1933. *Tetsuju rōjin: Kamakura yawa*. Tokyo: Gyūzandō Shoten.

Isoda Michifumi. 2003. *Kinsei daimyō kashindan no shakai kōzō*. Tokyo: Tōkyō Daigaku Shuppankai.

Iwasa Hiroshi, ed. 1987. *Yamaoka Tesshū sho no shishō: Iwasa Ittei*. Published by Iwasa Kiyoshi in Takayama City.

Iwasaki Sakae. 1945a. *Yamaoka Tesshū: kochū no maki*. Tokyo: Kaiseikan.

———. 1945b. *Yamaoka Tesshū: haha no maki*. Tokyo: Kaiseikan.

———. 1968. *Yamaoka Tesshū*. 5 vols. Kashiwa-shi: Hiroike Gakuen Shuppambu.

Izumi Masato. 1988. "*Kōbusho* ni tsuite." In the reprint of *Kōbusho* by Andō Naokata (1930). Tokyo: Jukai Shorin.

Jansen, Marius. [1961] 1994. *Sakamoto Ryōma and the Meiji Restoration*. Reprint. New York: Columbia University Press.

Jugen Seiki. 2003. "Gorin no sho o yomu." *Daihōrin* no. 70(7).

Kakei Yasuhiko 1967. *Chūsei buke kakun no kenkyū*. Tokyo: Kazama Shobō.

Kamikawa Taketoshi. 1997. *Daijō no ken: Tesshū, Kaishū, shōgun Yoshinobu*. Tokyo: Sōbunsha.

Katsu Kaishū. [1892–1896] 2000. *Hikawa seiwa*. Edited by Etō Jun and Matsuura Rei. Tokyo: Kōdansha.

Kendō Nihon, ed. 1981. "Iaijutsu: san ryūha ni miru jutsu no myō." *Kendō Nihon* no. 70.

Kensei Tsukahara Bokuden Seitan Gohyakunen-sai Kinen Jigyō Jikkō Iinkai. 1989. *Kensei Tsukahara Bokuden seitan gohyakunen-sai kinenshi*. Ibaraki-ken, Kashima-gun: Kensei Tsukahara Bokuden Seitan Gohyakunen-sai Kinen Jigyō Jikkō Iinkai.

Kikuchi Akira. 2005. *Kyōto Mimawarigumi shiroku*. Tokyo: Shinjimbutsu Ōraisha.

Kikuchi Akira, and Itō Seirō, eds. 1998. *Boshin sensō zenshi* (jō, ge). Tokyo: Shinjimbutsu Ōraisha.

King, Winston. 1993. *Zen and the Way of the Sword: Arming the Samurai Psyche*. New York: Oxford University Press.

Kodama Masayuki, and Ōtsubo Hisashi. 2001. "Yamaoka Tesshū no ken-Zen shugyōdō no kyokuchi ni itaru dōtei: shōji tokudatsu no engen e." *Gakujutsu Kenkyū Kiyō* no. 25.

Kōdansha, ed. 1983. *Nihon no budō: kendō* (jō). Tokyo: Kōdansha.

Kubo Michio. 2003. "Miyamoto Musashi no shōgai." *Daihōrin* no. 70(7).

Kuroda Tetsuzan. 1992. *Kenjutsu seigi*. Saitama-ken, Hatogaya-shi: Sōjinja.

———. 1997. *Kieru ugoki o motomete: Tetsuzan Pari gasshuku-ki*. Kanagawa-ken, Sagamihara-shi: Aiki Nyūsu.

Kuwata Tadachika. 2003. *Bushi no kakun*. Tokyo: Kōdansha.

Kuzuu Yoshihisa. 1929. *Kōshi Yamaoka Tesshū*. Tokyo: Kokuryūkai Shuppambu.

Maebayashi Kiyokazu. 1992. "Kinsei kenjutsu densho ni mirareru rinrikan: shoki kara chūki ni kakete." *Jimbun Gakubu Kiyō* no. 5.

———. 1995. "Kinsei bugei ni okeru kosumorojī to sono shisō-teki haikei." *Jimbun Gakubu Kiyō* no. 11.

————. 1999. "Waga kuni ni okeru dentō-teki ningen kensei ron (III): Sekiun-ryū ni okeru 'michi' to 'kokoro' o chūshin ni." *Jimbun Gakubu Kiyō* no. 18.

————. 2006. *Kinsei Nihon bugei shisō no kenkyū.* Kyoto: Jimbun Shoin.

Maebayashi Kiyokazu, and Watanabe Ichirō. 1988. "Kendō shugyō katei ni okeru shinteki hen'yō ni tsuite no ichi kōsatsu: shu toshite *Heihō kadensho* yori mitaru." *Tsukuba Daigaku Tai'iku Kagaku-kei Kiyō* no. 11.

Maekawa Shūji. 1977. *Ishizaka Shūzō kenkyū: shishi, sekiyunin toshite no ryōhansei.* Kashiwazaki-shi: Sanshūsha.

Maruyama Bokuden. 1918a. *Zenshōan kiroku bassui.* Tokyo: Zenshōan.

————. [1918b] 1962. *Tesshū koji no shimmemmoku.* Reprint. Tokyo: Zenshōan.

Matsuura Rei. 1968. *Katsu Kaishū.* Tokyo: Chūō Kōronsha.

Mayama Seika. [1940–1942] 1975. *Mayama Seika zenshū.* Tokyo: Kōdansha.

Minamoto Norinaga. [1843] 1995. *Gekken sōdan.* In *Shimpen bujutsu sōsho.* Enlarged edition by Budōsho Kankōkai. Tokyo: Shinjimbutsu Ōraisha.

Miyachi Masato. 2009. "Shinsengumi no ronjikata." In *Shinsengumi no ronjikata: Shinsengumi shiryō fōramu kara.* Published by Shinsengumi Shiryō Fōramu Jikkō Iinkai.

Mori Yoshikazu. 2005. "Hikone-han Ii-ke shoshi no seikatsu to kyōyō keisei: kinsei chūkōki shoshi yōiku seido no seiritsu to tenkai." In *Buke no seikatsu to kyōyō.* Edited by Murai Yasuhiko et al. Hikone-shi: Hikonejō Hakubutsukan.

Morikawa Ryōichi. 1983. *Mutō-ryū hiroku: Kagawa Zenjirō den.* Kannonji: Kagawa Zenjirō Den Kankōkai.

Moriyasu Osamu. 2003. "Miyamoto Musashi no gaji." *Daihōrin* no. 70(7).

Murakami Ichirō. 1975. "*Gorin no sho* ni okeru hōhō ishiki." *Kokubungaku: kaishaku to kanshō* no. 40(1).

Murakami Yasumasa, ed. 1999. *Ittō Shōden Mutō-ryū kaiso Yamaoka Tetsutarō-sensei nempu.* Published by the editor in Kanazawa City.

Nabekura Takeyoshi. 1991. *Taisei Yamaoka Tesshū.* Tokyo: Nihon Shuppan Hōsō Kikaku.

Nakabayashi Shinji. [1983] 1988. "Nihon kobudō ni okeru shintai-ron." In *Budō ronkō*, by Nakabayashi Shinji. Tsukuba: Nakabayashi Shinji Sensei Isakushū Kankōkai.

Nakamura Tamio. 1999. "Bakumatsu Kantō kenjutsu ryūha dempa keitai no kenkyū (2)." *Fukushima Daigaku Kyōiku Gakubu Ronshū Shakai Kagaku Bumon* no. 66.

————. 2001a. "Bōgu (kendō-gu) no rekishi (jō)." *Kendō Jidai* no. 344. Online version: http://www2.educ.fukushima-u.ac.jp/~kuro/nakamura/kendo001.html (accessed on October 20, 2011).

————. 2001b. "Bōgu (kendō-gu) no rekishi (ge)." *Kendō Jidai* no. 344. Online version: http://www2.educ.fukushima-u.ac.jp/~kuro/nakamura/kendo002.html (accessed on October 20, 2011).

Nakamura Toshio. 1981. *Supōtsu no fūdo: Nichi-Ei-Bei hikaku supōtsu bunka.* Tokyo: Taishūkan Shoten.

Nanjō Norio. 1978. *Yamaoka Tesshū* (jō, ge). Tokyo: Bungei Shunjū.

Naruse Kanji. 1940. *Tatakau nihontō.* Tokyo: Jitsugyō No Nihonsha.

Nihon Kobudō Kyōkai, ed. 1997. *Nihon kobudō sōran.* Revised edition. Tokyo: Shimazu Shobō.

————, ed. 2002. *Dai 25 kai Nihon kobudō embu taikai* (pamphlet). Tokyo: Nihon Kobudō Kyōkai.

Nihonshi Kōjiten Henshū Iinkai, ed. 1997. *Nihonshi kōjiten.* Tokyo: Yamakawa Shuppansha.

Nippon Budōkan, ed. 2008. *Nihon Kobudō Kyōkai: 30 nen no ayumi.* Tokyo: Nihon Kobudō Kyōkai.

Nishiyama Matsunosuke. 1982. *Iemoto no kenkyū.* Tokyo: Yoshikawa Kōbunkan.

Nojima Jusaburō, ed. 1987. *Nihonreki seireki gappi taishōhyō.* Tokyo: Nichigai Asoshiētsu.

Odaka Nobuyuki. 2004a. *Saitama no rōshi tachi: "Rōshigumi" shimatsuki.* Saitama-shi: Saitama Shimbunsha.

————. 2004b. "Rōshigumi no jitsuzō: Kiyokawa-ra no tsūsetsu o kenshō." *Rekishi Tokuhon* no. 49(12).

Ogasawara Nobuo. 1995. *Nihontō no kanshō kiso chishiki.* Tokyo: Shibundō.

Ogino Dokuon. 1889. *Yamaoka Tesshū koji den.* Published by the author in Kyoto.

Ogino Dokuon, and Obata Buntei. [1890] 2002. *Kundoku kinsei zenrin sōhō den* (jō, ge). Reprint. Kyoto: Zen Bunka Kenkyūjo.

Oimatsu Shin'ichi. 1968. "Bakumatsu ni okeru kenjutsu kaikoku shugyō ni tsuite: Nobeoka-han Suzuki Sakae no nikki o chūshin ni." *Juntendō Daigaku Hoken Tai'iku Kiyō* no. 11.

Ōkuma Miyoshi. [1973] 1995. *Seppuku no rekishi.* Reprint. Tokyo: Yūzankaku Shuppan.

Ōmori Nobumasa. 1974. "Kinsei ni okeru kenjutsu densho no shisō ni kansuru ichi kōsatsu: Shinkage-ryū kenjutsu to Bukkyō no kankei." *Risshō Daigaku Kyōyōbu Kiyō* no. 7.

————. 1976a. "Kinsei shotō no kenjutsu densho ni kansuru ichi kōsatsu: *Heihō kadensho* to Bukkyō no kankei." *Risshō Daigaku Kyōyōbu Kiyō* no. 9.

————. 1976b. "Kinsei shotō no kenjutsu densho ni kansuru ichi kōsatsu: 'Ittō-ryū' densho (mokuroku) to Bukkyō no kankei." *Risshō Daigaku Kyōyōbu Kiyō* no. 10.

————. 1991. *Bujutsu densho no kenkyū: kinsei budō-shi e no apurōchi.* Tokyo: Chijinkan.

Ōmori Sōgen. 1970. *Yamaoka Tesshū.* Enlarged edition. Tokyo: Shunjūsha.

Ōtake Risuke. 1975. "Ken no hihō." *Tōken Bijutsu* no. 218.

————. 1977-1978. *Mukei bunkazai Katori Shintō-ryū [The Deity and the Sword: Katori Shintō-ryū]*. 3 vols. Tokyo: Minato Risāchi.

————. 1979. "Chiba ni ikiru: Tenshin Shōden Katori Shintō-ryū." *Aiba* no. 67.

————. 1981. "Kensei Iizasa Chōisai Ienao-kō." *Chiba Kyōiku* no. 288.

————. 1985a. "Katana no kōzō to kinō." *Kendō Nihon* no. 111.

————. 1985b. "Koryū ni miru tōhō no jissai." *Kendō Nihon* no. 111.

————. 2007. *Katori Shintō-ryū [Katori Shintō-ryū: Warrior Tradition]*. Berkeley Heights, NJ: Koryu Books.

————. 2009a. "Heihō Tenshinshō-den Katori Shintō-ryū: kenjutsu 'omote no tachi.'" *Budō* no. 509.

————. 2009b. "Heihō Tenshinshō-den Katori Shintō-ryū: kenjutsu 'gogyō,' 'ryōtō,' 'kodachi.'" *Budō* no. 510.

Ōtsuka Tadayoshi. 1995. *Nihon kendō no rekishi*. Tokyo: Madosha.

Ōyama Kashiwa. 1988. *Boshin no eki senshi* (jō, ge). Enlarged and revised edition. Tokyo: Jiji Tsūshinsha.

Oyamatsu Katsuichirō. 1974. *Kiyokawa Hachirō*. Tokyo: Shinjimbutsu Ōraisha.

Ozawa Tomio. 2003. *Buke kakun ikun shūsei*. Enlarged and revised edition. Tokyo: Perikansha.

Ravina, Mark. 2004. *The Last Samurai: The Life and Battles of Saigō Takamori*. Hoboken: John Wiley & Sons, Inc.

Reid, Howard, and Michael Croucher. 1983. *The Way of the Warrior: The Paradox of the Martial Arts*. Woodstock, NY: The Overlook Press.

Saeki Ariyoshi et al., eds. [1942–1944] 1998. *Bushidō zensho*. 13 vols. Reprint. Tokyo: Kokusho Kankōkai.

Saigō Takamori Zenshū Henshū Iinkai, ed. 1976–1980. *Saigō Takamori zenshū*. 6 vols. Tokyo: Daiwa Shobō.

Sakai Toshinobu. 2005. *Nihon seishin-shi toshite no tōken-kan*. Tokyo: Dai'ichi Shobō.

Sakura Magozō. 1893. *Yamaoka Tesshū den*. Tokyo: Fukyūsha.

Sakurai Kōdō. 1989. "Sesshō kara ken no keijijō-ka e: Niten Ichi-ryū Miyamoto Musashi no heihō ni tsuite." *Nihon Oyobi Nihonjin* no. 1593.

Sasaki Suguru. 1977. *Boshin sensō: haisha no Meiji ishin*. Tokyo: Chūō Kōronsha.

Sasama Yoshihiko. 1985. "Tōken bugu no hattatsu to waza no hensen." *Kendō Nihon* no. 111.

Sasamori Junzō. 1965. *Ittō-ryū gokui*. Tokyo: Ittō-ryū Gokui Kankōkai.

Satō Hiroshi. 2002. *Yamaoka Tesshū: bakumatsu ishin no shigotonin*. Tokyo: Kōbunsha.

Satō Kenji. 1950. "Miyamoto Musashi no kū-kan." *Daihōrin* no. 17(7).

Satow Ernest. 1921. *A Diplomat in Japan: The Inner History of the Criticial Years in the Evolution of Japan When the Ports were Opened and the Monarchy*

Restored, Recorded by a Diplomatist who Took an Active Part in the Events of the Time, with an Account of His Personal Experiences during that Period. London: Seeley, Service.

Seimiya Hidekata. 1877. *Hokusō shishi.* Tokyo: Gyokuzandō.

Shibusawa Ei'ichi, ed. 1966. *Sekimu-kai hikki: Tokugawa Yoshinobu-kō kaisōdan.* Tokyo: Heibonsha.

Shiga Yoshinobu, ed. [1767] 1995. *Nihon chūkō bujutsu keifu ryaku.* In *Shimpen bujutsu sōsho.* Enlarged edition by Budōsho Kankōkai. Tokyo: Shinjimbutsu Ōraisha.

Shiina Ichie. 2008. "Oni Tetsu daigo." *Kendō Nihon* no. 389.

Shima Yoshitaka. 2000. "Tesshū to Chōmin to Goin to." In *Inoue Kowashi to sono shūhen.* Edited by Goin Bunko Kenkyūkai. Tokyo: Bokutakusha.

———. 2007a. "Yamaoka Tesshū to Zen ni tsuite." In *Teruya Yoshio-sensei koki kinen. Hikaku bunka no kanōsei: Nihon kindaika ron e no gakusaiteki apurōchi.* Edited by Ikeda Masayuki and Koga Katsujirō. Tokyo: Seibundō.

———. 2007b. "Yamaoka Tesshū no sho ni tsuite." *Shohō Kangaku Kenkyū* no. 1.

———. 2008a. "Yamaoka Tesshū to Zen, sho, ken." *Zen* no. 26.

———. 2008b. "Yamaoka Tesshū to Zen, sho, ken (2)." *Zen* no. 27.

———. 2008c. "Yamaoka Tesshū to Zen, sho, ken (3)." *Zen* no. 28.

Shimauchi Toshie, ed. 1912. *Tani Kanjō ikō* (jō, ge). Tokyo: Seikensha.

Shimokawa Ushio. [1925] 1986. *Kendō no hattatsu.* In *Kindai kendō meicho taikei,* Vol. 8. Edited by Imamura Yoshio et al. Kyoto: Dōhōsha Shuppan.

Shimura Kunihiro. 2003a. "Miyamoto Musashi no shisei-kan: nihonjin no daisukina 'Musashi' no ningenzō ni semaru. Ken ni iki, kokoro no tanren o kasaneta sue, nani o kiwameta no ka." *Daihōrin* no. 70(5).

———. 2003b. "Miyamoto Musashi to nihonjin." *Daihōrin* no. 70(7).

Shinjimbutsu Ōraisha, ed. 1994. *Nihon denshō bugei ryūha tokuhon.* Tokyo: Shinjimbutsu Ōraisha.

Shitō Seiya. 1967. "Miyamoto Musashi no *Dokugyōdō.*" *Gobun Kenkyū* no. 24.

Stevens, John. 1984. *The Sword of No-sword: Life of the Master Warrior Tesshu.* Boulder, London: Shambhala.

Sugie Masatoshi. 1974. "Kindai budō no seiritsu katei ni kansuru kenkyū: budō no kindai e no tekiō o meguru shomondai ni tsuite no ichi kōsatsu." *Budōgaku Kenkyū* no. 6(2).

———. 1984. "Kendō yōgū to gijutsu no hensen." In *Tai'iku-shi kōgi.* Edited by Kishino Yūzō. Tokyo: Taishūkan Shoten.

Suzuki Daisetsu (Daisetz). 1938. *Zen Buddhism and its Influence on Japanese Culture.* Kyoto: The Eastern Buddhist Society.

———. 1959. *Zen and Japanese Culture.* Tokyo: Tuttle Pub.

Suzuki Kunio. 2006. "Miyamoto Musashi *Gorin no sho* ni tsuite: 21 seiki no ningenzō no moderu toshite." *Ōbirin Gengo Kyōiku Ronshū* no. 2.

Suzuki Masaya. 2000. *Katana to kubitori: sengoku kassen isetsu.* Tokyo: Heibonsha.

Tada Kōmon, ed. [1927] 1968. *Iwakura-kō jikki.* Revised edition (jō, chū, ge). Reprint. Tokyo: Hara Shobō.

Takano Kiyoshi. 2004. *Kiyokawa Hachirō no Meiji ishin: sōmō no shishi naru ga yue ni.* Tokyo: Nihon Hōsō Shuppan Kyōkai.

Takemura Eiji. 2002. "Bushiteki tokumoku to kōi, sono kōsatsu e no shiza: Yamaoka Tesshū o daizai ni." *Hikaku Hōshi Kenkyū* no. 10.

———. 2005. "Yamaoka Tesshu, a swordsman for peace: His deeds and the education of the samurai." *21 Seiki Ajia Gakkai Kiyō* no. 3.

Tamon Masahisa. 1841. *Taihei bubishi.* Preserved in the National Diet Library of Japan.

Tanaka Hiroshi. 2001. "Miyamoto Musashi *Gorin no sho* ni tsuite 1: Yagyū Munenori *Heihō kadensho* to hikaku shinagara." *Kinsei Shoki Bungei* no. 18.

———. 2002. "Miyamoto Musashi *Gorin no sho* ni tsuite 2: Yagyū Munenori *Heihō kadensho* to hikaku shinagara." *Kinsei Shoki Bungei* no. 19.

———. 2003. "Miyamoto Musashi *Gorin no sho* ni tsuite 3: Zeami *Fūshika-den*, Yagyū Munenori *Heihō kadensho* to hikaku shinagara." *Kinsei Shoki Bungei* no. 20.

———. 2004. "Miyamoto Musashi *Gorin no sho* ni tsuite 4: *Heihō kadensho narabi ni Heihō sanjūgo kajō* to hikaku shinagara." *Kinsei Shoki Bungei* no. 21.

———. 2005. "Miyamoto Musashi *Gorin no sho* ni tsuite, musubi: Yagyū Munenori *Heihō kadensho* to hikaku shinagara." *Kinsei Shoki Bungei* no. 22.

———. 2006. "Miyamoto Musashi *Gorin no sho* ni tsuite, ho'i 1: *Dokugyōdō* to no kanren o chūshin ni." *Kinsei Shoki Bungei* no. 23.

———. 2007. "Miyamoto Musashi *Gorin no sho* ni tsuite, ho'i 2: *Ittōsai-sensei kempōsho* hoka to no hikaku." *Kinsei Shoki Bungei* no. 23.

Taniguchi Katsuomi. 1988. "*Gorin no sho* no sōjū kyōikuhō-teki ichikōsatsu." *Kōkū Daigakkō Kenkyū Hōkoku* no. R-42.

Taniguchi Shinko. 2005. *Kinsei shakai to hō kihan: meiyo, mibun, jitsuryoku kōshi.* Tokyo: Yoshikawa Kōbunkan.

Tateno Masahiro. 2003. "Miyamoto Musashi to *Dokugyōdō*: Michi no seishin-shi (1)." *Bungei Kenkyū* no. 91.

Terabayashi Shun. 2003. "Miyamoto Musashi to *Dokugyōdō*: itsu de mo tatakaeru kokoro no sonae." *Daihōrin* no. 70(7).

Terayama Katsujō. 1977. *Tesshū to shodō: shobi no honshitsu to sono shinka.* Tokyo: Gannandō Shoten.

———. 1982. *Sanshū oyobi Nanshū no sho.* Tokyo: Gannandō Shoten.

———. 1997. "Ken Zen Sho no kokoro: Yamaoka Tesshū no ikikata." *Ōkurayama Kōenshū* no. 6.

———— (Tanchū). 2003. "Zen no geijutsu: Tesshū no sho." *Zen* no. 11.

Tobe Shinjūrō. 1992. *Nihon kengō tan* (ishin hen). Tokyo: Mainichi Shimbunsha.

Tokuda Susumu.1991. "Koshahon *Yoshisada-ki* no shoshi-teki kenkyū: Eishō 12 nen koshahon o chūshin toshite." *Takasaki Keizai Daigaku Ronshū* no. 34(2).

————. 1992. "Yoshisada no saigo ni kansuru shomondai to *Yoshisada-ki* to no shōgō: toku ni Fujishima Jinja shahō no kabuto ni tsuite." *Takasaki Keizai Daigaku Ronshū* no. 35(3).

————. 1993. "*Yoshisada-ki* no seiritsu to kōsei." *Takasaki Keizai Daigaku Ronshū* no. 36(1).

Tōkyō-to Edo Tōkyō Hakubutsukan Toshi Rekishi Kenkyūshitsu, ed. 2001. *Katsu Kaishū kankei shiryō: bunsho no bu*. Tokyo: Tōkyō-to and other publishers.

Tominaga Kengo. 1972. *Kendō 500 nen shi*. Reprint. Tokyo: Shimazu Shobō.

Totman, Conrad. 1980. *The Collapse of the Tokugawa Bakufu, 1862–1868*. Honolulu: University of Hawai'i Press.

Tsumoto Yō. 1983. "Kobudō o tazuneru (jō)." Bungei Shunjū no. 61(11).

Umezu Heishū, ed. 1991. *Nikka seiten*. Kyoto: Ōyagi Kōbundō.

Uozumi Takashi. 2002. *Miyamoto Musashi: nihonjin no michi*. Tokyo: Perikansha.

————. 2005. "Miyamoto Musashi *Gorin no sho* no shisōshi-teki kenkyū." In *Nihon no kyōiku ni "budō" o: 21 seiki ni shin-gi-tai o kitaeru*. Edited by Yamada Shōji and Alexander Bennett. Tokyo: Meiji Tosho Shuppan.

————. 2008. *Miyamoto Musashi: "heihō no michi" o ikiru*. Tokyo: Iwanami Shoten.

Ushiyama Eiji, ed. [1937] 1989. *Yamaoka Tesshū sensei seiden: ore no shishō*. Reprint. Niigata-ken, Nishikubiki-gun, Ōmi-machi: Ogura Tetsuju-shi Kenshōkai.

————, ed. 1942a. *Yamaoka Tesshū den*. Tokyo: Nihon Seinenkan.

————, ed. 1942b. *Ore ga shishō Yamaoka Tesshū o kataru*. Tokyo: Ida Shoten.

————, ed. 1967. *Yamaoka Tesshū no isshō*. Tokyo: Shumpūkan.

————. 1974. *Yamaoka Tesshū: Shumpūkan dōjō no hitobito*. Tokyo: Shinjimbutsu Ōraisha.

————. 1976. *Teihon Yamaoka Tesshū*. Tokyo: Shinjimbutsu Ōraisha.

Vaporis, Constantine. 1994. *Breaking Barriers: Travel and the State in Early Modern Japan*. Cambridge, MA: Council on East Asian Studies, Harvard University.

Watanabe Ichirō. 1967. "Bakumatsu Kantō ni okeru kenjutsu sho-ryūha no sonzai keitai." *Tōkyō Kyōiku Daigaku Bungakubu Kiyō* no. 61.

Watatani Kiyoshi. 1971. *Nihon kengō 100 sen*. Tokyo: Akita Shoten.

Watatani Kiyoshi, and Yamada Tadachika, ed. 1978. *Bugei ryūha daijiten*. Revised and enlarged edition. Tokyo: Tokyo Kopii Shuppambu.

Waterhouse, David. 1996. "Notes on the *kuji*." In *Religion in Japan: Arrows to Heaven and Earth*. Edited by P. F. Kornicki, and I. J. McMullen. Cambridge: Cambridge University Press.

Yagyū Toshinaga. 1957. *Seiden Shinkage-ryū*. Tokyo: Dai Nihon Yūbenkai Kōdansha.

Yamada Jirōkichi. 1960. *Nihon kendō-shi*. Tokyo: Saikensha.

Yamaji Aizan, ed. [1913] 1976. *Kiyokawa Hachirō icho*. Reprint. Tokyo: Tōkyō Daigaku Shuppankai.

Yamaoka Tesshū (Tetsutarō). 1882. *Meiji Boshin Yamaoka-sensei to Saigō-shi ōsetsu hikki*. Published by Ōmori Hōkō in Tokyo.

Yano Sei'ichi. 1999. *San'yūtei Enchō no Meiji*. Tokyo: Bungei Shunjū.

Yatagawa Kokuzan, and Koike Naojirō. 1906. *Kashima-shi*. Published by Koike Naojirō in Kashima-machi.

Yokose Tomoyuki. 2000. *Nihon no kobudō*. Tokyo: Nihon Budōkan.

Yoshida Tomoo. 2007. "Ono-ha Ittō-ryū ni tsuite: Ono-ke densho (Shumpūkan Bunko) to Tsugaru-ke densho kara ukagaeru ryūgi no tōhō to sono ishi oyobi Mutō-ryū e no keishō ni kansuru ichi kōsatsu." *Budō Supōtsu Kagaku Kenkyūjo Nempō* no. 13.

Yuasa Akira. 2000. "Kinsei bugei-ron ni okeru shimpō no hen'yō ni tsuite: budō no renzokusei kaimei no tame no zentei." *Tenri Daigaku Gakuhō* no. 51(3).

Yuasa Yasuo. 1986. *Ki, shugyō, shintai*. Tokyo: Hirakawa Shuppansha.

Zenshōan, ed. 2009. *Yamaoka Tesshū: Zen and Swordsmanship from the Yamaoka Tesshū Archives*. Tokyo: Zenshōan.

Location of Cited Primary Sources

"Shumpūkan Bunko" collection, Tamagawa Library, Kanazawa City.
Zenshōan Temple, Tokyo.

Newspapers

Chōya Shimbun (1888/7/20)
Kōko Shimbun (1868/5/22)
Kōshi Zappō (1868/i4/7)
Mainichi Shimbun (2007/12/9; 2008/8/3; 2008/9/6; 2008/10/24)
Sankei Shimbun (2008/10/17)
Tōkyō Nichinichi Shimbun (1881/9/24, 26–27; 1888/07/21–22, 24–28; 1888/07/29)
Yomiuri Shimbun (2008/5/15; 2009/1/6)

Journals

Daisekai no. 9(2) (1954/2)
Jitsugyō No Nihon no. 59(12) (1956/5)
Nihon Oyobi Nihonjin no. 1650 (2004)
Sapio no. 12(18) (2000/10/25)
Shidankai sokkiroku, 101st collection (1901/4/12).
Shin Bummei no. 5(12) (1955/12)
Shūkan Asahi no. 103(13) (1998/3/27), 103(35) (1998/8/10)
Verdad no. 122–168 (2005/6–2009/4)

Index

Printed in Great Britain
by Amazon

83266371R00119